DA

Learning Disability
Physical Therapy, Treatment and Management

Learning Disability

Physical Therapy, Treatment and Management

A collaborative approach

Edited by

JEANETTE RENNIE, MPHIL, MCSP

Senior Physiotherapist, Learning Disability Service
Lothian Primary Care NHS Trust

W

WHURR PUBLISHERS

LONDON AND PHILADELPHIA

Chapter 11 © Patricia Odunmbaku Auty
Chapter 13 © Sally Smith and Debbi Cook
© 2001 Whurr Publishers
First published 2001 by
Whurr Publishers Ltd
19B Compton Terrace, London N1 2UN, England and
325 Chestnut Street, Philadelphia PA 19106, USA

Reprinted 2001 and 2004

British Library Cataloguing in Publication Data
A catalogue record for this book is available from the
British Library.

ISBN: 1 86156 192 X

Printed and bound in the UK by Athenaeum Press Ltd,
Gateshead, Tyne & Wear

Contents

Contributors

Patricia Odunmbaku Auty, MCSP
Physiotherapy Manager for Adults with Learning Disabilities, Community Health South London NHS Trust

Anneliese Barrell, MCSP
Superintendent Physiotherapist in Learning Disability, Plymouth Community Services NHS Trust

Jane Bruce, Dip COT, ISPA
Reflexologist and Aromatherapist with the elderly and people who have physical disabilities and learning disabilities

Lucy Clarke, Dip COT, D JABADAO
Senior Occupational Therapist, Deeside Community Hospital, North East Wales Trust

Debbi Cook, MCSP
Senior Physiotherapist, South Derby Community Team

Libby Davies, MCSP
Senior Physiotherapist, Learning Disability Service, Lothian Primary Care NHS Trust

Ann Findlay, MCSP
Head of Physiotherapy, Learning Disability Service, Lothian Primary Care NHS Trust

John Goldsmith
Director, The Helping Hand Company (Ledbury) Ltd

Liz Goldsmith, MCSP
Senior Physiotherapist, Premier Health Trust; Advisor, The Helping Hand
Company (Ledbury) Ltd

Jonathan Gray, Dip RG & RT, MCSP
Manager, The Keresford Centre, Barnsley

Helen Holme, MSC, MCSP
Senior Physiotherapist, Adult Learning Disability Services, Wirral and West
Cheshire Community NHS Trust

Angela Johnson, MA, MCSP
Physiotherapy Lecturer, Huddersfield University

Mohamed Megahed, MB, CHB, MRCPsych
Specialist Registrar in Psychiatry, The Royal London and St Bartholomew's
Scheme

Jeanette Rennie, MPHIL, MCSP
Senior Physiotherapist, Learning Disability Service, Lothian Primary Care
NHS Trust

James E Robb, FRCS
Consultant Orthopaedic Surgeon, Princess Margaret Rose Hospital and
The Royal Hospital for Sick Children, Edinburgh

Ian Silkstone, MCSP
Senior Physiotherapist, Learning Disabilities Services, Dewsbury Health
Care NHS Trust

Sally Smith, Dip RG & RT, MCSP
Senior Physiotherapist, Learning Disability Services, Nottingham Health
Care NHS Trust

Sue Smith, MRCSLT
Principal Speech and Language Therapist for People with Learning
Disabilities, Southampton Community NHS Trust

Sue Standing, MSC, MCSP
Superintendent Physiotherapist for People with Learning Disabilities,
Southampton Community NHS Trust

Mark Sterrick, JP, MB, ChB, GP(T), DFM
Associate Specialist, Formerly Lothian Primary Care NHS Trust, Learning
Disability Service

Alys Watson, MCSP
RDA Regional Therapist, South East Scotland

Preface

During the last 10 years, there has been an expansion of postgraduate diploma and higher degree courses in all the therapies and nursing. However, students starting out on projects and research studies relating to the physical treatment and management of people who have learning disabilities have discovered that the literature is very limited. Other professionals who are unfamiliar with the UK usage of the term 'learning disability', such as general medical practitioners (GPs), generic nurses, therapists and social workers, have had difficulty finding a comprehensive book that sets the presenting physical disability, whether long term or acute, in the context of learning disability and its associated conditions.

The authors of this book have based their writing on the available research and have many years' practical knowledge in their own areas of writing. They have also referred to some of the higher degree studies.

The book has been written as a resource for health professionals working with people (primarily adults) who have learning disabilities, social services staff and carers involved in their day-to-day management, and students. It also aims to address some of the many questions that are frequently asked or implied by other health, education or social services professionals who are confused by the multiplicity of terms such as 'mental retardation', 'mental handicap', 'learning difficulty', 'cognitive impairment' and 'learning disability'. It cannot answer all the questions or go into detailed treatment methods – it is hoped that the appendices and references will point readers in the direction of further study.

The term 'learning disability', which is used in the UK to mean 'mental retardation' (WHO, 1992, 1993), is favoured by most clients and their families. However, even this term can be misunderstood by other people who tend to assume that it is used only to mean 'very low intelligence' with which there are no other associated disabilities. Therefore, the need for teachers, and to a certain extent psychologists, speech and language therapists and occupational therapists, is apparent but people are frequently heard to question the need for doctors, nurses and physiotherapists.

Professionals working with people who have learning disabilities are also guilty of using 'verbal shorthand' and failing to mention that clients have one or more additional associated disabilities, for example, physical, psychiatric or behavioural problems, epilepsy or speech disorders.

Frequently asked questions include the following:

- Why do people with learning disabilities have physical disabilities?
- How do the various problems associated with learning disability affect each other?
- Why do physiotherapists work with people who have learning disabilities?
- How can I talk to someone with a learning disability – will he or she understand me?
- Where does a physiotherapist new to learning disability start?
- Why is it important that a range of professionals and care staff work together?
- How do you encourage people with learning disabilities to get fit and stay fit?
- Why do fully grown adults need to use special seating and equipment?
- What's the point of surgery for people with learning disabilities?
- What are 'normalisation' and 'inclusion'?

Since the 1950s, when therapists began to work with people who had a combination of learning disabilities and physical disabilities, four points have emerged: first, despite increased numbers of therapy staff, there have never been sufficient to meet the need; second, consistency of treatment is essential; third, individual therapy sessions cannot succeed without ongoing involvement of day-care staff and family or carers; and fourth, clients need to find out for themselves that therapy is fun, creates a sense of achievement and makes them feel better. In conjunction with moves from hospital to community care, treatment and management has had to be capable of being undertaken in a wide range of settings.

No book relating to learning disability can ever be written for one single profession; nor can it refer to only one profession's or one country's literature. Although many of these chapters have been written by physiotherapists, each includes involvement by other professionals and agencies.

The book is divided into three sections. Part I describes the theory underlying learning disability and its associated conditions. This begins with worldwide social policy developments that have influenced attitudes towards learning disability, and have therefore subsequently affected treatment and management of physical disabilities. Further chapters describe the following: the causes and categorisation of learning disability, treatment of associated conditions by medication, the side effects of medication and their impact on the clients' physical ability, and orthopaedic procedures. Part II focuses on assessment. It outlines the multiprofessional structure within which assessments are undertaken and describes communication skills that are a prerequisite of their success. Chapters 7 and 8 in this section are physiotherapy assessments and interpretation of results, but the underlying principles can be used by other professions. Part III describes eight different methods of managing and treating physical disability and improving physical fitness and general health of learning-disabled people.

Apart from the main chapter authors, there are many other people who have contributed in one way or another. I would like to thank the following people for their contribution to chapters: Colin McKay, Legal and Policy Advisor to ENABLE, Sheila Cozens, M. McPherson, J. Cunningham, Marjorie Tasker, Lynne Hewitt, Sue Jennings, M. Boreham, S.E. Bruce, A.L. Neale, P.A. Fenn Clark, I.L. Griffiths, L.M.C. Rees, Olive Gallagher and Riana O'Cofaigh (Ireland), Lisbeth Nielsen (Denmark), Sue Astwood (Bermuda), Brother Dike (Nigeria) and members of the Association of Chartered Physiotherapists for People with Learning Disabilities (ACPPLD) who responded to the original questionnaire and participated in discussions on assessment.

I would also like to thank the following people for their sustained support and for reading and discussing my own chapters: Dr Walter Muir, Department of Psychiatry, University of Edinburgh and Lothian Primary Care NHS Trust, Learning Disability Service; Dr Ros Lyall, Clinical Director; Margaret Owens, Senior Physiotherapist; Jane Neill McLachlan, Senior Speech and Language Therapist; and Fiona Wilkie, Community Nurse, Lothian Primary Care NHS Trust, Learning Disability Service. Where photographs of patients have been used, permission has been obtained from the patient or the patient's parent(s) or guardian(s).

Finally, I would like to thank the children and staff of Oslo Observasjonshjem og Poliklinikk for Åndssvake, Norway, who started me on this journey in 1964, and my husband who has patiently continued to encourage me.

PART I

LEARNING DISABILITY AND ASSOCIATED PROBLEMS THAT AFFECT PHYSICAL ABILITY

CHAPTER 1

What is learning disability?

An overview of worldwide policy development and its influence on physical ability of learning-disabled people

JEANETTE RENNIE

In the UK, the term 'learning disability' is used to mean 'mental retardation' (see Table 1.4 and Chapter 2). It is used throughout this book except where it is important to record the terminology of the period.

A number of writers have described the history of mental retardation, for example, Trent (1994), Scheerenberger (1987) and Morris (1969). This chapter examines the way that history has influenced treatment and management of the associated physical disabilities. It does not deal in depth with social and educational developments or specify work of individual voluntary agencies. Nor does it detail all legislation that impinges on learning disability.

The chapter is written under subheadings describing: the events and attitudes leading to the establishment of institutions and organisational developments within them; the concept of community care for people with learning disabilities and its development; and the present legal aspects in the UK and recent changes in health and social care. The tables are used to show international influence on policy-making, UK legislation, development of definitions and terminology, and evolution of the definition of 'normalisation'.

A mix of politics, education, social policies and medicine

- Have ideologies, theories and practices benefited or deprived people with learning disabilities, with regard to facilities that would assist them to lead fulfilled lives?
- Have neurological and sensory impairments present in people with mild mental retardation (Fryers, 1997) been considered worthy of treatment or ignored as a vague associated clumsiness?
- Does the term 'learning disability', used in the UK to assist integration into normal society, promote misunderstanding among generic health-care professionals who associate 'learning' with 'education'?
- Does the term 'learning disability' hinder research between countries? For example, in the USA the term was introduced in 1962 to mean:

A disorder in one or more of the basic psychological processes involved in the understanding or in using language, spoken or written, which may manifest itself in an incomplete ability to listen, think, speak, read, write or spell, or to do mathematical calculations.

It includes:

. . . perceptual handicaps, dyslexia, developmental aphasia, brain injury, mid brain dysfunction.

It does not include motor handicaps or mental retardation. (Education for All Handicapped Children Act, Public Law 94 – 142, 34 CFR 300.5 [b] [9] in Brown and Aylwood, 1996.)

People with learning disabilities have produced many and varied reactions in those around them. They have also caused philanthropists, educational-ists, health professionals and sociologists to consider deeply how their needs may be met. The social and economic climate of the time has influenced the thinking of the period, which in turn has informed political decision-making, sometimes clashing with isolated progressive thought and sometimes reinforcing it. Many caring and progressive attitudes of previous years, interpreted today as selfish and condescending, were the building blocks for present policies. Key developments and interactions between countries in the developed world are listed in Tables 1.1–1.3.

Before the development of modern medicine, most profoundly learning-disabled children died in infancy in accordance with the natural law of survival of the fittest. In general, therefore, the literature refers to people who would now be regarded as having mild-to-moderate learning disability.

Table 1.1 Key developments worldwide

France

1801	Itard published his book *The Wild Boy of Aveyron*. It described innovative treatment of a 'mentally defective' boy (Lane, 1977)
1806	Pinel published his paper 'Treatise on alienism'. 'Defectives' had the ability to be trained to their level of intelligence but no further (Trent, 1994)
1846	Seguin published *The Psychological Treatment, Hygiene and Education of Idiots*, a handbook for institutional care (Kanner, 1964)

USA

1820–60	The Depression, ideas from Europe and Britain and the Civil War led to the end of 'outdoor relief' and the development of 'indoor relief'
1848	Seguin moved to the USA
1856	Schools for feebleminded children became residential asylums for training feebleminded adults and idiots. Medically trained superintendents replaced head teachers
Late 1800s	Wilbur categorised mental defectives (see Table 1.4)
1958	Anthony Dexter conceived a 'social system concept'
1961	President Kennedy appointed a President's Panel on mental retardation
1969	Concept of 'normalisation' introduced by Bank Mikkelsen and Bengt Nirje (see Table 1.5)
1970	The Developmental Disabilities Services and Facilities Construction Act
1971	International League of Societies for the Mentally Handicapped endorsed philosophy of normalisation
1987	The Developmental Disabilities Assistance and Bill of Rights Amendments included people with mental retardation

Switzerland

1839	Guggenbuhl established a 'colony' on the Abendberg

Italy

1870s	Lombroso suggested that inherited factors caused criminal tendencies
1978	Law passed to replace all institutions with community care

Denmark

1959	The Government passed 'An Act Concerning Care of the Mentally Retarded and other Exceptionally Retarded Persons' (see Table 1.5)

Canada

Early 1970s	Responsibility for people with mental handicap transferred from health to social welfare and educational ministries

Australia

1970s	Several states acted on reports recommending that mentally handicapped people be transferred to the community

Table 1.1 (contd)

UN	
1971	Declaration on the Rights of Mentally Retarded Persons
1975	Declaration on the Rights of Disabled People
WHO	
1980	*International Classification of Impairments, Disabilities and Handicaps* (see Table 1.3)
Sweden	
1990	Recommended that all institutions close

Compiled from Morris (1969), Scheerenberger (1987) and Trent (1994).

Table 1.2 UK: key reports and legislation

1713–14	Vagrancy Acts: 'apprehension of those who might be dangerous'
1774	Madhouses Act: 'provision of minimum standards of care and for the control of private madhouses'
1808	County Asylums Act: public asylums in England replaced private madhouses
1908	Report of Royal Commission on Care and Control of the Feebleminded
1913	Mental Deficiency Act: people with mental deficiency dealt with as a specific group. Segregation introduced. Mental defectives classified (see Table 1.3)
1914	Mental Deficiency Act: local authorities to protect mentally defective patients by providing accommodation
1927	Mental Deficiency Act: creation of separate institutions for the mentally ill and mentally handicapped
1946	National Health Service Act: minimum standard of care available for all who needed it
1948	The National Health Service Act (as amended) standardised mental subnormality hospitals in accordance with general hospitals
1959	Mental Health Act repealed all previous legislation. Emphasis placed on voluntary instead of compulsory admission to hospital. Civil rights of patients recognised, including access to a Health Service Commissioner
1961	Minister of Health proposed start of 'running down' mental hospitals
1971	'Better Services for the Mentally Handicapped'
1975	The National Development Group and National Development Team for the Mentally Handicapped established
1978	'Helping Mentally Handicapped People in Hospital'
1978	Warnock Committee Report on special educational needs
1979	Jay Report: policy based on principles of normalisation. Special help would be required from their communities and the professional services. Advocacy recommended 'A Better Life' (Scotland). Concept of community care endorsed, gradual progress recommended
1980	SHAPE (Scottish Health Authorities Priorities for the Eighties)
1981	Education Act for Children with Special Education Needs and Education (Scotland) Act. Education should be fitted to the child's requirements as far as possible. Statement of needs and needs assessments proposed

Table 1.2 (contd)

1983	The All Wales Strategy
1983	Mental Health Act
1984	Mental Health (Scotland) Act
1986	Disabled Persons Act (Tom Clarke Act). Right to representation, assessment, information, consultation. Carers have a right to ask for assessment of disabled person's needs and carers' ability to care to be taken into account
1987	Report by the Department of Health and Social Security: 'Mental Handicap: Progress, Problems and Priorities: A Review of Mental Handicap Services in England since the 1971 White Paper'
1988	Community Care: Agenda for Action (Griffiths Report)
1988	SHARPEN (Scottish Health Authorities Review of Priorities for the Eighties and Nineties)
1989	White Paper 'Caring for People: Community Care in the next Decade and Beyond'
1990	NHS and Community Care Act. Confirmed proposals in 1989 White Paper
1995	'The Health of the Nation' including 'A strategy for people with learning disabilities and their carers'
1998	'Signposts for success'
1999	Health Act

Table 1.3 Development of terminology

Year	Country	Terminology
Late 1890s	USA	Wilbur's categories of mental defectives (see Table 1.4)
Late 1890s	UK	Feebleminded, imbecile, idiot
1913	UK	Moral imbecile, feebleminded, imbecile, idiot
1921	USA	Mental retardation
1927	UK	England: moral defective replaced moral imbecile
1959	UK	Legal terminology, England and Wales: subnormal, severe subnormal. (Also used 'mental handicap' and 'severe mental handicap') Scotland: mental deficiency, severe mental deficiency
1968	WHO	Mental retardation: mild, moderate, severe, profound
1978	UK	Education terminology, England and Wales: moderate and severe learning difficulties replaced moderate and severe educationally subnormal
1980	WHO	Mental retardation – all people with IQ of < 70
1981	UK	Education terminology: one category – learning difficulty
1983	UK	England and Wales: mental impairment, severe mental impairment Scotland: mental handicap, severe mental handicap
1995	UK	Learning disability accepted terminology. Medically, used in conjunction with more specific definition and diagnosis (see Chapter 2 and Table 1.4)

Writings such as the Arthurian legends and Shakespearean plays automatically refer to people 'possessed' or with 'second sight' who influenced everyday occurrences and major battles. Such people were either venerated, or locked up and maltreated (Morris, 1969; Scheerenberger, 1987; Trent, 1994). In the early fourteenth century in the UK, differentiation was made between learning disability (people who were born 'fools') and mental illness (people who became 'mad'), on the basis that the former could never become 'normal' but the latter may regain their sanity:

> . . . born fools could not inherit property, the King as parens partrie assumed rights over the fool and his property as if he were an infant
> O'Connor and Tizard (1956) (in Morris, 1969)

Comparison with infants led to a protective and humane attitude towards the more severely learning disabled. It was also possible, however, for anyone to sue for the guardianship and administration of a 'fool's' estate — 'to beg for a fool' (Schwarz, 1993). In the sixteenth and seventeenth centuries, various tests were devised to verify 'fools', both to protect them and to gain their property rights.

Before the industrial revolution, however, known local people with learning disabilities were an accepted part of life. This probably contributed to the success of outdoor relief given as direct aid to 'worthy' dependants in the USA before 1820 (Trent, 1994).

Until France produced pioneers such as Itard and Pinel in the early nineteenth century, positive treatment or teaching had been deemed impossible. Itard's use of warm baths as sensory stimulation to train 'defectives' and Pinel's humanitarian, psychological approach were the first steps towards enabling 'defectives' to learn and to grow in self-esteem.

Spa treatment was being used throughout Europe for a variety of medical conditions and the term 'hydrotherapy' was an accepted description for specifically medical treatment in England. However, Itard appears to have used baths for training purposes only and not to improve physical abilities in 'mental defectives'.

Development of institutions

During the mid-nineteenth century two parallel strands developed:

1. An awareness that 'defectives' had an ability to learn and that it was society's duty to provide education and security for them.
2. The proposal that low intellectual ability was an entirely inherited factor – the 'degeneration' theory which later gave rise to eugenics.

In 1839, a colony for the cure of cretinism was established by Guggenbuhl on the Abendberg in Switzerland. It was closed 20 years later as a result of the failure to discover a 'cure'. However, the principle of the 'colonies', and Guggenbuhl's treatment theories of a sensible diet, massage and physical exercise, spread to other countries in Europe, the UK and the USA.

At the same time, Seguin opened his centres in Paris for 'physiological and moral training' (Kanner, 1964).

In the UK, philanthropic reformers began to found institutions to replace the asylums where mentally ill and learning-disabled people were kept together. For example, Dr and Mrs Brodie (Henderson, 1964) founded the Edinburgh Idiot Asylum in 1855. It transferred to Stirlingshire and became the Scottish National Institution for the Education of Imbecile Children and subsequently the Royal Scottish National Institution for Mental Defectives, the first institution purely for 'mental defectives'. In conjunction with this, a small school was established where Dr Ireland began to develop a special educational system for children with learning disability.

In the Republic of Ireland, Stewart's Hospital in Dublin was opened in 1869. This was a private charitable institution administered on a voluntary basis by a committee of management who were supported by the state through revenue allocations and capital grants.

The USA responded to pressure from local officials, parents and superintendents by ending outdoor relief and following the UK's government-driven programme of building large centralised hospitals for 'idiots' and the 'feebleminded'.

Gradually, medically trained superintendents and medical terminology became normal practice in the residential institutions, and an increasing number of physicians were employed. Despite this development, all study and research appear to have been directed towards assessing and categorising 'idiots' into different levels by intellectual ability.

Categorisation

Categorisation was made using new tests, notably the Binet–Simon (Savage, 1970). The tests were revolutionary but assumed that intelligence could be tested in isolation without reference to an individual's social and environmental conditions and physical disabilities. They therefore reinforced the theory of hereditary transmission, which fostered fear of further increases in numbers of people with a learning disability. In the late nineteenth century, this fear led to the development of the eugenics movement and custodial care of people with learning disability.

Segregation

In 1908, the first edition of Tredgold's renowned book, *Textbook on Mental Deficiency*, was published. In 1909, in an article in the *Eugenics Review*, he referred to the high inheritance factor in mental deficiency and a relatively high birth rate among poor and handicapped people. It has been suggested that this influenced the addition of a Statutory Instrument to the Mental Deficiency Act 1913. The Act segregated 'mentally deficient' people from the general population and from the opposite sex to prevent an increase in 'mental deficiency . . . as a protection of society as a whole'.

One of the effects of segregation was to retain children and adults who had a combination of physical disabilities and learning disability in hospitals specialising in learning disability. Staff were not equipped to treat their physical disabilities and were, on the whole, unable to recognise the impact that such disabilities made on communication, mobility and daily living skills, and subsequently the frustration that resulted in aggressive behaviour.

Photographs from large UK and US hospitals, however, showed that active exercise was provided for physically able people with learning disabilities, in the same way as social reformers such as Robert Owen provided 'exercise classes for the moral and physical development of his young workers' (Barclay, 1994).

The institutions grew in size and numbers and segregation continued, but gradually attitudes towards aims of treatment within the institutions changed. For example, Dr Chislet, the first medical superintendent of Lennox Castle Hospital, Glasgow, wrote in 1936 that treatment should consist of:

> Custodial care for those who require such for life i.e. the lower grades of defectives and an endeavour by treatment and training to render certain defectives fit to take their place in the general community.

Suggestions and instructions regarding the developing 'colonies' included the:

> . . . necessity of a rural setting away from danger
> . . . adequate classification according to sex, age, ability, medical condition and behavioural problems.
>
> Loudon (1992)

However, institutions that were isolated were liable to have difficulty attracting specialist staff to deal with medical conditions and behavioural problems. They therefore tended to become self-contained units largely ignored by the rest of the nursing and medical professions, and society as a whole.

The 1948 National Health Service Act (as amended) required:

- Appointment of appropriately qualified senior doctors
- Local authorities to remove 'persons in need of care and attention to suitable premises'
- Local authorities to provide temporary accommodation where necessary

This produced rapid expansion of both the number of hospitals for people with learning disability and the number of patients that they could accommodate.

New thoughts about institutions

In the UK, the Mental Deficiency Act 1913 had introduced a category of 'Moral Defective' to cope with offenders who were considered to be guilty but who lacked full understanding of their crime. This was beneficial to people for whom life imprisonment would have been detrimental. However, it also resulted in compulsory life-time hospitalisation for people who appeared to be potential criminals, such as borderline learning-disabled people, angry and frustrated teenagers, and sexually promiscuous adults.

During the 1950s, publicity about such hospitalisation led to the Royal Commission on the Law Relating to Mental Illness and Mental Deficiency (1957) and the Mental Health Act 1959. This Act introduced informal admission to learning disability hospitals and changed terminology. It created a greater awareness of 'mental handicap' and mental illness, although 40 years later confusion still arises between the two in the mind of the general public.

At this time, there was a worldwide search for a more appropriate definition and method of care. The medical model was increasingly considered inappropriate because it was recognised that people with learning disability were not ill and did not have a disease. A 'social systems concept' was first proposed by Lewis Anthony Dexter in 1958. He viewed the 'cost and trouble' caused by 'mental defectives' in society as a result of both

> . . . society's expectations of the mentally defective and the mental defectives' learned role as to what was expected of them.
>
> Scheerenberger (1987)

It gradually became acknowledged that only the most severely 'subnormal' people required skilled nursing care and few needed the support of custodial care. However, appropriate nursing care for the most severely 'subnormal' who also had severe physical disabilities was considered to be palliative and protecting, and not stimulating and enabling patients to achieve their maximum potential.

Access to a range of treatments for children with physical disabilities and normal intelligence was being developed by people like Karel and Bertha Bobath in England in the 1930s (Bobath and Bobath, 1975). In Hungary in the 1940s, Andreas Peto was developing conductive education (Hari and Akos, 1988). Infants with physical disabilities and learning disability were usually excluded on the grounds of lack of understanding and short life expectancy. In the UK, treatment was made available through special schools such as Trefoil, founded in 1939, Westerlea 1948 and Craig-y-Park, Drummonds and Thomas de la Rue, 1955. Many paediatric services began to provide pre-school treatment either at hospital outpatient departments or on a domiciliary basis.

Introduction of the concept of community care

Mention was first made of community care in a statutory report of midwives in 1955 but the Danish Government's Parliamentary Act acted as the major catalyst for change (see box).

---

5 June 1959: Danish Government passed The Act of 'normalisation'

The Act profoundly affected the lives of people with learning disabilities throughout the world.

At that time the Danish Government was accused of abdicating responsibility for the mentally retarded by:

• Permitting children to go to normal schools
• Permitting adults to leave their parents' home and be trained, taught and employed

---

In the USA, four alternative methods of care were proposed in the 1960s (Scheerenberger, 1987):

• The least restrictive alternative allowed equal protection under law, including the right to deny as well as accept treatment and the necessity for informed consent by the individual or guardian.
• The developmental model: mentally retarded children and adults were capable of growth, learning and development.

- Mainstreaming recommended integration of mentally retarded children into mainstream schools, but offered no additional assistance.
- Normalisation.

In 1961, the President's Panel set up by President Kennedy for recommendations for mental retardation included ideas for research, preventive health measures and production of a new legal as well as social concept of the retarded. However, the concept of normalisation was not introduced to the USA by Nirje until 1969. It was followed in 1970 by an Act that gave Federal authorisation to

> . . . 'assist' States to ensure that people with disabilities were enabled to receive the necessary care treatment and other services to live their lives to the maximum.
>
> Scheerenberger (1987)

Although community care was first recommended for people with learning disability in the UK in 1961, partly as a cost-cutting exercise (Scrivens, 1986), the number of residents in large institutions peaked at about 52 000 in the early 1970s (Brown, 1992). A number of factors lay behind this statistic, including the following:

- Statutory obligation of the National Health Service (NHS) to meet the need for care for the whole population.
- NHS supported by central funding which removed dependency on local rates or charitable donations.
- Prevailing medical and social opinion, which was that the most appropriate form of care was sheltered living offered by hospital services.
- People with learning disability living longer.

This was the period in which therapists began to expand their work in hospitals for people with learning disability. For example, occupational therapy started at Gogarburn Hospital, Edinburgh, in 1964, physiotherapy in 1966, and speech therapy was seconded from the Scottish Council for Spastics (now Capability Scotland) in 1966. Recreation was recognised as an important part of rehabilitation (Luckey and Shapiro, 1974) and remedial gymnasts began to organise sporting activities (see Chapter 15). Elsewhere, physiotherapy, occupational therapy, speech therapy and psychology were available for children and young adults at Oslo Observasjonshjem og Poliklinikk for Åndssvake, Norway, in the 1950s, physiotherapy and occupational therapy started at St Michael's House in Dublin in 1955, physiotherapy started in Denmark in the early 1960s, and in Bermuda at about the same time. In the former Eastern Region of Nigeria, people with learning disabilities were treated in small general hospitals and specialist parts of large general hospitals in the 1970s, and day centres and special education centres began to be established.

The first attempts were made to quantify the number of therapists working in this field in the UK in 1970.

England

- Occupational therapists 77 (others 212)
- Physiotherapists 37 (others 4)
- Speech therapists 18
- Chiropodists 20
- Other therapists 285 (in 1971)
- Psychologists 54 (DHSS, 1987)

Scotland

- Occupational therapists 0.22 per 100 patients
- Physiotherapists 0.17 per 100 patients
- Speech therapists 0.06 per 100 patients
- Chiropodists 0.06 per 100 patients
- Other therapists 0.27 per 100 patients
- Psychologists 0.07 per 100 patients (Scottish Home and Health Department, 1970).

In many hospitals, residents were encouraged and supported to live as full a life as possible but this failed to achieve full individual development. In other hospitals, residents lived in restricted and repressive conditions. A series of scandals resulted in the publication of *Better Services for the Mentally Handicapped* (DHSS, 1971).

Internationally, in 1971 the United Nations published *The Declaration on the Rights of Mentally Retarded Persons*:

> They should have 'to the maximum degree of feasibility the same rights as other human beings' and a right to a qualified guardian.

UK Central Government support for community care began with publication of *Better Services for the Mentally Handicapped* (DHSS, 1971):

- Multiprofessional teams encouraged to support and enable people with 'mental handicap' to live more normal lives in the community.
- Links encouraged between health and local authorities.
- Community integration strongly recommended.

Search for common definitions and terminology

Wolfensberger's reworded principle of normalisation and his introduction of the term 'social integration' encouraged worldwide progress towards care in the community. In the 1970s, this included Canada and Australia (Loudon, 1992).

Social integration

Living as an integrated member of the local community, partici-pating in local activities with the general population.

However, multiprofessional and interagency work has always been impeded by variations in terminology both nationally and internationally (Table 1.4 and see Chapter 2). An attempt to reduce frequency of change in terminology was made by the American Association on Mental Retardation in 1973. When it revised its definitions, it also defined aims for future develop-ment and standardisation of a common base for classification of terminology.

Table 1.4 Development of definitions

Late 1800s USA	Wilbur's categories
	Simulative idiots: could be prepared for ordinary duties and enjoyments of humanity
	Higher-grade idiots: would attend common schools to be qualified for civil usefulness and social happiness
	Lower-grade idiots: could become decent in their habits, educated in simple occupations, capable of self-support under judicious management in their own families, or in public industrial institutions for adult idiots
	Incurables: aim to achieve some education (Trent, 1994)
1921 USA (AAMR)	American Association on Mental Retardation (AAMR) published the first edition of the *Manual on Terminology and Classification in Mental Retardation*
1973 USA (AAMR)	'Mental retardation refers to significantly subaverage general intellectual functioning existing concurrently with deficits in adaptive behaviour and manifested during the developmental period' (Grossman, 1973)
1980 WHO	*International Classification of Impairments, Disabilities and Handicaps*
	Impairment: musculoskeletal abnormality and organ misfunction
	Disability: the resultant functional ability
	Handicap: the disadvantage arising from impairment or disability
	Intellectual impairments include intelligence, memory and thought, but exclude language and learning
	Impairments of intelligence include: 'disturbances of the rate and degree of development of cognitive functions, such as perception, attention,

Table 1.4 (contd)

	memory, and thinking, and their deterioration as a result of pathological processes' Mental retardation Mild: IQ: 50–70 – individuals who can acquire practical skills and functional reading and arithmetic abilities with special education, and who can be guided towards social conformity Moderate: IQ: 35–49 – individuals who can learn simple communication, elementary health and safety habits, and simple manual skills, but do not progress in functional reading or arithmetic Severe: IQ: 20–34 – individuals who can benefit from systematic habit training Profound: IQ: < 20 – individuals who may respond to skill training in the use of legs, hands, and jaws (WHO, 1980)
1983 USA (AAMR)	Definition of mental retardation (Scheerenberger, 1987)
1983 UK (England and Wales)	'Mental impairment': 'a state of arrested or incomplete development of mind which includes a significant impairment of intelligence and social functioning and is associated with abnormally aggressive or seriously irresponsible conduct on the part of the person concerned' (Mental Health Act for England and Wales 1983)
1983 UK (Scotland)	Mental handicap replaced mental deficiency but had the same general meaning (Mental Health (Scotland) Act 1984)
1992 WHO	*International Classification of Impairments, Disabilities and Handicaps* ICD-10: mental retardation accepted terminology, but definition updated (see current terminology in Chapters 2 and 3)
1992 USA (AAMR)	Mental retardation: accepted terminology but definition updated (see current terminology in Chapters 2 and 3)
1994 USA (APA)	American Psychiatric Association DSM-IV: mental retardation: accepted terminology (see current terminology in Chapter 2)
1995 UK	Learning disability accepted terminology. Used generally to mean mental retardation: impaired intelligence and impaired social functioning . . . a reduced ability to understand new or complex information and learn new skills and a reduced ability to cope independently. Learning disability is a condition that starts before adulthood and has a lasting effect on development (Department of Health, 1995). Medically used in conjunction with ICD-10, AAMR or DSM-IV

AAMR, American Association on Mental Retardation; ICD-10, *International Classification of Disease*, 10th revision (WHO, 1992); DSM-IV, *Diagnostic and Statistical Manual of Mental Disorders*, 4th edn (APA, 1994).

Acceleration of community care

Acceleration towards community care was further assisted by the UN in 1973 with the 'Declaration on the Rights of Disabled People' (1975). It included the following among its 13 statements:

Disabled persons have the inherent right to respect for their human dignity. Disabled persons, whatever the origin, nature and seriousness of their handicaps and disabilities, have the same fundamental rights as their fellow-citizens of the same age, which implies first and foremost the right to enjoy a decent life, as normal and as full as possible.

Progress could be seen by developments in both private and charitably run facilities and in the long-stay hospitals. For example, in the Republic of Ireland, St Michael's House, Dublin, was extending its services to: support learning-disabled children in integrated education, provide appropriate further education through developmental day centres, give back-up support and training for clients in open employment, and provide residential services for very small groups in ordinary homes. Also in Dublin, Stewart's Hospital began to develop: clinical services with family support and respite for children and adults, courses for sports and leisure, and an introduction to additional skills of parenting, budgeting and advice on nutrition. Their residential numbers decreased and their services both on the campus and leased in the city became more available to clients in the community.

In the UK, the National Development Group and Development Team for the Mentally Handicapped were established to facilitate progress from hospitals to the community. A series of consultation documents have continued to be issued and Parliamentary Bills passed. These are listed in Table 1.2.

Community care was also stimulated by:

- Increasing awareness among families
- Growth of voluntary organisations
- Realignment of funding from Central Government
- Increased involvement of social services departments
- The Warnock Report (1978) on special educational needs:
  - a named link with relevant professionals and parents became 'key worker' system for adults
  - voluntary and pressure groups led to campaigns for related issues for adults

Development of health services working practice

The unexpected opportunities given to many people with learning disabilities meant that health-care staff had to learn how to work closely with people whose background was socially, and not medically, orientated. It was essential to find work space. It was also essential to ensure that social services and voluntary agency staff understood that appropriate equipment supplied by therapists was necessary to enhance quality of life and was not reinforcement of a disability.

In 1977 the numbers of therapists working with learning-disabled people in England had risen to:

- Occupational therapists 113 (helpers 484)
- Physiotherapists 103 (helpers 62)
- Speech therapists 32
- Chiropodists 23
- Other therapists 269 (decrease)
- Psychologists 140 (DHSS, 1987)

The clients' view

While reformers were working hard to integrate people with learning disabilities into normal society, they themselves were not necessarily acquiescent of the principle. At a National (American) Conference on Normalisation and Contemporary Practice in Mental Retardation in 1980, representatives of the People First International, an organisation of disabled persons, stated that:

> . . . consumers need a group identity. They need a culture, a history and their own heroes. They need each other so that they're able to develop what the rest of society has. . . . Groups give a special meaning and identity.

They saw themselves as any other minority group in the USA and normalisation as a way in which they would become isolated within the 'normal' community (Scheerenberger, 1987). Table 1.5 shows how Wolfensberger, one of the main proponents of normalisation (Wolfensberger and Thomas, 1983), attempted to answer their concerns by gradually redefining the concept of normalisation.

Provision of services in the community

Between 1967 and 1982, the number of residents in large institutions in the UK fell by over 40%. In 1983, the All Wales Strategy was published. This emphasised development of community services underpinned by the principles of normalisation and has been referred to in many studies.

By 1987 it was recognised that (DHSS, 1987):

- Most people with learning disability lived at home.
- Of the few children not living at home, most were older and had profound learning disabilities.

Table 1.5 Normalisation and beyond

1959	Danish Act of Parliament: 'Whatever facilities are open to all other citizens must, in principle, also be available to the mentally retarded'
1969	Bank Mikkelsen and Bengt Nirje: '. . . making available to the mentally retarded patterns and conditions of everyday life which are as close as possible to the norms and patterns of the mainstream of society'
1972	Wolfensberger: 'Utilization of means which are as culturally normative as possible, in order to establish and/or maintain personal behaviours and characteristics which are as culturally normal as possible'
1981	O'Brien's five essential accomplishments for quality of life: community presence, choice, competence, respect and community participation (Tyne and O'Brien, 1981)
1983	Wolfensberger redefined normalisation as Social Role Valorisation (SRV): 'The enablement, establishment, enhancement, maintenance, and/or defence of valued social roles for people – particularly for those at value risk – by using, as much as possible, culturally valued means' (Wolfensberger and Thomas, 1983)
1987	Kristiansen and Ness's (1987) additional accomplishments for quality of life: expression of individuality and experience of continuity in one's own life
1992	Wolfensberger differentiated between valuing a person for him- or herself and ensuring that that person filled a valued role

- Multiprofessional 'community mental handicap teams' were developing.
- Good community services could improve quality of life for individuals and their families, and help to ensure that residential care was only for those with greatest need.
- There were concerns:
  - regarding the level of help and priority for people with learning disability by generic services
  - regarding respective roles of health and local authority services in service provision
- Response to concerns had been made by:
  - increased requests for specialist staff to support generic staff in the community and to work directly with people with learning disability and their families
  - some social services departments employing health-care staff
  - some learning disability nurses undertaking domiciliary work from a hospital base

These trends and the first report by the Development Team for the Mentally Handicapped were endorsed by White Papers for England and Scotland in 1988. They also recognised that education of the general public, families of people with learning disability and health service providers would be required, and that hospital residents would need to be re-educated. Appropriate community facilities and resources would have to be in place before any changes occurred.

Caring for People (Department of Health, 1989) placed responsibility for assessing and providing for people's needs with local authorities. They could provide services themselves or contract or buy them in from other agencies. Voluntary organisations and families would assume some responsibilities previously provided by Social Services. Residential care was recommended for people with special medical or nursing needs.

By 1993, it was reported from a joint meeting of the Forum on Learning Disabilities and the Centre for Physiotherapy Research that physiotherapists in England and Wales were starting to join multiprofessional teams. From this meeting, 533 were identified and the survey showed that, of the 427 who responded, about one-third were working in a hospital, one-third from a community base, and the remainder from day centres or a variety of settings. They tended to be experienced senior clinicians who had additional areas of specialisation (Partridge, 1994).

Consultation

Problems of interpreting views of people with learning disability about their future needs continued to be discussed. The necessity for accurate and acceptable terminology, which did not reflect professional or ideological bias, was highlighted in meetings organised by the British Institute of Mental Handicap and the Department of Health (Harris, 1991). Cullen (1991) reflected the dichotomy that can arise and the problems of over-simplification. He suggested that 'Normalisation and social role valorisation had suffered at the hands of those who yearn for a simple approach to life' and quoted Mesibov (1990):

> Some of the commonly held tenets of normalisation are vague and unattainable; inappropriate practices are often carried out in the name of normalisation, for example, discouraging contact between people with disabilities; many advocates of normalisation have been over zealous and this over zealousness has resulted in distrust and antagonism

Such confusion raised concerns among health-care professionals about community facilities for the management and treatment of physical disabilities of residents leaving long-stay hospitals.

These concerns were confirmed by data based on 108 Community Care Plans in 1993–94 throughout England (Turner, Sweeney and Hayes,

1995). Proposed community facilities had not been established and resources were still needed for long-stay hospitals, for example:

- Widespread plans for development of day-care provision including: employment, training, respite care, education, leisure and advocacy.
- Only three plans anticipated completion of resettlement by 1993.
- Average numbers of long-stay residents were 3.6/10 000 population.
- Independent sector had increased provision in at least half of the areas. Provision by nursing homes and hostels together equalled the total of group homes and ordinary houses.

In Scotland, where hospital reprovisioning was progressing more slowly, *Recommendations of the Future of Mental Handicap Hospitals* (Loudon, 1992) appeared to provide answers to many of the concerns. These included:

- Facilities with high standards should be available before hospitals closed.
- Individuals and their families should be involved in a pre-transfer assessment of needs.
- Guidelines should be issued for residential care to meet the special clinical needs of people with mental handicap and serious behaviour problems and/or major psychiatric illness and/or multiple handicap.
- All health boards are expected to ensure access to a full range of services.
- The Social Work Department, Education Department and employers are expected to provide opportunities for recreation, education and high-quality work.

In 1995, the UK Government published a strategy *The Health of the Nation* (England and Wales) and publicly adopted the term 'learning disabilities'. A *Strategy for People with Learning Disabilities* was accompanied by a booklet specifically for the client group (Department of Health, 1995). This defined 'learning disability' (see Table 1.4) and listed related problems including: obesity, poor cardiovascular fitness, and behavioural, psychiatric, orthopaedic and mobility problems.

Restructuring of the NHS in the late 1990s led to concerns about allocation of health service resources for people with learning disabilities. However, it also alerted relevant committees to their needs. *Signposts for Success* (Lindsey, 1998) stated that community learning disability health services should:

- Offer a wide range of coordinated support and advice for people with learning disabilities, their families and carers.
- Provide therapeutic services.
- Offer training for people with learning disabilities, their families, carers and staff of other organisations.
- Work closely with other agencies.
- Help the development of good practice in relation to health promotion and health care.
- Facilitate access to general health services.

In practice, these aims have been partially met, but coordination of services is still the greatest stumbling block:

- Development of multiprofessional teams has improved management of physical disabilities in people with learning disabilities (see Chapter 5).
- Well-planned joint working provides new opportunities for effective treatment and management.
- Care in the community has provided opportunities for training parents and carers individually in handling older people with profound disabilities.
- Use of community facilities enables adults with learning disabilities to carry their treatment and management into everyday life, but closure of specifically designed physiotherapy treatment areas and hydrotherapy pools can limit the range of treatment offered to adults with profound physical and learning disabilities.
- Parents and carers of people with profound multiple disabilities have difficulties working with health and social services to find day, respite and future long-term care.
- General health services do not always have sufficiently long appointment times to accommodate people with learning disabilities.
- The move from day centres to individual packages of care involves time-consuming arrangements for therapy sessions, increased travelling time for therapists and reduced client contact time.
- Attempts to include people with learning disabilities only in 'normal' community activities deprives them of participating in therapy-led peer group work.

The Health Act 1999 has sought to improve coordination of services for everyone in the UK. It has given rise to the 'Partnership in Action' agenda which encourages improvement of services through flexible interagency work, a practice of seamless working that has long been attempted on an ad hoc basis for the benefit of people with learning disabilities. However, this Act proposes support of local flexible working practices by allowing agencies working together on specific packages of service to pool their budgets. Further discussions are continuing at central and local levels. People with learning disabilities may also be affected by the Arbuthnot Report in Scotland, which reflects the need for redistribution of the health budget to take account of unique problems found in scattered rural populations.

In some areas of the UK, it has been suggested that delivery of services for people with learning disabilities might be progressed along the lines of Western Australia's 'Local Area Co-ordination'. In this model, local area coordinators hold a budget from which direct payments can be made to clients and their families to select and pay for their own services (The Disability Services Commission – Western Australia, 1998).

The ideals that developed into the principles of normalisation and inclusion of people with learning disability in everyday activities have developed into locally accepted codes of practice and relevant legislative provision with enabling powers. Few of these ideals have, however, been translated into laws specifically for the benefit of people with learning disability.

Ethics and the UK law

All professionals are ethically bound by their code of conduct which includes confidentiality in verbal, written and photographic records.

A professional who delegates tasks to an assistant has a professional obligation and duty of care to ensure that that member of staff is individually trained (Parry and Vass, 1997; Saunders, 1997a, 1997b). Carers should be requested only to undertake specific areas of client treatment or management and should be trained for that task. A written record should be kept of what has been taught and a carer should not be expected to instruct other care staff. Guidelines for delegation of tasks are published by the relevant professional bodies (Chartered Society of Physiotherapy, 1996b; College of Occupational Therapists, 1996; United Kingdom Central Council for Nursing, Midwifery and Health Visiting, 1998a). Manual handling should be undertaken in accordance with the Health Services Advisory Committee (1998), the Chartered Society of Physiotherapy (1998) and statutory training for the relevant hospital or community trust and social work services. A risk assessment should be undertaken for individual clients who require any assistance in moving. This should be area specific and take account of the differing skills of carers. The 'Care Plan' should allow for changes in the client's ability.

Nurses and physiotherapists, who of necessity see clients unclothed, and speech and language therapists, who are in close communication with clients, should be aware of the signs of child and elder abuse, and the procedures to take in cases of concern.

All professionals should be aware that people with learning disability have a legal right to assistance from an advocate who is not involved with them in a professional capacity and can speak independently on their behalf (Disabled Persons Act 1986).

All staff working in multiprofessional teams will be indirectly involved with legal aspects such as the holding power, compulsory admission, informal admission (Mental Health Act for England and Wales 1983) and respite care (Chronically Sick and Disabled Persons Act 1970).

Treatment and management of physical disabilities in people with learning disability are most commonly affected by consent to treatment, and restraint.

Consent to treatment

Before commencing treatment with a new client, it is always wise to consult with medical and nursing staff who have a greater knowledge of the client's ability to give consent and when possible with parents or carers:

- Consent to medical treatment by an adult with learning disability is valid only if they understand the significance of the consent. An ability to understand cause and effect of simple exercise treatment is not indicative of understanding the significance of proposed surgery and hospitalisation (see Chapter 6).
- In Scotland, the only person who can give consent for an adult with a learning disability is a tutor dative. Parents may not give consent unless they have been appointed tutor dative. There is no comparable system in England.
- For hospital residents, treatment may be given with a second medical opinion.
- Treatment may be given without consent if it is either life-saving or reversible and immediately necessary to prevent serious deterioration, alleviate serious suffering or prevent the patient from being dangerous to himself or others (Mental Health Act 1983, Mental Health (Scotland) Act 1984).

Care must be taken to ensure that people who have learning disabilities are not denied the right to necessary medical treatment.

Restraint

> There is an underlying presumption in the law that it is wrong to interfere with
> the actions of another adult without lawful excuse.
>
> McKay (1998)

The question repeatedly arises as to whether seating harnesses and other
positioning equipment used by people with physical and learning disabilities constitute restraint. There is no specific piece of legislation setting out
what is lawful in a care setting and what is not. It would be wise therefore
to examine the case for each piece of equipment against the criteria of
whether it breaches any statutory provision or any principle of criminal or
civil law.

Criminal law

• Assault
• Cruel and unnatural treatment
• Unjust imprisonment

Civil law

• Assault
• Unlawful detention/wrongful apprehension/wrongful imprisonment
• Force and fear

This may be answered through the following questions:

• Is the individual's physical condition liable to deteriorate if the equip-
  ment is not used?
• Is the individual's general health improved by use of the equipment?
• Does the equipment help to relieve pain?
• Does the equipment enable greater mobility?
• Does the equipment enable greater communication?
• Does the equipment improve overall quality of life?

Seating harnesses are **not** designed to prevent overactive people or
people who wander from moving out of a chair.

Conclusion

Ideologies, theories and practices have both enhanced and reduced the
lives of people with learning disabilities who also have physical disabili-

ties. For example, fear and protection of them led to segregation. This deprived many people of progressive treatments and of recognition of neurological impairments and sensory disabilities in people with mild mental retardation. Normalisation and the term 'learning disability', used in the UK, have assisted development of self-respect and opportunities for many people. Supported flats and small group homes, which the principle has generated, enable people to live in the community but need careful management to allow opportunity for everyday exercise and freedom of movement. Proponents of inclusion need to recognise the value of therapy-led group work with the clients' own peer group, as well as inclusion in local activities with the general community.

Inconsistent terminology still leads to misunderstanding among health, educational and social service professionals who are not directly involved in this area, and between colleagues internationally.

Work to enable people with learning disabilities to lead an increasingly full and active life is being progressed by politicians, educationalists, social services and health-care professionals today. It is presently undertaken through person-centred planning and inclusion, multiprofessional and interagency work and self-advocacy. Management and treatment of physical disability sustained in conjunction with learning disabilities between birth and 16–21 years (Accardo and Capute, 1998) or acquired later in life are in accordance with the standards laid down by the individual professional bodies. Aims of treatment are achieved whilst working in a variety of socially accepted settings and while encouraging all people with learning disabilities to enjoy a healthy lifestyle. Treatment and management of their physical disabilities will continue to develop in conjunction with the increased life expectancy of people with learning disabilities (Fryers, 1997; Herge and Campbell, 1998).

CHAPTER 2

Learning disability, aetiology and associated conditions

JEANETTE RENNIE AND MARK STERRICK

This chapter describes the classification and aetiology of learning disability and gives a brief overview of associated neurological conditions that present with physical disabilities or impinge on physical ability. These include cerebral palsy, motor delay and epilepsy. This chapter does not include normal development or neuroanatomy.

The three internationally recognised methods of classification and the 'two group' theory have been described because reference is made to them throughout clients' medical records and team meetings, and in the relevant literature.

In the UK, the term 'learning disability' (Department of Health, 1995) is used to mean 'mental retardation' (WHO, 1992, 1993) or 'mental handicap'.

It should not be confused with the US definition of learning disability, which in the UK is known as 'specific learning difficulties' or 'specific learning disabilities' and includes problems such as dyslexia (see Chapter 1).

Prevalence

Estimated prevalence ratios are mild-to-moderate 30/1000, severe 3/1000 and profound 0.5/1000 (Fraser and Green, 1991). However, studies show that these can vary from year to year, by age and time and by socio-economic group (Murphy et al., 1998). It was estimated that, by 1998, the largest cohort would be aged 30–34 years. Records for mild 'mental retardation' vary greatly between populations, largely because of cultural differences that preclude standardisation of data collection (Fryers, 1997).

Classification

Defining the concept of learning disability has frequently caused misunderstanding between professionals from different theoretical backgrounds. Some social services, education authorities and voluntary agencies in the UK aim to dispense with any definition or classification, regarding it as a form of labelling and stigma. However, a definition and criteria are necessary to guard against incorrect assumptions and to ensure that appropriate treatment and management can be offered to the individual and that research can be undertaken for the benefit of all people with learning disabilities. It should not be used as a label, which assumes that a child or adult cannot develop further. In fact, the American Association on Mental Retardation (AAMR) considered that an individual could meet the recognised criteria for 'mental retardation' at one time in life and not another, as a result of alterations in intellectual functioning, adaptive behaviours and the expectations of society (Grossman, 1973). Current methods of classification go a long way to clarifying the complex heterogeneous group of conditions causing and associated with learning disability.

The criteria for 'mental retardation' used in three internationally recognised classifications *International Classification of Disease*, 10th revision (ICD-10: WHO, 1992, 1993), AAMR classification (Luckasson et al., 1992) and *Diagnostic and Statistical Manual of Mental Disorders*, 4th edn (DSM-IV: American Psychiatric Association, 1994) are:

- Intellectual impairment (IQ <70) (AAMR 70–75)
- Diminished social adaptive functioning
- Onset during the developmental period (usually regarded as no later than 18 years)

The level of severity is broadly classified by ICD-10 and DSM-IV as IQ <70 mild, <50 moderate, <30 severe or profound (see, for example, Muir, 1998). AAMR does not refer to levels of severity (Luckasson et al., 1992).

ICD-10 states that mental retardation is a condition of arrested or incomplete development of mind, which is particularly characterised by impairment of skills manifested during the developmental period, which contributes to the overall level of intelligence. It can occur with or without other mental or physical disorders. ICD-10 has been used, and is expanded on, in Chapter 3.

Both AAMR and DSM-IV use a multiaxial method of classification. In 1992 AAMR incorporated this approach by changing its 1973 definition (see Chapter 1) to require 'significant delay in two or more of ten areas of adaptive functioning' which include 'daily living skills, self care and communication' (Luckasson et al., 1992).

DSM-IV is best defined by use of its guidelines (adapted from Muir, 1998):

- Axis I: clinical disorders and conditions including specific learning disorders.
- Axis II: personality disorders and mental retardation (UK: learning disability).
- Axis III: aetiology and related general medical problems.
- Axis IV: psychosocial and environmental problems.
- Axis V: the global assessment of adaptive functioning.

In research, DSM-IV is used at least as frequently throughout the UK as the ICD-10.

Causes

Learning disability is a heterogeneous group of disorders. Although it is frequently of unknown aetiology, it also includes organic causes, such as genetic and chromosomal abnormality and infection, and trauma that affects the developing brain (Fryers and Russell, 1997; Murphy et al., 1998).

Before the introduction of the 'axis system', the causes of learning disability were divided into two groups predisposing to mild or severe learning disability. Mild and severe learning disability were based on distribution of the IQ within the general population. This method was used as the primary basis for further investigations. IQ alone is no longer considered to be an adequate basis for continuing investigation. The 'two group' theory, however, still gives a good overview of causes and risk factors of learning disability and for that reason is described in this chapter.

IQ 50–70 (mild)

Over 50% of people with an IQ of 50–70 have no known organic cause, 15–20% are caused by perinatal hypoxia, 10% are congenital abnormalities and 5% are defined genetic syndromes including trisomies (Muir, 1998). Accardo and Capute (1998) estimated that only 24% of children in this group have a known organic cause. Learning disability with no known organic cause is referred to as 'sociocultural', 'psychological' or 'having a familial or cultural basis'. A study by Murphy et al. (1998) on mental retardation described the underlying basis for this as 'risk factors'. 'Risk factors' do not necessarily lead to learning disability but increase the possibility of it occurring. Fourteen studies were cited which, between them, produced the following risk factors:

- More boys than girls have learning disability (1.4 : 1).
- Low socioeconomic status measured by: parental educational level, family income, father's occupation, quality of home learning environment, or a combination of two or more factors.
- In the USA, there appeared to be an association between non-white children and learning disability, but at least half of this could be accounted for by socioeconomic factors.

IQ <50 (moderate and severe)

The smaller group who have an IQ of less than 50 (10–20% of the learning-disabled population) usually have an organic cause:

- Prenatal: genetic, maternal behaviour during pregnancy, intrauterine infection.
- Perinatal: infections, asphyxia, low birthweight.
- Postnatal: environmental contaminants, infections, injury.

In this group, the largest proportion of known causes is genetic conditions – more than 500 known conditions (Murphy et al., 1998).

People with an IQ of 50–70 and no recognised organic cause for their learning disability tended to be offered fewer investigations than any other group of people with learning disability. However, recent studies reviewed and reported in Accardo and Capute (1998), Muir (1998) and Murphy et al. (1998), suggested that organic factors could also be present in this group. This caused Accardo and Capute to recommend careful investigations for children with developmental delay and mild as well as severe learning disability.

The broad-based multiaxial system used by AAMR and DSM-IV gives greater opportunities for full investigation than the 'two group' theory which is based purely on level of IQ.

Associated conditions

Conditions associated with learning disability include developmental delay, cerebral palsy, epilepsy, and behavioural and psychiatric disorders. Many of the syndromes and associated conditions require direct physiotherapy intervention and multiprofessional management for physical disability. Epilepsy and psychiatric and behavioural disorders can impinge on that treatment and management. Conditions relating to old age may be apparent as early as the mid to late 40s (Herge and Campbell, 1998). Anecdotal evidence reports that fractures resulting from osteoporosis are on the increase.

Motor delay, developmental coordination disorder and cerebral palsy are described only briefly in this chapter, because a considerable amount of literature is easily accessible to health, Social Services and educational professionals elsewhere, for example, Levitt (1977), Bobath and Bobath (1984), Illingworth (1987), and Cogher et al. (1992).

Epilepsy is described in more detail because it is a subject that is rarely studied by therapists or nurses during their general training. It is the most common serious neurological condition in the general population, with a prevalence of between 0.5% and 1% (Goodridge and Shorvon, 1983). However, in the learning-disabled population, a higher proportion of people have epilepsy and often their condition is of a severe and intractable nature. Specifically, in learning disability, epilepsy has a prevalence of 21% in those who do not have a concomitant cerebral palsy and 50% in those who do (Richardson et al., 1979; Kerr et al., 1996). As such, epilepsy has an important impact on the physical, social and emotional well-being of people with learning disability as a whole. Moreover, it has important repercussions, at a 'local' level, for carers and families of sufferers and, at a more general level, for communities and society itself. Yet, epilepsy is often 'hidden from sight' because of the perceived, and actual, stigma that has a habit of accompanying it. It is important, therefore, for health professionals to realise that they have an essential role in supporting individuals with epilepsy, their families and their carers, as well as in educating the wider public.

Genetic and chromosomal causes, behavioural and psychiatric disorders, specific developmental delays, and their treatments are described in Chapter 3.

Motor delay

Simple motor delay is delayed attainment of motor milestones such as sitting, standing and walking. Muscle tone is low and there may be associated congenital heart defects and chronic respiratory conditions. It can be caused by the organic and 'sociocultural' causes of learning disability or by sensory and perceptual defects and apraxias. It is most easily recognised in people with Down's syndrome.

Developmental coordination disorder

The term has been used synonymously with motor delay, perceptuomotor dysfunction and developmental dyspraxia. One school of thought suggests that it is caused by motor delay. More commonly, it is thought to result from damage to the sensory system – vestibular, visual or proprioceptive or a combination of two or more (Willoughby and Polatajko, 1995). It is not thought to be caused by any other physical disability. It manifests itself as delayed motor coordination which is below the intellectual ability of the child or young adult. Although it is seen in children with average or higher than average intellectual ability, it can also be present in people with learning disability.

Cerebral palsy

Cerebral palsy (CP) caused by brain damage around the time of birth is subclassified as follows:

- spastic
- dyskinetic
- ataxic
- mixed.

Terminology for disorders arising from damage to the basal ganglia has evolved over the past thirty years. This is primarily because CP now tends to be global rather than specific to any one area of the brain. Children with purely athetoid CP are rarely seen and so this category has been replaced by dyskinesia (literally, difficult or abnormal movement). Dystonia (including chorea and athetosis) is sometimes used as a subdivision of dyskinesia or as an independent category.

These subclassifications relate to the most severely damaged area of the brain. The distribution of spasticity is frequently described as being hemiplegic when one side of the body is affected, quadriplegic when all four limbs are involved to the same degree or diplegic when lower limbs are more involved than the upper limbs. Some authorities describe double hemiplegia as involving the upper limbs more than the lower limbs (Minear, 1956; Ingram, 1964; Levitt, 1977; Gage, 1991; Cogher et al., 1992).

It is a non-progressive condition that affects normal developmental reactions, postural reflexes, muscle tone and motor development. These in turn affect growth and structure of muscle and bone (O'Dwyer et al., 1989; Gage, 1991) which recent studies suggest lead to muscle fibre atrophy and changes in their contractile ability. Symptoms of the condition change as:

- the injured brain grows
- the individual grows in height and weight
- external forces react on the body

- living and working conditions change and individuals wish to participate in the same activities as their non-CP peer group.

There is a very high potential for contractures and deformity in spastic or mixed CP which frequently require special equipment, orthosis and orthopaedic intervention (see Chapters 4, 9 and 10). Studies are also currently being undertaken to validate findings that neuromuscular electrical stimulation (NMES) is effective in strengthening hypotrophic muscle and therefore assists in prevention of deformity and reduced mobility (Croal, 1999). The potential for deformity and abnormal muscle tone means that eating and drinking disorders are closely associated with CP.

Epilepsy

Epilepsy may be simply defined as a tendency to recurrent seizures. It is not a disease in itself, but merely a symptom of some underlying problem with the brain's ability to regulate its electrical discharge processes on an intermittent, brief and usually spontaneous basis.

Given the right stimulus, everyone is capable of having a seizure but this does not mean that everyone has epilepsy. About 1 in 20 people will have a single, non-febrile seizure at some time in his or her life, but only half of these people will go on to have another seizure (Goodridge and Shorvon, 1983). To qualify as epilepsy, there must be recurrent seizures. Someone withdrawing quickly from a chronic and excessive consumption of alcohol may have several withdrawal seizures over time, but this, again, does not warrant a diagnosis of epilepsy because there is no intrinsic brain disturbance conferring an automatic tendency to recurrent seizures. The seizures are provoked by the withdrawal of alcohol and will settle when the person's body has adjusted to the change. In comparison, recurrent seizures arising from a damaged area of the brain as a consequence of low oxygen concentration at birth will be regarded as epilepsy, because the cause is intrinsic to the brain and not external to it.

In general, in 61% of people with epilepsy, the underlying cause of the tendency to recurrent seizures is not identifiable and this situation is often referred to as cryptogenic (or, sometimes and erroneously, idiopathic) epilepsy (Sander et al., 1990). However, in epilepsy specifically affecting people with learning disability, the underlying problem is usually more readily identifiable because it often arises as part of a neurological disorder. This is referred to as symptomatic epilepsy. For example, epilepsy often accompanies cerebral palsy in the context of learning disability. Table 2.1 reveals the causes of epilepsy from a learning disability perspective. It will be noted that genetic conditions play an important part

Table 2.1 Causes of epileptic seizures from a learning disability perspective

Causes	Examples and subdivisions
Genetic causes	Metabolic disorders, e.g. phenylketonuria
	'Structural', e.g. tuberous sclerosis
	Some primary generalised epilepsies
	Mitochondrial disorders
Developmental disorders	For example, arteriovenous malformations
Intrauterine and perinatal	
injury including anoxia	
Infection	For example, encephalitis
Trauma	
Vascular	
Tumour	
Dementia and neuro-	
degenerative disorder	
Metabolic	For example, hypoglycaemia
Toxic	For example, alcohol

Abridged from Betts (1998).

in the aetiology of learning disability epilepsy, and certain syndromes are almost invariably associated with learning disability, e.g. West's syndrome, Lennox–Gastaut syndrome and severe myoclonic epilepsy in infancy.

The *International Classification of Seizures* (International League Against Epilepsy, 1981) divides seizures principally into generalised and partial. Generalised attacks essentially involve the whole of the cerebrum in the epileptic discharge, whereas partial attacks involve an area that is somewhere short of this. When the electrical discharge of a partial seizure remains relatively well circumscribed to one lobe, the person is likely to retain consciousness and this is classified as a simple partial seizure. However, where the discharge has begun to spread, perhaps to involve the whole of one lobe or even two lobes, the consciousness becomes impaired (but not necessarily lost) and this is classified as a complex partial seizure (one form being what is referred to as 'temporal lobe epilepsy'). Partial seizures can take many forms depending on the lobes of the brain that are affected, for example, a frontal lobe discharge may give some form of 'motor' seizure incorporating a series of jerks affecting one arm. A partial seizure can spread so widely that it may ultimately affect the whole cerebrum and this is then referred to as a secondarily generalised seizure. However, generalised seizures may begin anew and do not always appear to be dependent on spread of discharge from a partial focus. These attacks are therefore known as primary generalised seizures. Generalised seizures are further classified into absence (typical and atypical), myoclonic, clonic, tonic, tonic–clonic and atonic seizures. The hallmark distinction between a partial and generalised seizure is that in a generalised seizure there is a loss of consciousness, which is usually sudden. All seizure types usually begin spontaneously and end equally spontaneously, but occasionally an episode may develop into a situation involving the onset of serial seizures and status epilepticus. The latter is a medical emergency and people with learning disability and epilepsy have a higher tendency to experience this type of progression.

People who have epilepsy within the context of learning disability are especially likely to suffer from complex partial seizures. However, it can be difficult to recognise these because of the presence of concomitant neuropsychological problems in people with severe learning disabilities and developmental disorders. In addition, behavioural difficulties and mood disturbances may be genuinely associated with seizure episodes, but may be mistaken for separate psychiatric conditions and treated erroneously. Therefore, in order to achieve an accurate diagnosis, it is essential to have a suitably detailed eyewitness account of the attacks under question. However, it is also important for carers and health professionals to have an appreciation of the effects that seizures may have on a person's lifestyle as well as the effects that a person's lifestyle may have on his or her seizures.

Seizures can be physically, socially and emotionally disabling for the sufferer, both acutely and chronically, but it should not be forgotten that parents, spouses and carers may also be similarly affected because of the impact of caring for someone with intractable epilepsy on top of a learning disability. In addition, the effects of medication may interfere with an individual's ability to concentrate, and to learn and perform certain tasks. Some medications such as phenobarbitone (phenobarbital), carbamazepine and the diazepam-type drugs have sedative properties, and close monitoring and adjustment of doses may be necessary, especially during initial titration of these drugs, if an individual is not to be further handicapped by adverse drug effects. On the other hand, lamotrigine may have a mood-lifting effect and may help to increase concentration and learning ability. Occasionally, these medications may cause significant mood and behavioural disturbances in people with learning disabilities. It is therefore important for doctors to adopt a philosophy of 'start low–go slow' which ensures that drugs are introduced at the lowest practicable dose and are increased in small increments. This seems to be especially important in some people with Down's syndrome who appear to be more sensitive to these medications. Often, combinations of medications are necessary to increase the chances of control, but these must be carefully monitored because an additional drug load may exacerbate toxicity with little further to offer by way of seizure control. Therefore, assessment of side effects from medication is very important, especially where there is the use of polypharmacy. However, it is occasionally difficult to assess the efficacy of medications because the recording of seizure frequency and type can be inadequate given the difficulties that some people with learning disabilities have with communication and expression (see Chapter 6). Further, non-epileptic seizures are not uncommon in people with learning disability and can cause protracted difficulties in the diagnostic and management processes.

A person's lifestyle circumstances may also have an effect on his or her epilepsy control. Thus, alcohol, 'late nights' and stress may have significant adverse effects. Physical stresses by way of infections and other medical diseases may have a drastic but short-lived effect on the seizure rate. However, emotional stress is also significant. Some activities that may be expected to be pleasurable, such as going to a party or even going on holiday, may be stressful enough to provoke extra seizures. In addition, being pushed 'to the limit' physically, emotionally or educationally, by well-meaning but over-zealous parents, carers or professionals, may have a triggering effect on seizures for people with a learning disability. The concomitant use of psychotropic medication for a variety of psychological and psychiatric conditions (not uncommon in learning disability) may also lower the seizure threshold, as may a lack of compliance with medication, for whatever reason.

As far as prognosis is concerned, generally speaking, up to 80% of people with epilepsy will become seizure free on medication (Betts, 1998). The other 20% will continue to display seizures despite medication, but will probably have had some benefit from it by way of a reduction in seizure frequency and/or a reduction in the intensity of individual seizures. Unfortunately, many people with epilepsy within the context of learning disability will fall into this continuing seizure group. Although they do achieve benefits from their antiepileptic medications, many will never be totally free from seizures despite best efforts at manipulating the medication. In turn, these people appear to be at an increased risk for disorders of cognitive function such as memory impairments or attentional difficulties, although significant problems appear to affect only a small minority. There are, in addition, techniques that can help to reduce the impact of a weak memory on daily functioning. In recent times, there has been a rekindling of interest in the use of neurosurgery for intractable epilepsies and every 2 years or so we see the introduction of new, and sometimes better, antiepileptic drugs. Also of importance is the increase in death rate among people with epilepsy. Most deaths in epilepsy result from the underlying cause (Klenerman et al., 1993). Some deaths may result from trauma sustained during a seizure or from accidental drowning in the bath at the time of a seizure. However, a small number of people with epilepsy are found to have died unexpectedly. The mechanism of death in these cases is uncertain and postmortem examinations often fail to demonstrate a clear cause. It has been postulated that these deaths may have been caused by arrhythmia-producing effects of intraictal anoxia on the heart, although this is an area that has yet to be fully researched.

Much can be done to improve the physical, emotional and social well-being and status of people with learning disability and ongoing epilepsy. Health-care professionals do not have a monopoly in this area, but they do have an important role, and their actions and attitudes towards people with epilepsy and their carers will often inform the perceptions and reactions of the wider community.

Conclusion

Learning disability can be identified only when the criteria of intellectual impairment, diminished social adaptive functioning and onset before the age of 18 years are met.

The cause may be organic or unknown, but recent studies indicate that organic factors are present more frequently than had previously been realised. Where the cause is of an organic nature, it is likely that associated conditions will be present.

The associated neurological conditions described in this chapter may present with physical disabilities as in motor delay, developmental coordination disorder and cerebral palsy or, as the learning disability itself. They may impinge on the treatment and management of a physical disability, as in epilepsy.

Prevalence ratios show that the number of people with learning disability, compared with those without, is not large. However, the numbers are still substantial and the criteria and associated conditions show that an individual with learning disability is liable to need considerable support throughout life. In the case of people with profound complex needs, they will require treatment and management from a range of health-care professionals.

CHAPTER 3

Psychiatric and behavioural disorders in people with learning disabilities

MOHAMMED MEGAHED

The association between learning disability and psychiatric disorders is a focus of growing research interest. Indeed, de-institutionalisation has increased interest in the field of 'dual diagnosis of learning disability and psychiatric disorders'. Until recently, a large proportion of people with learning disabilities lived in institutions as a direct consequence of a perceived behavioural or psychiatric disorder. It was thought that behavioural concomitants of learning disability and learning disability itself were inseparable. Nowadays, admission to psychiatric wards is almost always reserved for specialised assessment and treatment of a recognised psychiatric illness.

The term 'mental retardation' is still used in modern psychiatric classification systems. In the UK, this term has largely been replaced in everyday practice by 'learning disability' (see Chapters 1 and 2). The *International Classification of Diseases*, 10th revision (ICD-10: WHO, 1992) states that:

> The prevalence of psychiatric and behavioural disorders is at least three to four times greater in people with learning disabilities compared with the general population.

There is clear evidence for this finding in surveys of children and adults with learning disabilities. Table 3.1 describes the prevalence of associated psychiatric and behavioural disorders in people with learning disabilities. Different explanations have been proposed for this high prevalence: one theory is that a possible genetic aetiology or brain disease may account for both the psychiatric disorder and the learning disability. This explanation is supported by the degree of specificity of certain psychiatric and behavioural presentations in a number of syndromes of learning disability. Table 3.2 outlines the common psychiatric and behavioural disorders in some of these syndromes. Psychosocial theories have also been proposed, for example, some psychiatric and behavioural disorders may be a consequence of psychological abnormalities such as impaired attention and lack of social skills. There may also be a reaction to the stigma of the learning disability.

Table 3.1 Prevalence of psychiatric disorders in people with learning disabilities

Study	Age	Method and sample	Percentage of psychiatric disorders among cases	Percentage of psychiatric disorders among controls
Rutter et al. (1976)	9–11	Comparative assessment of the entire age cohort in the Isle of Wight	30–42	6–7
Gillberg (1986)	13–17	Comprehensive assessment of representative cohort	57 mild, 64 severe	5
Lund (1985)	Over 20	Comprehensive assessment of sample from Danish register for learning disabilities	27	Non-comparative
Gastason (1985)	20–60	Comprehensive assessment of sample from Swedish register	33 mild, 71 severe	23
Patel et al. (1994)	Over 50	Comprehensive assessment	21 (11.4 dementia)	Non-comparative

Earlier studies suggested that the higher prevalence of dual diagnosis is an artefact, because an individual with learning disability as well as a psychiatric disorder is more likely to come to the attention of the services than another individual with either disorder. This explanation was not supported by more recent population studies.

Common psychiatric and behavioural disorders among people with learning disabilities

The range of specific psychiatric and behavioural disorders encountered in people with learning disabilities varies markedly according to their level of intelligence. All varieties of dual diagnosis occur, but the pattern of

Table 3.2 Syndromes of learning disability, their associated intellectual impairment, behavioural phenotypes and psychiatric vulnerabilities

Syndrome	Aetiology	Learning disability	Behavioural phenotype and psychiatric vulnerabilities
Aicardi's syndrome	Possibly X-linked inheritance	Most die in infancy; rest develop learning disability	Aggression, self-injurious behaviour, lethargy
Angelman's syndrome	Chromosomal abnormality	Present	Laughing at minimal provocation, inquisitiveness
Brachmann–de Lange syndrome	A possible locus is on chromosome 3	Usually moderate-to-severe learning disability	Explosive outbursts, stereotypical movements and self-injurious behaviour
Cerebral palsy	Perinatal brain damage	Majority of below-average intelligence, athetoid type more commonly associated with an average IQ	Various forms of challenging behaviour depending on the level of intellectual impairment
Cretinism	Iodine deficiency, thyroid atrophy	Usually present, altered by early diagnosis and thyroxine treatment	Lethargy, psychomotor retardation, challenging behaviour
Down's syndrome	Trisomy 21	Mean IQ 50, most individuals performing at moderately retarded range	Mood disorders, Alzheimer's disease, challenging behaviour
Foetal alcohol syndrome	Excessive alcohol consumption during pregnancy	Mean IQ 70	Hyperactivity, poor attention span, giving the impression of hyperkinetic disorder

(contd)

Table 3.2 (contd)

Syndrome	Aetiology	Learning disability	Behavioural phenotype and psychiatric vulnerabilities
Fragile X syndrome	FMR-1 gene (X-linked inheritance)	Usually mild to moderate, accounts for 4% of cases with mild learning disability in males	Features of avoidant personality, some features of autism, schizotypal disorder, hyperkinetic disorder
Joubert's syndrome	Autosomal recessive inheritance, genetic locus has not yet been identified	Usually severe	Abnormal breathing sound, autistic features, self-injurious behaviour
Klinefelter's syndrome	XXY karyotype	Mean IQ 90, but a slight increase in mild learning disability	Passive–compliant during childhood, may show aggressive behaviour in adult life
Lesch–Nyhan syndrome	X-linked recessive inheritance leading to error of purine metabolism	Severe learning disability	Self-mutilation, in > 85% some form of aggressive behaviour
Neurofibromatosis	Autosomal dominant inheritance	Learning disability in minority	Symptoms depend on site of neurofibromas
Noonan's syndrome	Phenotypically related to Turner's syndrome (XXX genotype), but occurs in both sexes	Present	Challenging behaviour, stubbornness, problems in peer relations, preservation
Prader–Willi syndrome	Microdeletion of the long arm of chromosome 15	Variable, some have normal IQ, most have mild-to-moderate learning disability	Impulse control problems, mood symptoms, obsessional and compulsive symptoms, sleep problems, self-injury (spot picking)

(contd)

Table 3.2 (contd)

Syndrome	Aetiology	Learning disability	Behavioural phenotype and psychiatric vulnerabilities
Phenylketonuria	Autosomal recessive inheritance leading to an error of metabolism	Present (neonatal diagnosis and dietary management alter the course of illness)	Hyperactivity, impulse control problems, features of bipolar illness
Rett's syndrome	May be an X-linked dominant disorder	Initial period of normal cognitive development, followed by intellectual retardation	Language impairment, autistic features, stereotypical movements and self-injurious behaviour
Smith–Magenis syndrome	Microdeletion in chromosome 17	Moderate learning disability	Hyperactivity, autistic features, aggressive behaviour, self-injurious behaviour, sleep disturbance
Tuberous sclerosis	Autosomal dominant	Learning disability in 70% of cases	Autistic features and hyperactivity
Velocardiofacial syndrome	Microdeletion of chromosome 22	Present (can be mild)	Features of schizophrenia, challenging behaviour
Williams syndrome	Microdeletion of chromosome 7	Present	Symptoms of hyperkinetic disorder and anxiety

psychiatric and behavioural disorders is usually coloured by the intellectual deficit. Table 3.3 outlines some of the differences between the various intelligence quotient (IQ) ranges and the associated behavioural and psychiatric disorders.

Table 3.3 IQ ranges and associated behavioural patterns

IQ range	ICD-10 code and diagnosis	Obsolete terms	Associated behavioural patterns and psychiatric morbidity
50–69	F70: mild mental retardation	Feebleminded Moron Mild oligophrenia High-grade defect	More closely akin to those found in general population. All psychiatric disorders are diagnosed in this IQ range
35–49	F71: moderate mental retardation	Imbecile Moderate oligophrenia	Limited conceptual capacity and poor language development render the diagnosis of psychiatric disorders difficult, increase in challenging behaviour, sometimes serving communicative function. Associated epilepsy
20–34	F72: severe mental retardation	Severe oligophrenia	Marked motor impairment renders the quality of challenging behaviour different compared with the above groups. Associated epilepsy. In practice, schizophrenia never diagnosed
<20	F73: profound mental retardation	Profound oligophrenia Idiocy	IQ is difficult to measure. Formal psychiatric disorders extremely difficult to diagnose

Schizophrenia

Schizophrenia is diagnosed in 1% of the general population, and in about 3% of people with learning disabilities. Schizophrenic disorders are characterised by fundamental and characteristic distortions of thinking and perception, associated with inappropriate affect (WHO, 1992). In the general population, the picture of schizophrenia varies from episodic remittent illness with good response to antipsychotic medications and psychosocial interventions to a more continuous disorganised illness. Schizophrenia in people with mild learning disability is closely akin to that found in people of normal intelligence. In those with an IQ of less than 45, schizophrenia is extremely difficult to diagnose. The 10 most common symptoms of acute schizophrenia in the general population are shown in Table 3.4. The following points outline some of the ways in which schizophrenia can be modified by coexistent learning disability.

Table 3.4 The 10 most frequent symptoms of schizophrenia in the general population

Symptom	Frequency (%)
Lack of insight	97
Auditory hallucinations	74
Ideas of reference	70
Suspiciousness	66
Flat affect	66
Second person hallucinations	65
Delusional mood	64
Delusions of persecution	64
Thoughts spoken aloud	50
Thought alienation	42

Disorders of thought content

Delusional thoughts are a common presentation of schizophrenia. A delusion is defined as a false, fixed belief which is not correctable by reasoning and not consistent with the prevailing culture. Delusions can present in various degrees of sophistication from simple persecutory ideas to well-formed delusional systems. In people with learning disabilities, delusions are usually less elaborate. Unexplained agitation, avoidance, altered behaviour and situation-related anxiety can indicate the presence of delusional thoughts. Normal fantasy in individuals with learning disabilities can give the impression of underlying delusional thoughts.

Hallucinations

A hallucination is a false sensory perception in the absence of real external stimulus. Hallucinations occur in about three-quarters of people with acute schizophrenia, most commonly auditory in modality and frequently in the third person. In patients with mild learning disabilities, hallucinations can occasionally be difficult to ascertain. In patients with moderate-to-profound learning disability, any abnormal perceptual experience can pass unrecognised as a result of the limited ability to express morbid experience.

Disorder of the form of thought

This usually occurs in people with disorganised schizophrenia. It includes loosening of association, derailment of thoughts on to a subsidiary thought, disordered mixture of constituent parts of one complex thought and a fusion of elements of thoughts. Formal thought disorder is difficult to diagnose in people with moderate-to-profound learning disabilities, who may show an unusual intermixture or disruption of thought process without suffering from schizophrenic formal thought disorder.

Catatonia

Catatonia is defined as a state of increased muscle tone at rest, abolished by voluntary activities. Catatonic symptoms include excitement, posturing, negativism, preservation and stupor. It is a psychiatric syndrome caused by a large variety of disease processes and not specific to schizophrenia. It can also be a complication of treatment with some psychotropic medications. Motor mannerisms seen in people with learning disabilities can be misinterpreted as catatonic symptoms. These mannerisms usually run a continuous course and may respond to behavioural interventions. Catatonic symptoms are mostly episodic with clear onset and good response to electroconvulsive therapy.

Negative symptoms of schizophrenia

These include motor retardation, blunted affect and poverty of thought. These symptoms are usually slowly progressive and develop during an early stage of life. In a person with learning disability, a long-standing pattern of social withdrawal, poverty of thought and constricted affect may be misinterpreted as a schizophrenic illness with negative symptoms.

The international classification of mental and behavioural disorders suggests that the diagnosis of schizophrenia should be guided by a significant and consistent change in the overall quality of behaviours. This diagnosis should not be made in the presence of overt brain disease, in which case the diagnosis of organic delusional disorder should be made.

Affective (mood) disorders

Categories of mood disorders include the following:

- Depressive episode
- Recurrent depressive disorder

- Manic episodes (including hypomania and mania)
- Bipolar affective disorder (manic depressive illness)
- Persistent mood disorder

Until recently, mood disorders in general have rarely been diagnosed in people with learning disabilities. It was thought that some syndromes of learning disabilities preclude the development of certain types of mood disorders (e.g. Down's syndrome and mania). In 1989, Szymanski and Crocker suggested that the under-diagnosis is a result of three factors: first, that people with learning disabilities have limited conceptual capacity and are therefore thought to be unable to experience and express mood symptoms; second, they lack the expressive language capabilities necessary to describe the emotional state; and, third, depression is less likely than other psychiatric disorders to induce behavioural consequences, which normally trigger referral to psychiatric services. More recent studies suggest higher prevalence of mood disorders among people with learning disabilities (approximately 15%).

Depressive symptoms

As with schizophrenia, clinical manifestations of depressive disorders are largely dependent on the level of intellectual impairment. People with learning disabilities are less likely to complain of mood changes. Behavioural concomitants of mood changes are more noticeable, including agitation, withdrawal and aggression. Cognitive symptoms of depression, including ideas of hopelessness, helplessness, worthlessness and guilt, are less frequently encountered. Diurnal variation of mood is an important symptom of depression: those suffering from depressive disorders tend to complain of feeling more depressed in the morning than at other times of the day. Diurnal variation of behaviour is a similar presentation in depressed people with learning disabilities: more agitation, aggressive outbursts, lethargy and perplexity are noticed early in the morning. Other biological symptoms of depression occur and are generally similar to those experienced by depressed patients with average IQ. They include appetite changes, weight loss, disturbed sleep and reduced concentration.

Alexithymia is defined as difficulty in awareness, or description of one's own emotions. This symptom is commonly encountered in people with borderline intelligence. A common consequence of alexithymia is somatisation in which a depressed patient may complain of repeated unexplained somatic symptoms.

Suicide may be less common in people with learning disabilities (Vitiello and Behar, 1992). It has been reported in those suffering from depressive illness, bipolar disorder and adjustment disorders with depressive component. Suicide attempts are usually poorly planned.

Mania and hypomania

These present with episodic excitement, hyperactivity, sleep disturbance, sexual disinhibition, weight loss and pressured speech. Grandiose delusions are common in patients with mania and an average IQ. These types of delusion are less frequently diagnosed in people with learning disabilities. Secondary mania occurs in people with learning disabilities and can be precipitated by a number of physical conditions and medications, including frontal lobe tumours, endocrine disorders, and steroid and anticonvulsant therapy. The clinical picture of secondary mania does not necessarily typify that of classic manic episodes. As mania in learning disability can also present with atypical features, it is particularly important to exclude causes of secondary illness in these cases. In manic illness, symptoms are more severe and persistent compared with hypomania. The presence of delusions and/or hallucinations precludes the diagnosis of hypomania.

Neurotic and stress-related disorders

The following are common neurotic and stress-related disorders:

- Phobic anxiety disorders
- Generalised anxiety and panic disorders
- Obsessive–compulsive disorder
- Reaction to severe stress, and adjustment disorders

Neurotic disorders are defined as psychiatric conditions that arise in the absence of gross brain abnormalities, and are not associated with delusions, hallucinations or reality distortion. The term 'neurosis' has fallen out of favour recently, although it is still used by ICD-10 to describe a class of mental and behavioural disorders. In the field of learning disabilities, neurotic disorders present in a wide range of behavioural manifestations. There is no simple consistent relationship between some of these disorders and a specific behavioural pattern. It is thought that some of the management strategies for people with learning disabilities concentrate on the behaviour consequences of a neurotic disorder rather than addressing the disorder itself, leading to under-diagnosis of these conditions.

Phobic anxiety

This is a group of disorders in which anxiety is precipitated mainly by certain situations, resulting in a characteristic avoidance behaviour. It includes agoraphobia, social phobias and specific phobias. All phobic disorders have been described in people with learning disabilities. In a study by Novosel (1984), these disorders were detected in 57% of consecutive admissions with mild-to-severe learning disabilities. Social aloofness in autistic spectrum disorders can be misinterpreted as social phobia; characteristically, autistic spectrum disorders present with unresponsiveness to social overtures rather than actual fear of social situations.

Panic disorders

These present with recurrent attacks of severe anxiety, alternating with periods of comparative freedom from anxiety symptoms. Anxiety is not restricted to a particular set of circumstances. Dual diagnosis of learning disability and panic disorder can also be overlooked. Malloy (1998) argued that, in assessing people with learning disabilities for psychiatric disorders, clinicians should be alert to the possibility of panic disorder if patients who report vague somatic complaints, such as people with learning disabilities, can symbolically somatise their emotional states.

Obsessive–compulsive disorder

Obsessive–compulsive disorder (OCD) is diagnosed in patients presenting with recurrent intrusive thoughts of an unpleasant nature. These thoughts are usually accompanied by unsuccessful resistance. Obsessive–compulsive disorder can also present with repeated rituals that are perceived by the sufferer as a senseless symbolic attempt to avert a perceived danger or other unpleasant feeling. In people with learning disabilities, symptoms of OCDs include more compulsive rituals than obsessional thoughts, for example, stereotypical movements, compulsive self-injurious behaviour, compulsive ordering, checking and touching. Features of OCDs are frequently found in a variety of syndromes of learning disabilities, including Rett's syndrome, tuberous sclerosis and Prader–Willi syndrome.

Stress-related disorders

These include acute stress reaction, adjustment disorder and post-traumatic stress disorder (PTSD). They develop as a reaction to a stressful life event, but the severity of the stressor, onset and reaction pattern varies. The precipitating stressful event tends to be milder in cases of acute stress reaction and adjustment disorders; in fact it can fall within the range of normal experience (e.g. moving to a new social environment). Post-traumatic stress disorder arises as a reaction to an exceptionally threatening or catastrophic life event (e.g. rape, serious accident or witnessing a crime). The onset of symptoms varies from within a few hours of the stressor in acute stress reaction, to within 6 months in PTSD. Post-traumatic stress disorder is characterised by repeated reliving of the threatening event in intrusive memories and dreams. There is an autonomic component to this disorder, because it also presents with hypervigilance and enhanced startle reaction. It has been suggested that PTSD in people with learning disability can present only with behavioural changes and self-mutilation. Post-traumatic stress disorder is thought to be a disorder of high functioning, learning-disabled people (Hardan and Sahl, 1997). Bereavement reaction is a type of adjustment disorder that was systematically studied by Hollins and Esterhuyzen in 1997. Bereaved learning-disabled individuals tend to present with irritability, lethargy, hyperactivity, stereotypy and inappropriate speech. In the general population, the most common symptoms are numbness, pining for the deceased and depression.

Specific personality disorders

A personality disorder is an enduring pattern of inner experience and behaviour that deviates markedly from the expectations of the individual's culture, is pervasive and inflexible, has an onset in adolescence or early adulthood, is stable over time and leads to distress and impairment (APA, 1994).

ICD-10 types of specific personality

- Paranoid personality disorder
- Schizoid personality disorder
- Dissocial personality disorder
- Emotionally unstable personality disorder (including borderline personality disorder)
- Histrionic personality disorder
- Anankastic personality disorder
- Anxious (avoidant) personality disorder
- Dependent personality disorder

The American *Diagnostic and Statistical Manual of Mental Disorders* (DSM-IV) describes two other types of specific personality disorders: schizotypal and narcissistic types (APA, 1994).

Virtually all types of personality disorder have been described in people with learning disabilities (Szymanski and Crocker, 1989). Corbett (1990) found that the prevalence of personality disorders in adults receiving services for people with learning disabilities was 25.4%. This population makes a significant demand on psychiatric services. Personality disorders can lead to greater problems in the diagnosis and management of other psychiatric disorders among people with learning disabilities. Diagnosis is usually based on a long-standing pattern of disharmonious attitudes and behaviour, which affect the individual in various spheres of life and give rise to severe personal distress and impaired social performance. The onset of personality disorders is usually early in life and the course is stable in some types (schizoid, schizotypal and obsessive–compulsive) or remits with age in other types (antisocial and borderline disorders).

Paranoid personality disorder

This is characterised by suspiciousness, reluctance to confide in others and conspiratorial explanation of events. It accounts for about 15% of all cases of personality disorder among people with learning disabilities.

Schizoid personality and schizotypal disorder

Both conditions have a number of common features similar to negative symptoms of schizophrenia. These diagnoses also overlap with the diagnosis of autistic spectrum disorders. All these conditions are characterised by emotional coldness, detachment, flat affect and a tendency to solitary activities. The main differentiating features are that schizotypal disorder is associated with odd beliefs, magical thoughts and unusual perceptual experiences, whereas autistic spectrum disorders are associated with social aloofness, language impairment and ritualistic behaviour. Schizoid personality disorder is characterised by a pattern of emotional indifference and excessive preoccupation with fantasy.

Anankastic (obsessive–compulsive) personality disorder

This is characterised by preoccupation with details, rigidity, stubbornness and excessive doubts. This pattern of symptoms also manifests in people with autistic spectrum disorders, and in those suffering from fragile X syndrome.

Dissocial personality disorder

This is characterised by a failure to conform to social norms, aggression and callous unconcern for the feelings of others. It is usually preceded by conduct problems during childhood and adolescence. Different dissocial traits have been associated with specific reading disorders and with hyperkinetic disorders.

Emotionally unstable (borderline and impulsive) personality disorder

This is characterised by recurrent episodes of deliberate self-harm, emotional outbursts and efforts to avoid abandonment. It tends to be diagnosed more frequently in people with milder forms of learning disabilities. Sufferers usually present considerable management difficulties. Self-harming behaviour can present among various groups of people with learning disabilities without the emotional and cognitive components of emotionally unstable personality disorder.

Histrionic personality disorder

This is characterised by exaggerated expression of emotions, continual seeking of appreciation by others, over-concern with physical attractiveness and inappropriate sexual seductiveness.

Dependent personality disorder

This is characterised by difficulty in making decisions, feelings of inferiority to others and a constant need for nurture and support. It is rarely diagnosed in people with learning disabilities because of the difficulty in distinguishing between a dependent state precipitated by the disability and a truly dependent personality.

Anxious (avoidant) personality disorder

This is characterised by the avoidance of interpersonal contact and a preoccupation with being criticised or rejected in social situations. Features of avoidant personality disorder are seen in cases of fragile X syndrome.

Narcissistic personality disorder

This is characterised by a pervasive pattern of grandiosity and preoccupation with fantasies of unlimited success. It is uncommon, and research into its association with learning disabilities is generally lacking.

Dementia

People with learning disability are living longer as a result of treatment of their medical complications; consequently, a higher proportion tends to experience dementing illness.

Dementia in Alzheimer's disease

This is the most common type, as it is in the general population. It is characterised by an insidious onset of cognitive impairment associated with higher cortical dysfunction (aphasia, agraphia, alexia and dyspraxia). Down's syndrome has a particular association with Alzheimer's disease. This association is explained genetically through the role of the β-amyloid precursor protein gene on chromosome 21. In patients with Down's syndrome, pre-existing intellectual impairment can lead to a delay in the diagnosis of an added dementia. Recently developed standardised assessment tools and brain imaging techniques can aid the diagnosis.

Cortical Lewy body disease

This is a type of dementia that clinically manifests with intellectual impairment similar to that seen in Alzheimer's disease. It is usually accompanied by motor disorders suggestive of Parkinson's disease and hallucinatory experiences.

Vascular dementia

This is characterised by memory decline and deficits in attention, language, verbal skills and motor control. It occurs after a stroke or as a gradual progression from small asymptomatic infarcts. Depression occurs in about 20% of sufferers.

Childhood disintegrative disorder (dementia infantalis)

This is a dementing illness that occurs at an early stage of life. It is characterised by impoverishment, then total loss, of speech and language, accompanied by behavioural disintegration. This disorder has been associated with inborn errors of metabolism.

Disorders of psychological development

These constitute a group of disorders that commonly present to psychiatric clinics for people with learning disabilities. Some of these conditions are associated with lower levels of intelligence. The onset is always in infancy or childhood and the course is steady. Disorders of psychological development include the following.

Specific developmental disorders of speech and language

These include speech articulation disorder, expressive language disorder, receptive language disorder and acquired aphasia with epilepsy (Landau–Kleffner syndrome). Landau–Kleffner syndrome is a disorder that occurs between the ages of 3 and 7, after a period of normal development. Characteristically, it presents with seizure activity and paroxysmal abnormalities on the EEG. There is loss of language development, particularly evident in receptive language. It can progress to complete mutism.

Specific developmental disorders of scholastic skills

These include specific reading disorder, spelling disorder and specific disorder of arithmetical skills. Specific reading disorder occurs when the child's performance is significantly below the expected level for age, general intelligence and school placement. The term was introduced to replace the term 'specific reading retardation'; the latter was coined to replace 'dyslexia'. Like most disorders of psychological development, specific reading disorder is more common in males.

Pervasive developmental disorders

These include childhood autism, Asperger's syndrome, high functioning autism, Rett's syndrome and an over-active disorder associated with mental retardation and stereotypical movement. Childhood autism is the best-recognised pervasive developmental disorder. It is usually diagnosed during the first 36 months of life. Features of autism include aloofness from others, unresponsiveness to social overtures and extremely poor attachment behaviour. Autism also presents with speech delay and approximately half of autistic individuals do not acquire useful speech. There are difficulties in social use of language (pragmatics), meaning (semantics) and structure (syntax). It is also characterised by repetitive behaviour, which gives the impression of obsessionality. Some develop true obsessions, especially in adolescence. About half of those affected with autism have an IQ below 50, whereas only 30% have an IQ in the borderline range or above. Asperger's syndrome is another type of pervasive developmental disorder that typifies autism in the quality of social interaction. It is not associated with delay in language or cognitive capacity. People with Asperger's syndrome may show a high degree of achievement in circumscribed interests. There is controversy about whether Asperger's syndrome can occur at all in people with learning disability. Rett's syndrome is a pervasive developmental disorder that is being found almost exclusively in girls. It can produce autistic-like behaviour associated with stereotypical hand movements, trunk ataxia, scoliosis and seizures. Characteristically, this disorder leads to severe learning disability.

Hyperkinetic disorders (attention deficit disorders)

This is a group of disorders characterised by a combination of over-activity and poor attention. They are associated with learning difficulties in a large minority. Hyperkinetic disorders always start within the first 5 years of life. Added to hyperactivity and inattention, they present with impulsivity, lack of perception of danger, social disinhibition and recklessness. These features occur in certain syndromes of learning disabilities including Williams syndrome, fragile X syndrome and foetal alcohol syndrome.

Secondary complications include low self-esteem and antisocial behaviour.

Gilles de la Tourette's syndrome

This syndrome is characterised by multiple motor and vocal tics, which usually develop at an early stage of life (in some cases as early as 2 years). It runs a lifelong course and is diagnosed more commonly in males. Other features of Gilles de la Tourette's syndrome include coprolalia (repetitive obscene utterances), distractibility, impulsivity and depressed mood. In most, vulnerability to this syndrome is transmitted in an autosomal dominant fashion. Individuals with the non-genetic form tend to have an associated psychiatric and developmental disorder (e.g. pervasive developmental disorders and hyperkinetic disorders).

Challenging behaviour in people with learning disabilities

Challenging behaviour is defined as manners that seriously disrupt the individual's life or that of people around them, and include behaviours out of their usual context, violence to self and others, and generally inappropriate conduct. Most studies of challenging behaviour produce a prevalence rate of 20%, but variations depend on the definition of challenging behaviour, degree of intellectual impairment and research setting. Challenging behaviour includes the following:

- Mannerisms, rocking and other apparently purposeless activities.
- Self-injurious behaviour.
- Violence to others, including hitting, biting, property damage and tantrums.
- Challenging behaviour of a sexual nature, including public masturbation and exposure.
- Unusual eating behaviour and excretion habits.
- Production of unusual noises.

Behaviours that create the biggest impact for care include aggression, wandering away, disturbing noises, temper tantrums and sexual delinquency (Lowe and Felce, 1996). The cause of challenging behaviour varies from being a reaction to a social misunderstanding to being a reflection of physical or psychiatric symptoms. It can serve an important communicative function, particularly in individuals with impaired language development.

Effects of medication on client behaviour

Between 20% and 50% of institutionalised people with a learning disability receive psychotropic medication. A similar or slightly lower proportion of those living in the community also receive these drugs (Fraser and Deb, 1994). In practice, some non-psychotropic medications are also used in the treatment of various psychiatric and behavioural disorders, among which are vitamins, minerals and amino acids. Table 3.5 describes the different classes of medications used in people with learning disabilities.

Table 3.5 Classification of psychiatric medications used in the field of learning disabilities

Class of medications	Examples	Uses
Typical antipsychotics (neuroleptics, first generation antipsychotics)	Haloperidol (Serenace) Trifluperazine (Stelazine) Chlorpromazine (Largactil) Perphenazine (Trilafon) Fluphenazine (Modecate) Pipothiazine (Piportil Depot)	Schizophrenic psychosis Mania and hypomania Rapid tranquillisation in cases of severe psychomotor agitation Anxiety states (in small dose)
Atypical antipsychotics (second and third generation)	Sulpiride (Dolmatil) Olanzapine (Zyprexa) Risperidone (Risperdal) Quetiapine (Seroquel) Clozapine (Clozaril)	Schizophrenia (positive and negative symptoms) Clozapine in treatment-resistant schizophrenia
Antidepressants	Imipramine (Tofranil) Clomipramine (Anafranil) Amitriptyline (Tryptizol) Fluoxetine (Prozac) Paroxetine (Seroxat) Venlafaxine (Efexor)	Depressive disorders (acute treatment and prophylaxis) Anxiety disorders Obsessive–compulsive disorder Self-injurious behaviour Autistic rituals
Mood stabilisers	Lithium salts Carbamazepine (Tegretol) Valproate (Epilim)	Acute treatment of mania and prophylaxis of manic depressive disorders Treatment-resistant depression Aggressive behaviour

(contd)

Table 3.5 (contd)

Class of medications	Examples	Uses
Anxiolytics	Diazepam (Valium) Lorazepam (Ativan) Chlordiazepoxide (Librium) Buspirone (Buspar)	Anxiety disorders Alcohol withdrawal symptoms Rapid tranquillisation in cases of psychomotor agitation
Hypnotics	Temazepam Zopiclone (Zimovane) Zolpidem (Stilnoct)	Insomnia
Psychostimulants	Dexamphetamine (Dexedrine) Methylphenidate (Ritalin)	Hyperkinetic disorders Narcolepsy
β Blockers	Propranolol (Inderal) Atenolol (Tenormin)	Anxiety Impulsivity and rage outbursts
Opiate antagonists	Naloxone Naltrexone	Self-injurious behaviour
Anticholinergic/ antiparkinsonian	Procyclidine	Pseudo-parkinsonism Dystonia
Anti-libidinal	Cyproterone Benperidol	Hypersexuality Inappropriate sexual behaviour not responsive to psychological interventions

Antidepressants

Antidepressant medications are used not only in the treatment of detectable depressive disorders, but also in a number of other psychiatric disorders. Clomipramine is a serotonergic tricyclic antidepressant that is used for the treatment of phobic states and in OCD. Self-injurious behaviour is sometimes treated with clomipramine. In autistic spectrum disorders, clomipramine is used and is thought to be effective in reducing rituals (Gordon et al., 1993). Antidepressant medications are also used in people with learning disabilities to treat hyperactivity, agitation and tantrums, whether or not associated with depressive illness.

Antipsychotics

Antipsychotic agents are drugs that tranquillise without impairing consciousness and without causing paradoxical excitement. This group of drugs is indicated in the following.

Positive symptoms of schizophrenia

All antipsychotics have been proved to have antidelusional, antihallucinatory effects.

Negative symptoms of schizophrenia

These show better response to atypical antipsychotics.

Therapy-resistant schizophrenia

Clozapine is the only antipsychotic proved to be effective in this condition, which is defined as the type of illness that fails to respond to different classes of antipsychotic medications in adequate doses, after adequate duration of treatment.

Manic episodes

All antipsychotic medications are used in the treatment of manic episodes. They are effective in controlling persistent elevation of mood, irritability, pressure of speech, increased tempo of thinking, distractibility, delusions and hallucinations.

Motor tics associated with Gilles de la Tourette's syndrome

They are treated in part by haloperidol and pimozide.

Psychomotor agitation, excitement and violence or dangerously impulsive behaviour

Antipsychotics are used for short-term management.

Adjunctive management of anxiety

Some antipsychotics – for example, thioridazine – are used in the treatment of anxiety symptoms. The dose sufficient for treatment of these symptoms is usually less than the antipsychotic dose.

Inappropriate sexual behaviour

Neuroleptic medications are also used along with anti-libidinal medications in the management of inappropriate sexual behaviour among people with learning disability.

Mood stabilisers

These are medications used for prophylaxis as well as the acute treatment of bipolar illness. They include:

* Lithium carbonate and citrate
* Antiepileptics: carbamazepine, sodium valproate, gabapentin and lamotrigine
* Calcium channel blockers: verapamil

Research provided evidence for the efficacy of lithium carbonate in aggressive episodes and in aggression associated with hyperactivity. In the field of forensic psychiatry, lithium is also thought to have a significant effect in reduction of aggressive behaviour among prisoners and individuals with learning disability. Carbamazepine is a mood-stabilising antiepileptic related chemically to some antidepressants. It is used alone or with lithium in severe and rapidly cycling bipolar illness (four or more episodes of illness in 1 year). It is effective against impulsive and aggressive behaviour. There are also reports suggesting its usefulness in the treatment of attention deficit hyperactivity disorder. Calcium channel blockers have also been used in stuttering, violent behaviour and Gilles de la Tourette's syndrome.

Opiate antagonists

Recently, there has been an increasing interest in the use of opiate antagonists for the treatment of self-injurious behaviour. It was suggested that self-injurious behaviour leads to the release of endogenous opiates, causing a euphoric state. This assumption provided a rationale for the treatment of self-injurious behaviour using these medications. Some laboratory studies suggested that there were higher levels of endogenous opiate derivatives in individuals with autism and self-injurious behaviour. It has also been reported that autistic patients treated with opiate antagonists showed some improvement in aggression, negativism, physical contact, eye contact and communication.

Medications in attention deficit disorder

Drugs are useful in the treatment of severe hyperkinesis or in those resistant to non-drug measures. Medications commonly used in attention deficit disorders include stimulants (methylphenidate and methamphetamine), clonidine, haloperidol and antidepressants. They have some effect in reducing demonstrable inattention, motor over-activity, impulsivity and recklessness.

Side effects of psychotropic medications

Behavioural side effects

Table 3.6 outlines the most common behavioural side effects in people receiving psychotropic medication.

Table 3.6 Behavioural and psychiatric side effects of psychotropic medications used in learning disability

Side effect	Medications precipitating the side effect
Agitation	Anxiolytic (benzodiazepine) withdrawal
	Fluoxetine (possibly occurs in 9% of those treated with fluoxetine)
	Other SSRIs (reported with paroxetine and citalopram)
Aggression	Psychostimulants (amphetamine, methylphenidate)
	Benzodiazepines (paradoxical effect)
	Withdrawal of SSRIs (case reports)
Depressed mood	Antipsychotics
	β Blockers
	Benzodiazepines
Hallucinations	Psychostimulants
	Benzodiazepine withdrawal
	Tricyclic antidepressants (rarely reported)
	Zopiclone
Delusions	Psychostimulants
Manic features	Antidepressants
	Psychostimulants
Delusional thoughts	Psychostimulants
Tics	Psychostimulants

SSRIs, serotonin-specific reuptake inhibitors.

Neuromuscular side effects of psychotropic medications

Akathisia

This is subjective or objective motor restlessness that presents in the form of walking, pacing or shifting posture. It is commonly accompanied by a feeling of inner tension. Akathisia can be confused with agitation or psychosis. Treatment of akathisia is difficult, β blockers and benzodiazepines commonly being used.

Pseudo-parkinsonism

This occurs in 15–50% of patients receiving antipsychotic medications. It results from blockade of dopamine receptors in the negrostriatal system of the brain (extrapyramidal effect). Symptoms include muscular rigidity, resting tremors and bradykinesia. These symptoms usually occur within 5–90 days of treatment initiation, and are dose related. Management includes the administration of anticholinergic/antiparkinsonian agents, reducing the dose of antipsychotic medications or switching from older high-potency antipsychotic medication to ones with less extrapyramidal effect.

Tardive dyskinesia

This is a syndrome of involuntary movements that develops during long-term treatment with antipsychotic medications. It is characterised by choreic (semi-purposeful) or athetoid (snake-like) movements of the face, limbs or trunk. The typical syndrome is mainly seen in elderly patients, most frequently as lingual and masticatory dyskinesia. These abnormal involuntary movements, if severe, can lead to problems in swallowing and speech. Individuals with gross brain morphological abnormalities, including some of those with learning disabilities, are particularly susceptible to tardive dyskinesia. Tardive dyskinesia can also present with choreic movements of the hands (piano playing), pelvic thrusting or rocking of the legs.

Respiratory dyskinesia

This is motor disorder characterised by irregularity of rhythm and depth of breathing. It is a rare complication that occurs in those receiving antipsychotic medications.

Dystonia

This presents as sustained involuntary muscular rigidity, resulting in twisting of the neck, limbs and trunk. Two types of dystonia exist: acute and tardive types. Acute dystonia develops in the early course of treatment. It is reported in 5–20% of those receiving antipsychotics. Tardive dystonia can present with similar features, but occurs late in the course of treatment.

Myopathy

In psychiatric practice, this disorder can be precipitated by lithium and β blockers. The presenting features are muscle cramps and mild weakness. These symptoms are usually reversible on cessation of treatment.

Neuroleptic malignant syndrome

This is a life-threatening complication of antipsychotic treatment. It has also been reported in a small number of patients receiving other classes of psychotropic medications. The presenting features are muscular rigidity, altered consciousness and hyperpyrexia. Neuroleptic malignant syndrome is usually treated with supportive measures, including the administration of antipyretics and neuromuscular blocking agents. It has a mortality rate of about 25%.

Myoclonic twitches

Twitches and tremors of the tongue and extremities are fairly common in those receiving antidepressants and antipsychotic medications.

Epilepsy

Most psychotropic medications are known to lower seizure threshold, precipitating fits in those who are predisposed. Medications known to have high risk for causing seizures include the following:

- Antipsychotics: chlorpromazine and loxapine
- Antidepressants: maprotiline and bupropion
- Mood stabilisers: lithium
- Benzodiazepine withdrawal

Myasthenia gravis

Benzodiazepines are known to worsen states of muscle weakness and are usually given with extreme caution. Progressive muscular weakness in cases of myasthenia gravis can also occur in those receiving antipsychotic medications. Zolpidem and zopiclone are two novel hypnotic agents that are contraindicated in this disorder.

Conclusion

There is a growing research interest in the association between learning disability and psychiatric disorders, and with it improved accuracy of diagnosis. However, diagnosis is still made difficult by the limited ability of people with learning disability to express thoughts and mood symptoms and their tendency symbolically to somatise their emotional states. Further difficulties arise when neurological disorders associated with learning disability are also present. As with the general population, there can be side effects from psychotropic medication, which necessitate especially careful monitoring in people with learning disabilities.

Psychiatric and behavioural disorders and the effect of their medication will benefit from psychology, speech and language therapy, occupational therapy, art therapy, complementary therapies and physiotherapy appropriate to the specific disorder. These disorders and the side effects of their medication impact on the whole of the client's life, including treatment for other conditions associated with learning disability and other medical conditions and recent injury.

CHAPTER 4

Orthopaedic aspects of learning disability

JAMES E ROBB

There is a wide spectrum of orthopaedic disorders associated with learning disability, some as a consequence of the underlying condition and others incidental to it. There is little information available on the orthopaedic aspects in the literature and so the information discussed in this chapter is based on conditions encountered over the last 10 years in an orthopaedic clinic devoted to problems in adults with learning disabilities.

Assessment

Patients with learning disability may not be able to explain their particular problem and may rely on their relatives or carer to give this information. Explanations of the condition and its possible treatment may not be as easily achieved as for the non-learning-disabled person. It may not be possible for the clinician to present information about the benefits and risks of a particular line of management in a form that is readily understood. (See Chapter 1 for a more detailed discussion of the issues of consent.)

It is preferable to see the patient in surroundings familiar to him or her so as to minimise any distress. This also has the advantage that the patient can be accompanied by the physiotherapist and carers, and one can thus obtain a better perspective of his or her functional difficulties. However, there is the logistical problem of holding a clinic in an environment where there is no ready access to radiography, which may necessitate another hospital visit for the patient and carer. When hospital admission is required, communication between the patient's usual carers and hospital staff is invaluable. For people who are long-stay hospital residents, we have found it extremely helpful to have a member of their care team to assist in their ward care and subsequent rehabilitation. This requires a good working relationship between hospitals and the various disciplines involved. It may also help in the early transfer of the patient back to their more familiar surroundings.

As many of these patients may have multiple problems, it is helpful to identify the principal area of concern to the patient, relative or carer. These may not always coincide and it is important that decisions are not taken from a 'snapshot' view of the patient. For example, a patient with cerebral palsy who is able to walk may be concerned about the posture of the feet. This could result from excessive internal femoral torsion rather than a problem within the feet themselves. Equally, the tendency to walk by holding the foot in an equinus position could result from a limb length inequality or a hip flexion contracture rather than from shortening of the calf muscles. Similarly, a patient could have severe windsweeping at the hips, but this might be irrelevant to that particular consultation because the functional problem might be, for example, severe equinus precluding the fitting of footwear.

It also helps to define specific aims of management. For example, the presence of severe knee flexion contractures in a non-walking patient with cerebral palsy may not have an adverse effect on his or her ability to sit and for this reason treatment would not necessarily be required. But, if the aim of the patient's management programme were to include the use of a standing frame, there could be justification in surgical treatment of the knee contractures if they precluded its use.

Pain in patients who have learning disability is often difficult to quantify or localise. In severe cerebral palsy, gastro-oesophageal reflux, constipation and hip dislocation can coexist. All may produce 'abdominal' pain. Carers may confirm that the pain is worse when moving the legs at pad-changing time, thus implicating the hip as the probable source of pain. Abdominal examination may help in determining whether or not the patient is constipated and further investigations such as radiographs or an upper gastrointestinal endoscopy may help further.

Requests for treatment of what initially appears to be a cosmetic problem are also made. For example, in severe hemiplegic cerebral palsy, patients may have concerns about a hemiplegic hand, compare it with the sound side and request surgical treatment. Closer questioning often establishes that the problem is not just one of cosmesis, but also of difficulties with volar skin crease hygiene and clothing. Under these circumstances, it is justifiable to offer surgical correction of that particular deformity which does not usually have any functional gain.

Review of patients

The following information derives from a clinic held at Gogarburn Hospital for people with learning disabilities. From an organisational point of view, it had been traditional for an orthopaedic surgeon to visit the hospital over the years to provide a consultation service for inpatients and outpatients associated with the hospital. Until recently, most patients seen were residents of the hospital because of either severe motor and physical disability or significant psychiatric morbidity. More recently, because of political changes, a larger number of patients who might have formerly been residents now live in the community. This has resulted in fewer residents attending the clinic, but a greater number of outpatients. It could now be argued that, as the majority have to travel to the clinic, they might be better seen in a conventional hospital setting where ancillary investigations are readily available.

The cases of the most recent 117 patients with learning disabilities aged between 19 and 89 years, and seen personally by the author, have been reviewed to give an indication of the type of pathologies seen in this particular setting. In 25, there was no specific associated diagnosis. In those who had a specific diagnosis associated with learning disability, the majority had cerebral palsy, perhaps a reflection of a particular interest in neuromuscular conditions. The associated conditions were as shown in Table 4.1.

Table 4.1 Associated conditions seen at Gogarburn Hospital

Condition	Number
Cerebral palsy	69
Autism	1
Multiple congenital anomalies	1
Cortical dysplasia	1
Hydrocephalus	2
Hypocellular dwarfism	1
Microcephaly	5
Primary osteoporosis	1
Myelodysplasia	4
Mucopolysaccharidosis	1
Traumatic brain injury	1
Idiopathic scoliosis	2
Schizophrenia	2
Rett's syndrome	3
No specific associated diagnosis	25

Cerebral palsy: walking patients

In the 36 patients who were able to walk (age range 20–87, mean 38 years) the presenting problems were as shown in Table 4.2.

Table 4.2 Problems in walking patients with cerebral palsy

Problem	Number
Foot problems	19
Deteriorating mobility	5
Crouch gait	5
Hip pain	3
Gait assessment	2
Wrist pain	1
Backache	1

For those presenting with foot problems, seven were provided with adapted shoewear, four with ankle–foot orthoses, three with gastrocnemius lengthenings for equinus, and two received fusions – one of the first metatarsophalangeal joint for a severe bunion and the other a subtalar joint for a fixed hindfoot valgus – and two no specific treatment. Foot pain, particularly in spastic diplegia, is a well-recognised cause for a patient to go off the feet, and foot problems were the most common cause for consultation.

Crouch gait in patients with diplegia presents either as a flexed hip, knee and ankle pattern or as a flexed hip, knee and excessively dorsiflexed ankle pattern. The first pattern was seen in these five patients. One did not require any treatment because the problem was mild, but the remainder all received surgical treatment. This consisted of intramuscular lengthenings of psoas and gastrocnemius in the first, hamstring and gastrocnemius in the second, psoas adductor and hamstring in the third, and a femoral extension osteotomy in the fourth. Surgical management was appropriate in this group because all had severe functional problems. There were no postoperative complications.

The hemiplegic patient presenting with wrist pain was treated with a wrist fusion because the pain was associated with a severe flexion deformity and skin hygiene problems. The 45-year-old patient complaining of mechanical backache had a diplegia and an associated hyperlordosis. He did not require surgical treatment.

In this group, 35 of the 36 patients had a mobility problem necessitating a consultation. Those seven patients presenting specifically with a deteriorating gait and for a gait assessment (age range 26–38) represented a group who had been mobile without undue difficulty in their late adolescent years, but who were now facing increasing difficulty. Although there is little information on the longer-term outcome of gait efficiency in the older patient with cerebral palsy, there is a clinical impression that walking efficiency seems to deteriorate with time. There is a range of potential causes for deteriorating walking efficiency, which may include hip or foot instability, contractures, prolonged sitting, muscular weakness, increasing weight and pain arising from the lower back, patellofemoral joint or feet. Foot problems – both postural and pain – were the most common reason for presentation in this group. This can be a complex problem because often the underlying cause may not actually lie in the foot but in a more proximal area, and the presenting foot problem is a compensation for this. For example, pes valgus may be secondary to an external tibial torsion, which might in turn be associated with excessive internal femoral torsion. Under these circumstances, one may have to accept that correction of these multiple level problems is not a practical proposition for the foot problem. There is an increasing interest in correcting torsional problems in the younger hemiplegic and diplegic patient, but it is not known whether or not this will have a protective effect on foot function in adult life.

Cerebral palsy: non-walking patients

The presenting problems in the 33 patients who were unable to walk (age range 17–76, mean 32 years) were as shown in Table 4.3.

Table 4.3 Problems in non-walking patients with cerebral palsy

Problem	Number
Spinal deformity	8
Seating problems	7
Hip dislocation	7
Foot problems	6
Wrist pain	4
Perineal access difficulties	2
Hip pain	2

Clearly, in this group there was some overlap of presenting features because some patients with spinal deformity also had a hip dislocation. The main problem has been recorded above.

The patients with spinal problems all had a severe fixed neuromuscular scoliosis that was beyond surgical correction. All were provided with a detachable, lightweight, thermoplastic, underarm orthosis the aim of which was to improve trunk stability and head control.

The seven patients who had a seating problem all went on to have a formal seating assessment from the local bioengineering centre. They all received adaptations to their existing seating system and none required a moulded seat. Usually, it has been possible to adapt a commercially available chassis for the individual's needs.

Seven patients had a hip dislocation and in four the dislocation was painless. Three had modifications of their seating to accommodate hip posture. The fourth had adductor and psoas tenotomies, the aim of which was to improve hip abduction sufficiently for seating purposes, but not to reduce the hip as this would have entailed a much more complex procedure. Three patients had a painful dislocation. In the first, hip reduction was achieved by pelvic and femoral osteotomy. The remaining two patients both had a proximal femoral excision for high-riding, painful, irreducible hips.

Successful outcomes in terms of seating and hip pain were seen in all those undergoing surgery. No attempt was made to treat fixed pelvic obliquity and associated severe scoliosis. It is easier technically to reduce a hip surgically if there is reasonable acetabular and femoral morphology, and there is a good case for intervening early where the hip is clearly symptomatic and dislocating. The difficulty lies in the case of patients who have a painless dislocating hip and no functional deficit, to decide whether or not prophylactic intervention is justifiable before the hip becomes unreconstructable. It has been reported that about 50% of institutionalised patients with severe cerebral palsy go on to develop a painful hip dislocation (Cooperman et al., 1987). For this reason, it is important to be able to distinguish between a painful and a non-painful dislocated hip and whether or not the hip is reconstructable. The views of the patient's carer help greatly in deciding management. The painless dislocated hip can be treated by an abduction osteotomy to improve perineal access and seating posture, if this is a problem. However, if the joint is painful, a different approach is necessary – either hip reduction or excision. In the dislocated hip, there is usually a combination of femoral and acetabular deformity. On the femoral side, the deformity may consist of either lateral flattening of the head caused by pressure of the glutei or flattening on the medial side resulting from pressure from the dislocated hip abutting against the side wall of the pelvis. In addition, the head can be notched by the psoas tendon. On the acetabular side, there is usually a saucer-shaped elongation of the acetabulum in the direction of the dislocating femoral head. The aim of reduction is to produce a pain-free mobile joint.

Perineal access problems were seen in two patients who had congruent hip joints. These were both treated by anterior obturator neurectomy and division of the adductor longus and gracilis. Two patients had hip pain caused by hip subluxation and these were treated successfully with femoral varus derotation osteotomy. It is essential before undertaking these major procedures to ensure that the source of pain is correctly identified and that the likely functional gains for the patient are considered from the point of view of the patient and carers.

Six patients had severe foot deformities. Five underwent surgical treatment to give a foot that could be accommodated in a shoe and the sixth received adapted footwear. Even though these patients were non-walkers, they required footwear that could be fitted and also a foot posture that would allow the foot to rest comfortably on the foot plate of their wheelchair.

Wrist pain was seen in four patients and all four had, in addition, hygiene problems with their flexor wrist creases. In all, there was no useful hand function and all underwent a flexor release and wrist fusion.

A recent report has studied the expectation of cerebral palsy patients reaching the age of 40 years. It was shown that 85% of patients with total body involvement could expect to achieve this in the absence of severe epilepsy, which worsened the outlook (Crichton et al., 1995). This suggests that there is a cerebral palsy population who will require long-term care and for whom survival to midlife is a very real possibility. This has resource implications and is also a justification for treatment to improve function in order to assist the patient and his or her carers.

Learning disability and non-specific orthopaedic problems

Twenty-five patients had no recognised orthopaedic problem associated with their condition. Unlike the cerebral palsy groups, these patients were very likely to reflect the type of orthopaedic problems that might occur in the population at large. Their orthopaedic conditions were much more in keeping with those seen in routine adult practice. Three had Dupuytren's contracture and all were on medication for epilepsy – there is a well-recognised association between the two conditions. One presented with a flexed knee walking pattern (although in the absence of any upper motor neuron lesion suggestive of cerebral palsy) and another presented with knee hyperextension associated with generalised joint laxity.

Five older patients aged 55–84 presented with osteoarthritis of the hips. In three, the pain was severe enough to justify a hip replacement. From a technical standpoint, it was important to recognise that none of these three patients would be able to cooperate with a standard hip replacement rehabilitation regimen, so allowances had to be made for this. A lateral surgical approach to the hip was used and a prosthesis with a large diameter head was selected to minimise the risk of dislocation. All three rehabilitated well and none suffered a dislocation. Good pain relief was obtained in all. However, one man developed profuse ectopic bone formation around the hip, which limited the range of movement of the joint, but this remained painless.

One elderly man presented with osteoarthritis of the shoulder, another with spinal stenosis and a third with scoliosis. None required surgery.

One patient presented with an intracapsular fracture neck of femur that had occurred some time earlier and another with a loose hip replacement that had been inserted for a femoral neck fracture some years earlier. Both required surgery.

Ten patients had the foot problems shown in Table 4.4. All patients received functional foot orthoses and modified footwear where necessary. One schizophrenic patient presented with bunions that were managed with footwear adaptations. One patient who had primary osteoporosis and another who had a mucopolysaccharidosis had gait assessments.

Table 4.4 Foot problems among patients

Problem	Number
Bunions	1
Metatarsalgia	1
Mild equinus	2
Idiopathic club feet	1
Pes cavus	1
Valgus hypermobile feet	4

Learning disability and associated orthopaedic conditions

Two patients had hydrocephalus: one presented with a hyperlordotic lumbar spine that did not require any specific treatment and the other with severe bunions that were treated by first metatarsophalangeal fusions. One patient with hypocellular dwarfism and epilepsy developed mild equinus, which was treated with serial plaster casts.

Five patients had microcephaly and severe learning difficulties. Two were non-walkers and of these one required an underarm jacket for a neuropathic scoliosis; the other required footwear adaptations for a mobile valgus foot. One, who was a therapeutic walker, required a seating assessment, another, who was fully ambulant, advice for hip pain and one required footwear adaptations for a mild equinus.

Four patients had myelomeningocele. Three were non-walkers and had mid-thoracic paraplegias. All had a significant spinal deformity that was not amenable to surgical correction and received an underarm spinal jacket. The fourth, who was a walker, had a crouch gait associated with a low lumbar lesion and benefited from the provision of floor reaction ankle–foot orthoses.

Three patients had Rett's syndrome. Two had a spinal deformity, one of which was managed with an underarm orthosis and the other by spinal fusion. The third had developed a mild equinus, which was treated with a heel raise.

The last patient had a traumatic brain injury and developed severe hip, knee and ankle contractures that precluded stable sitting. He underwent multiple level surgery to produce a sitting posture.

Case studies

Osteoarthritis of the hip

The patient, a 64-year-old woman, was a long-term resident at Gogarburn Hospital. She had severe learning difficulties and behavioural problems consisting of screaming, pinching and poking other individuals, was unable to communicate her needs and required supervision of all her day-to-day activities. She was normally able to walk out of doors under supervision. In the preceding 2 years, she had been noted to develop a painful left-sided limp and limitation of her walking, so that latterly she would no longer go outside. In addition, it was noted that she appeared to have pain when her left leg was moved by her carers.

Examination and subsequent radiographs confirmed advanced osteoarthritis of her left hip. After discussion with her carers and her brother and sister, it was decided to offer a hip replacement. This posed several potential problems. First, the patient was unlikely to have any understanding of the proposed procedure and would not be able to cooperate with a standard postoperative rehabilitation programme after hip replacement; second, she was likely to be at a greater risk of dislocation of the hip; and third, she would be noisy in an open ward and probably upset other patients also undergoing elective orthopaedic surgery.

It was decided to use a prosthesis with a larger diameter head than usual to minimise the risk of dislocation. She was looked after in a side room so as to minimise any disturbances on the ward, and an early return to her normal environment at Gogarburn Hospital was planned for her own well-being. In addition, there was excellent coordination between the nursing staff of both hospitals, and nursing staff from Gogarburn came to the orthopaedic ward to assist with her care. No attempt was made to follow a conventional rehabilitation programme and the patient mobilised at 48 hours without difficulty. She made surprisingly good progress and was well enough to return to her usual environment 5 days after surgery. Her subsequent progress was uneventful: her walking pattern improved, her limp resolved and her carers noted that she did not appear to have hip pain. Her progress has been maintained 2 years after surgery.

Wrist pain in patient with hemiplegia

The patient, a 37-year-old man, had a congenital hemiplegia and learning disability. He was unable to communicate verbally but appeared to have reasonable comprehension and lived with his elderly mother. There had been, over the years, a progressive flexion deformity of his right wrist and increasing wrist pain. He did not have any useful hand function but used the arm as a prop. In addition, he had increasing problems with hygiene of the flexor creases of the wrist.

After discussion, he was offered surgery to lengthen the forearm flexors and to fuse the wrist. This was carried out successfully 2 years ago and relieved him of his wrist pain and hygiene problem. There was no functional gain or loss. The pre- and postoperative appearances are shown in Figures 4.1–4.3.

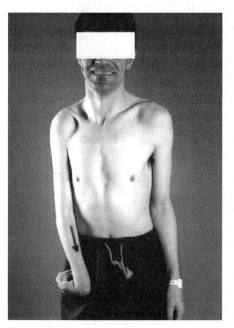 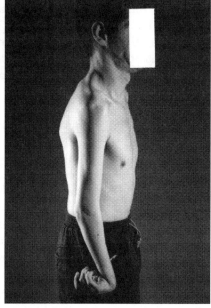

Figures 4.1 Preoperative appearances of the wrist.

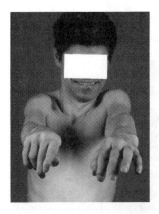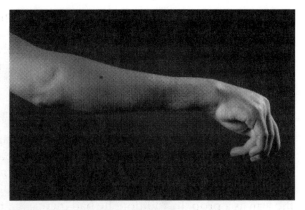

Figures 4.2 Postoperative appearances of the wrist.

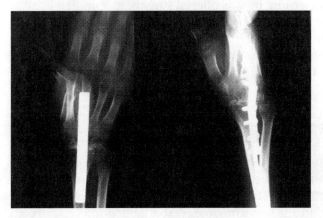

Figure 4.3 Postoperative radiological appearances; the wrist has fused and the plate has been used to align the third metacarpal to the radius and has been contoured to give some dorsiflexion.

Equinus in a patient with a chromosome disorder

The patient, a 35-year-old woman, had a severe learning disability and was unable to communicate verbally. She was able to walk using a rollator with assistance from day-care staff, but her ability to do so was hampered by a high-riding, long-standing, painless dislocation of the left hip and a progressive equinus of the left ankle (Figure 4.4). Her functional difficulty was an inability to contain her left foot comfortably in a shoe. This resulted in bottom-shuffling in a windswept posture as her chosen method of mobility. She was no longer able to walk and use a standing frame. After her mother's death she lived in a house run by the Cheshire Foundation.

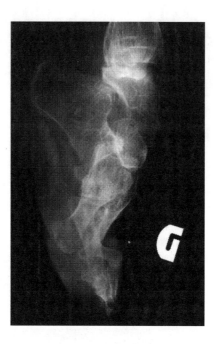

Figure 4.4 Lateral radiograph of the foot and ankle showing severe equinus.

After discussion with her tutor dative (see Chapter 1), it was decided to offer calf muscle surgery to improve the foot posture and to produce a plantargrade foot. The hip dislocation was painless and so did not require treatment and it was anticipated that she would require an ankle–foot orthosis and a compensatory shoe raise postoperatively.

She underwent an elongation of gastrocnemius, tibialis posterior and flexor hallucis longus of the left calf, which produced a plantargrade foot. Her postoperative recovery was uneventful; her foot posture and mobility have been maintained 2 years after surgery. She does not object to wearing her orthosis and is able to walk independently at her day centre using a rollator.

Seating difficulties in severe cerebral palsy

The patient, a 28-year-old man, was a long-term resident at Gogarburn Hospital. He had cerebral palsy with total body involvement and difficulties with seating. This was as a result of a combination of a severe scoliosis, a flexed and adducted right hip, and a fixed extension deformity of the left knee. He had severe equinovarus of the left foot and calcaneus of the right foot, and was able to wear only slipper socks. There were also severe flexion contractures of both elbows and wrists. He was unable to sit in any conventional form of seating and had a moulded seating device to accommodate his extended left knee. He had several other functional problems: difficulties of perineal access resulting from the fixed flexion deformity of the left hip of 80° and fixed adduction of 60°, hygiene problems with the elbows and wrists, and an inability to wear normal footwear.

The difficulties with perineal access and seating were identified as the dominant problems by his carers and, after discussion with them and the patient's father, it was decided to offer surgical treatment. This consisted of an abduction osteotomy of the right femur (Figures 4.5 and 4.6) and division of adductor longus, gracilis, the anterior obturator nerve and a left quadricepsplasty to gain knee flexion. This produced abduction of 5° on the right side and 90° of knee flexion on the left side. Both were sufficient to permit perineal access and the use of conventional seating rather than a moulded device. His severe scoliosis was inoperable. This surgery

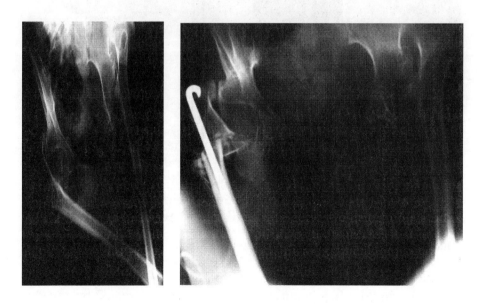

Figure 4.5 (Left) Preoperative radiograph of the pelvis. The right hip is in severe adduction and the hips are dislocated.

Figure 4.6 (Right) Appearances after the abduction osteotomy.

was undertaken 7 years ago and the postoperative position has been maintained (Figure 4.7).

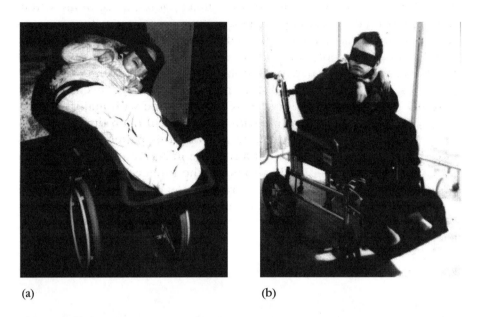

(a)   (b)

Figure 4.7 Clinical appearances (a) before and (b) after hip surgery.

One year later, it was felt by his carers that the hygiene problems of his elbows and wrists were causing a persistent disagreeable odour and surgical treatment was requested. These were long-standing deformities and it was felt that it would be possible to gain elbow extension to about 90° but no more, and that the wrist problems could be treated by wrist fusion. Both these procedures were carried out 6 years ago and have been successful in dealing with the hygiene problems.

Two years later, there were increasing concerns about the posture of his left foot and, because of severe equinovarus, the skin on the outer border of the foot had begun to ulcerate. This was treated by a wedge tarsectomy which produced a plantargrade foot. This, and the provision of an ankle–foot orthosis on the right side, enabled him to be provided with conventional footwear and to be able to rest both feet on the foot plate of his seating system.

This patient received the most surgery of all those seen in the clinic. Such procedures are justifiable if clearly defined problems and goals of treatment are identified.

Conclusion

There was inevitably a spectrum of patients seen in this environment. Some had orthopaedic conditions as a direct consequence of the condition producing their learning disability. Others were seen with conditions that were additional to their learning disability. Orthopaedic management, whether surgical or not, can be of benefit, providing that realistic aims and functional goals are set in conjunction with the patient's carers and therapists. Disability and age should not preclude treatment. Even the most severely handicapped patients were able to cope with major surgery. Having a long-established clinic with a tradition of open discussion and cooperation has been invaluable in assisting this patient group. It has already been shown that expectation of life in severe cerebral palsy has improved and this has implications for the longer-term care of more profoundly handicapped adults. More are now living in the community and it is not known what effect this may have on future referral patterns and morbidity.

PART II

ASSESSING PHYSICAL ABILITY AND PLANNING INTERVENTION

CHAPTER 5

The multiprofessional learning disability team

PATRICIA ODUNMBAKU AUTY AND JEANETTE RENNIE

Chapter 1 described the historical development towards multiprofessional team work with people who have learning disabilities. This chapter aims to describe benefits that can result from this working practice and problems that can impede its practical development.

For many years, different professionals have been involved in using their skills for the benefit of clients who have learning disability and associated disabilities. In a minority of hospitals, team work was routine practice. In many, however, departments or individuals tended to work in isolation with little consultation or cooperation with each other. Therefore, clients were unable to benefit from a coordinated programme, which is essential before the various skills can be focused in one smooth operation.

Working in isolation prevented treatment programmes (intervention, including treatment and management) from reaching their optimum level and achieving the desired outcomes. For example, if a physiotherapist established a programme of activity without knowing the linguistic skills, comprehension or sign language of the client, that programme was bereft of an essential component. This interfered with the client achieving his or her potential. Similarly, if an occupational therapist was not conversant with the programme for the client's challenging behaviour, that programme could not be completely effective.

This has now changed and multiprofessional working is the desired goal even if its interpretations take a variety of forms and the results range from excellent to indifferent.

Originally, the health-care element of community mental handicap teams (see Chapter 1) was drawn from nursing and therapy departments of the large hospitals as the clients moved into the community. Allan et al.

(1990) described the fears and misgivings felt by staff on being redeployed in the community. They noted that morale and confidence was affected by:

- change of work setting and environment
- job redefinition
- multiagency work
- training for a new service
- worries about staff recruitment
- new philosophical expectations

These were very real concerns, especially where clinical line management was no longer on site and where special equipment and large spaces were required for treatment, particularly for physiotherapy.

Examples of team configuration

Teams combined a number of different professions with different configurations. In 1991, Cheseldine wrote that:

> . . . the core membership of a Community Mental Handicap Team typically consists of a social worker, community mental handicap nurse and clinical psychologist.

Clients' needs may require involvement from other people including:

> . . . a consultant psychiatrist, occupational therapists, rehabilitation officers, home support workers, social work assistants, pre-school teachers, liaison health visitors and volunteer co-ordinators.

In other areas of the country, teams were developing along very different lines, obviously with a slant towards people with more severe physical disabilities (Hollins, in Craft et al., 1985). They included:

- Many nurses and a single physiotherapist or occupational therapist.
- A psychology manager, a predominance of psychologists and challenging needs specialists, and a single representative from different therapies.
- Equal number of different professions.

Teams ranged from a single professional representative of each health-care profession to three or more members of each. Many have always included a consultant psychiatrist. Social work representation varied according to the division between specialist and generic teams within the area.

Gradually, new government directives were enacted. Some have since been superseded, but all have influenced the development of multiprofessional work. They have included the role of Social Services, health authorities or boards as purchasers and not direct providers, GP fund-holding, the introduction of care managers (Macadam and Rodgers, 1997) and more recently the reformation of Health Service Trusts and the introduction of Primary Care Groups in England and Wales and Local Health Care Co-operatives in Scotland (Department of Health (England), 1997; Department of Health (Wales), 1997; The Scottish Office, 1997).

Team configuration has changed because the structure is led by client need, and resources are distributed proportionally to suit the local requirements. They may now include:

- a dietitian
- an art therapist
- a music therapist

depending on need and availability of staff. In some teams, community nurses operate an emergency on-call service.

Resources

Resources continue to be scarce in both finance and staff skills and experience. This can lead to professions that are small in staff numbers having to participate in more than one team and attempting to attend a number of team meetings. If care is not taken, they can begin to feel that they are not full members of any team. Conversely, a feeling of guilt may be generated if meetings seem to be attended at the expense of direct client contacts. It can also lead to the rest of the team neglecting that individual's potential contribution. In most areas, the problem of staff shortage is resolved by regarding the team as a coordinated group of professionals and accepting that all members are unlikely to be available to attend every meeting, so clients are deferred for discussion until such time as key staff are present. Everyone receives all minutes and correspondence.

Despite lack of resources, continuing development of community learning disability teams was clearly anticipated in a recent report from the NHS executive. It referred to the usual model of service delivery as:

... that of multidisciplinary community teams for people with learning disabilities. These provide a single point of access and assessment leading to a range of specialist provision on a peripatetic or outpatient basis.

It recognised that in a few areas specialist services had been integrated into uniprofessional teams or 'ordinary community services' (Lindsey, 1998). The concept of placing learning disability services in the primary and community care trusts was welcomed by MENCAP on condition that their specialist identity was preserved (Band, 1998).

> Team = a set of people working in combination = a coordinated group of professionals
>
> Schwarz (1993)

Establishing a team

The gathering together of a multiprofessional group of individuals does not constitute team working. Many steps are required before a truly coordinated group is established that can provide a holistic programme for the benefit of clients, without diminishing the unique contribution of each professional group. Underpinning any multiprofessional learning disability team is a shared philosophy, frequently expressed by O'Brien's five essential accomplishments for quality of life (see Chapter 1).

Communication and dynamics

Ignorance of each other's professional roles can present difficulties and sensitivities where professional boundaries overlap. To help to overcome this, many teams hold in-service training on roles and responsibilities. Some have resulted in the production of leaflets for the public which have enabled referrals to be directed to the appropriate services.

Establishing a base office is critical for success as a good working environment and administrative support is an important factor in effective work. Close proximity assists communication in the base. Multiprofessional working begins slowly, developing as friendship and respect grow.

Policy

A clear team operational policy, prepared and shared by all whilst respecting each set of professional standards, assists development of a successful service. It includes the general purpose of the team, its aims and priorities, membership, meetings, team leader role and professional management roles. It also includes case allocation and priorities. Some professions require their staff to make priorities by the referral issues, because they open the episode of care and assume legal responsibility at the point of contact with the referrer. Other professions make priorities after a meeting with the client and the referrer, and the episode of care and assumption of legal responsibility commence with the first treatment session. A strong operational policy also clarifies the issues surrounding shared or separate professional case files. Some trusts operate the system of 'integrated care pathways' as a flow chart to clarify a client's progress through the system and to specify who is responsible for decision-making at each stage of progression (Baldry and Rossiter, 1995).

Referral system

Referrals may be made by:

- The paediatric department
- Local general practitioners
- Social Services via social workers and day carers
- Residential care staff
- Clients and their families
- General hospitals and outpatient clinics
- Long-stay hospitals for people with learning disabilities as they move into the community

It is possible that only 30% of the team's caseload requires input from more than one professional. However, it may be that, after the initial assessment, other needs become apparent and other professionals are required. To share this information, a multiprofessional meeting at frequent and regular intervals is established. It is at this forum that difficulties can be discussed, support given and quality issues voiced. New referrals can be discussed and appropriate information on clients shared.

Once all this information is received and the client allocated to the appropriate profession, a screening takes place to make priorities of the client's needs.

Methods of making priorities

- Waiting lists
  - explicitly via a system of chronological referral
  - implicitly after discussion on the basis of clinical need
- Structured points system

The following example of a points system used in case-weighting was designed for physiotherapists. It could be transferred to other professionals or adapted for the team as a whole. Papathanasiou and Lyon-Maris (1997) based their system on the principles devised by Williams (1991) (Table 5.1).

Table 5.1 System of Papathanasiou and Lyon-Maris (1997)

- Clients are weighted by five factors:
  1. Type of input required
  2. Other support services involved
  3. Management of physical status
  4. Client/therapist interface
  5. Client/carer compliance
- Scores for each factor range from 1 to 5
- Minimum intervention would be required for a score of 1 point or less in each factor. Total case intervention score (CIS) of between 1 and 5. Maximum intervention would have a CIS of between 21 and 25
- The CIS is then classified by a case band A–E (minimum → maximum)
- Estimated physiotherapy intervention hours for case band A is 3 hours in 6 months and case band E is 48 hours in 6 months

In any system for determining priorities where there is also paediatric involvement, the team will be influenced by the assessment of the statement of needs or the needs assessment. This is especially important at the difficult transitional time.

Discussion at a multiprofessional meeting does not replace a case conference or planning meeting in which progress and problems are discussed in depth.

Case-load management

The number of people that the team can be expected to reach is estimated in a variety of ways in different areas of the country, for example, via a Learning Disability or Community Care Register. With pressure of clients, case-load management is essential to ensure that the clients who are treated receive quality interventions, that notes comply with clients' needs and legal responsibilities, and that discharge letters are written and statistical information is recorded before other clients are accepted.

Many professions have one or more recognised methods of estimating staff/client ratios. The most recent estimates for speech and language therapists indicate that most newly qualified staff spend 60% of their working hours in client contact time and 40% in indirect work. This will gradually shift from 60% to 40% in client contact time for more senior staff as training and lecturing responsibilities increase.

Table 5.2 is one interesting model which was produced by Joyce Wise and may be used as a basis for estimating physiotherapy staffing levels. It does not differentiate between levels of physiotherapy experience or conditions under which people are treated (hospital; community, centre based; community, domiciliary). As with speech and language therapists, direct client contact time will decrease with seniority as training, lecturing and management responsibilities increase. Table 5.3 is her model for physiotherapy case management. Both models in Table 5.3 may be multiprofessional, although this is less likely in the case of the therapeutic model.

Table 5.2 An example of staffing level requirements for physiotherapists for 1 year

Physiotherapist	**Patient contact hours**
1 whole-time equivalent	36 hours × 45 weeks = 1620 h/year
70% contact	1134 h (in learning disability, this can reduce to 50% as a result of clinics, meetings, telephoning and modifying seating and equipment, and in community work and travelling time)
Individual patient treatment hours/year	**Number of patients who can be treated**
Patient receiving recognised GP referral requirement of treatment	5 sessions at 0.5 h/session = 2.5 h in the year = 453 patients/year
Patient × 1 h in the year	1134 patients in the year
Patient × 5 h in the year	226 patients/year
Patient × 45 h in the year (many of the learning disability clients)	25 patients in the year

Joyce Wise, ACPPLD Conference (1998).

Table 5.3 Models of physiotherapy case management

Therapeutic model – largely gate kept by doctors
This is treatment that is in direct response to medical problems
    Assessment
    Intervention
    Episodic
    Discharge
        complete
        onward to wellness model

Wellness model – open referrals
    Maintenance of optimum health/fitness
    Preparation for therapeutic intervention
    Maximising and maintaining health gains obtained from therapeutic model
    Interface between childhood/adolescence and adulthood
    Multidisciplinary
    Multiagency
    Long term, seldom complete discharge

Joyce Wise, ACPPLD Conference (1998).

Joint working can be advantageous for clients
For example:

Eating and drinking referrals
Speech and language therapists, dietitian, physiotherapist and community nurse may have input from a psychologist and psychiatrist

Challenging behaviour
Psychiatrist, psychologist, community nurse, and speech and language therapist may have input from occupational therapist and on occasion physiotherapist

Housing needs and adaptations
Occupational therapists, physiotherapist and community nurse

Community nurses will be involved with health needs and liaison with local hospitals but will gather information which is appropriate to the specific episode or treatment from all who provide services to the client. Occupational therapists are involved with skills teaching and are closely linked to the Social Services and non-profit agencies.

Education and training

Training takes a large proportion of time. Appropriate skills are passed on from individual members of the immediate team to carers at home and in day centres and inclusion projects. Clients and staff are assisted to understand and carry out specific programmes such as those as described in various chapters in this book. However, current thinking questions the clinical effectiveness of attempting previously advocated larger scale skills transfer as it has been discovered in practice that the vast turnover of support staff often necessitates frequently repeated training and can result in ineffective outcomes.

It is also inevitable that the professionals learn from each other and develop a mutual respect for each other and for each other's professional skills. As teams develop into more cohesive units, they may invite informal speakers to their meetings or form their own journal club.

Members of the immediate multiprofessional team also learn from other professionals as they liaise with them over specific clients. For example, an audiologist's report influences the method by which speech and language therapists enable clients to achieve appropriate communication. More detailed examples are given in the case studies.

Reports

When it is appropriate, joint reports are written. These may be produced from case conferences and individual meetings around the clients in which all who provide a service participate. Any professional who is unable to attend will submit a report, which will be presented by a well-briefed colleague.

Each profession uses uniprofessional clinical audit and progress reports and has a tool for outcome measurement (see Chapters 7 and 8). Training of carers can be evaluated by a client and staff satisfaction scale.

Trying to find a measurement of outcomes to reflect an efficient, effective and beneficial team service to clients takes much thought and effort. Current methods include:

- Individual professions' outcome measures placed in the medical records.
- Simple rating based on the initial team assessment of needs using a scale of 0–2.
- Baseline assessment unique to the team followed by a written report after a specified time span.
- Recognised multiprofessional outcome measure (see Chapters 7 and 8).

Staff support

Increased stress levels can arise within a multiprofessional team. However, it is readily compensated for by mutual staff support from a group of people working together with the same client.

Teams tend to be coordinated by one of their members and managed by a nurse, therapist or psychologist who reports to a general manager.

> **Professionally**, staff need to retain their identity, have the opportunity for personal development and feel valued.
>
> This can happen only if the opportunity is afforded for **continuing education**.

Higgs and Titchen (1995) suggested that three types of knowledge were required as a basis for clinical reasoning. These were Continuing Propositional Knowledge gained through research, conferences, meetings and courses within the individual profession; Professional Craft Knowledge, practical expertise and skills that develop over the years, the type of knowledge that passes from experienced to less experienced staff and Personal Knowledge which is a deepening understanding of oneself and through that of others.

It is essential, therefore, that all professionals are encouraged and assisted to participate in relevant courses and conferences organised by their own professions. Opportunities should be strengthened by the introduction of 'clinical governance' which makes Chief Executives of trusts accountable for the quality of patient care in their trusts (National Health Services Executive, 1999). The service as a whole benefits if such encouragement and assistance is made known publicly whenever staff are being recruited.

It is also essential that all professions have access to appropriate clinical supervision and appraisal. In trusts that have maintained line management within professions in learning disability there should be no problems. Where professions have no clinical manager within learning disability support is reduced and there may be no obvious professional development structure. This can exacerbate recruitment difficulties. In such trusts structures may be established to allow supervision and appraisal by a therapist of the same profession in another specialty whilst concurrently developing peer assessment within learning disability in the local area. In some professions, discussions are being undertaken about the possibility of mentoring through the national clinical interest group of the professional body.

The strength and quality of the team is only achieved by the updated expertise of the members of each individual profession. However, growth of knowledge within individual professions can not replace multiprofessional training. They must be seen as complementary to one another and it is through training and working together that Personal Knowledge is most likely to become more fully developed.

Conclusion

Professionals work together as coordinated groups to reinforce each other's aims and objectives. They provide sound practical assistance for people with learning disabilities in their aim to lead an active life in the community. In stressful home and family situations, strong, coordinated support instead of indiscriminate attention from individuals is invaluable. In such situations joint voices are a powerful and influential tool.

Case studies

Case study 1: JA

Community support for Miss JA is illustrated in Figure 5.1.

Miss JA transferred to a home for elderly people from a long-stay hospital where she had lived for 35 years. She has a severe learning disability.

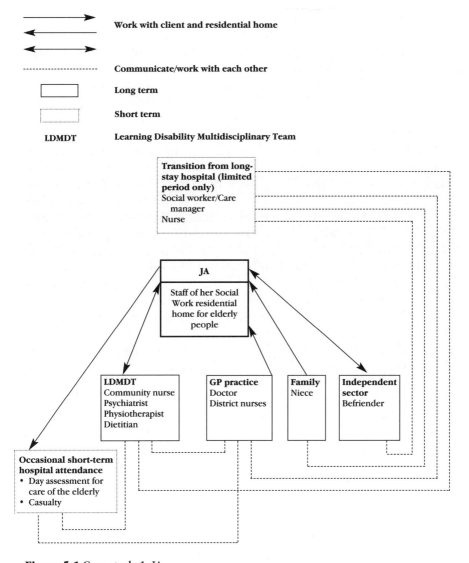

Figure 5.1 Case study 1: JA.

History

- A 69-year-old woman
- History of depressive illness, which can result in withdrawal and unwillingness to speak, eat or take medication
- History of tardive dyskinesia resulting in a slight parkinsonian tremor of the hands
- Prone to urinary tract infection and constipation

A comprehensive community care assessment was compiled by her Social Worker/Care Manager at the hospital in conjunction with the ward and all hospital departments with whom she had contact. This was used as the basis of her care plan.

During the transition from hospital to residential home, her care manager referred her to the local learning disability team psychiatrist and community nurse. Her residential home referred her to the district nurses and a voluntary befriender.

Three weeks after moving, she was referred to a physiotherapist in the team because of swollen and apparently painful hands. Before treatment a radiograph was requested. She resisted all attempts to take her to a radiography department until 6 weeks later. For 3 months, she resisted any contact other than gentle passive exercises undertaken in her chosen position, which was frequently walking round the building. It was established that she had psychoflexed hands. At one time, a fungal condition developed in the palm of her hands, which required daily treatment from the district nurse with assistance from the physiotherapist. The physiotherapist continues regular passive stretching (Jamieson, 1989) and, as Miss JA has become more amenable to having her hands touched, the home staff incorporate gentle finger movements during hand washing.

During the last 18 months she has had sharply fluctuating mood swings necessitating adjustment to her level of medication. She has undergone severe weight loss. The dietitian and community nurse have established food intake charts with the home staff and monitored her weight and body mass index (BMI) weekly.

Miss JA is routinely placed on a list for 3-monthly discussion at the team meeting. However, her variety of conditions and their impact on each other frequently necessitate an update discussion. This enables all staff to work in a concerted manner.

Case study 2: BH

Community support for BH is illustrated in Figure 5.2.

Mr BH married and moved into a voluntary agency 'Good Neighbour

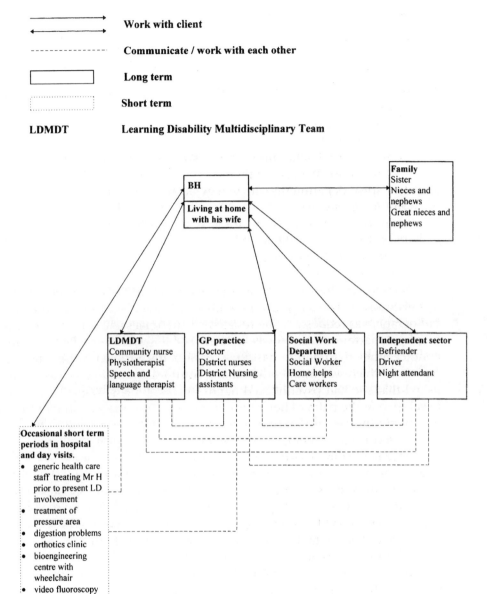

Figure 5.2 Case study 2: BH.

Scheme' flat from a long-stay hospital in 1983 when multiprofessional community care was becoming established. He was described as being in the 'dull–normal' range of intellectual ability and perhaps should not have been admitted to a long-stay learning disability hospital; his wife has moderate learning disability.

History

- A 73-year-old man
- Uncertain early history suggested postencephalitic syndrome
- Eventual diagnosis: ataxic diplegia with some extrapyramidal features presenting as pyramidal involvement of all four limbs, cerebellar incoordination of upper limbs, marked spasticity of lower limbs, facial grimacing and dysarthria, which was possibly cerebellar
- Reportedly walked at age 5.5 years
- Attended a special school
- Could become extremely frustrated and angry
- Aged 25 years and after the death of his father, admitted to a long-stay hospital
- On admission, still able to walk with a scissors gait pattern
- Five years after admission, he became confined to a wheelchair
- In 1968, he was referred for physiotherapy and speech therapy
- Treatment continued until he left the hospital
- Attended further education classes in and outside the hospital

The couple attended separate day centres three times a week. Mr BH ceased attending because it lacked stimulation. He was an active member of the 'Regional Rights Group and Division Planning Group for people with mental handicap' and was invited to discuss the proposals on the Disability Bill. He continued to expand his interests and activities in the community.

Daily contact was maintained with district nurses, home help, volunteer driver, befriender and neighbours, so formal contact with the learning disability team community nurse was regular but infrequent.

At the patient's request, all therapy ceased until 1987. On discharge from a general hospital, he was referred to the generic community physiotherapy department which re-referred him to learning disability physiotherapists. He participated in hydrotherapy sessions at his former long-stay hospital and subsequently self-referred whenever he felt that it was necessary.

In 1995, his learning disability team social worker referred him to the team physiotherapist. He was more frail and dependent, and required professional intervention to accelerate work on his wheelchair. Sadly, before this referral had been made, several months' retention of his wheelchair for major modifications had confined him to bed and resulted in an open pressure area.

It transpired that, between 1983 and 1995, he had periodically been admitted to a hospital for care of elderly people for treatment of a pressure area and had been treated for a right cervical neuropathy. Both upper limbs are now severely affected. Limb function is limited to pointing with his left arm.

Since 1995 he has participated in weekly physiotherapy at home. This has included: a short period of laser treatment in conjunction with a specific nursing regimen for his pressure area which has remained healed for 3 years; modifications to his wheelchair; regular positioning; and active and passive exercise and chest physiotherapy. His wife and carers have been taught how to position him correctly and undertake simple passive movements. The speech and language therapist, nurse and physiotherapist have worked together regarding mealtime positioning. His wife and home help have been shown how to position him at meal times. During this period he has sustained several transient ischaemic attacks which needed attention.

Despite his increasing level of dependence he continues to be the pivotal figure within his household and takes responsibility for his own decision making. However, he continues to need good community care and his multiplicity of needs necessitate frequent discussion at and between meetings.

Case study 3: KT

Community support for KT is illustrated in Figure 5.3.

Miss KT lives at home with her parents. She has a lively, very strong-willed personality. When first known to the team, she was emotionally labile. She has matured over the past 5 years.

History

- A 25-year-old woman
- Has moderate-to-mild learning disability
- Has moderate cerebral palsy, which was presenting with increasing problems in balance and diminishing walking distance
- Standard ankle–foot orthosis (AFO) supplied by generic physiotherapy service

On leaving school, Miss KT was referred to the community nurse in the team and later to a city-wide clinic for people who have physical disabilities in addition to learning disability. This was originally conceived to aid transition from the paediatric to the adult sector. It is primarily for people

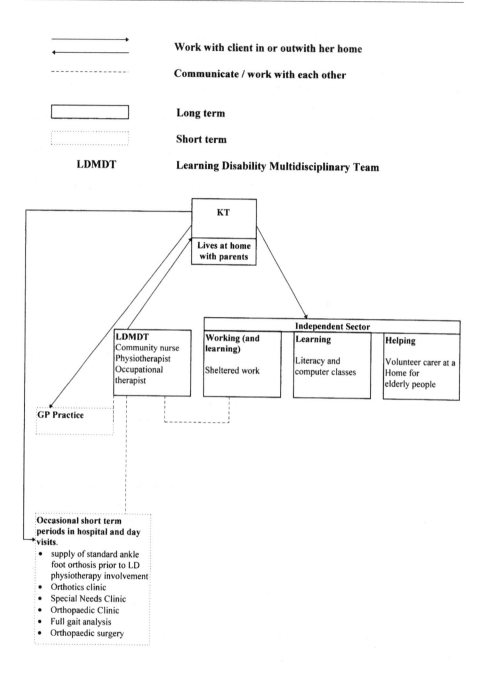

Figure 5.3 Case study 3: KT.

with severe learning disability, but can accommodate people who have multiple, although less severe, needs. It is run by a consultant psychiatrist in learning disability and attended by a community learning disability nurse and physiotherapist. It provides time and opportunity for full examination by the three professionals.

It was decided to continue to monitor her progress through the clinic and her learning disability team, encourage use of the standard AFO, undertake individual physiotherapy if the need arose, and refer her to her team occupational therapist.

Recommendations from the occupational therapist included the following:

- Increase domestic activities in the house
- Attend local groups/courses with own age group
- Continue classes to extend literacy and computing skills
- Work as a volunteer at a nursing home
- Continue search for respite care

Six months later, the team community nurse re-referred her to the team physiotherapist because of problems with the ankle–foot orthosis and concerns about deterioration in walking, which seriously affected her independent lifestyle.

She was referred to the orthopaedic clinic. Her walking pattern was considered to be secondary to calf muscle contractures and so she was referred for full gait analysis. This confirmed that she would benefit from gastrocnemius lengthening. She had a lengthening of bilateral gastrocnemius and the right tibial posterior tendon.

After her hospital discharge, physiotherapy continued with the learning disability team physiotherapist at home once weekly for 4 months. The main advantages of home treatment were that the whole family were involved and that it promoted discussion, which led to integration of daily exercises into a step routine and swimming with her mother. Physiotherapy reduced to 2-monthly visits for a further year with one visit 4 months later when a successful outcome was achieved with her discharge from physiotherapy. By that time she still had an abnormal gait pattern, but no longer required an AFO, rarely fell, negotiated stairs well at home and at work, travelled independently on the buses and went to the cinema with friends.

She continues to be seen by the team community nurse in relation to her new sheltered work and relationships with boyfriends. She can be re-referred to other members of the team when required.

CHAPTER 6

First steps in getting to know and communicating with people who have learning disabilities

SUE STANDING AND SUE SMITH

A therapist meeting a person with learning disabilities for the first time is faced with many challenges. First, their own perception of learning disability: what does it mean to them? Their own beliefs, values and experience will dictate the way in which they react. Second, fear of communication difficulties may lead to the embarrassment of misunderstanding. Third, the inability to identify the client's need accurately could lead to inappropriate goals and plans being developed which will promote failure rather than achievement.

Examination of the therapist's perception of learning disability

Professionals often state that they hold positive beliefs about people with learning disabilities because they have had appropriate training and clinical experience. This can be challenged. First, their response may reflect Oppenheim's (1992) opinion that people answering questions conform to the most socially desirable views. Second, if offered the chance, would you change places with a person with learning disabilities?

Despite these two reservations, Gething (1993) found that the accepted view was largely true with regard to physiotherapists. She discovered that their attitudes towards people with disabilities were more positive than those of the general population, a fact that she attributed to pre-registration disability awareness training and in-service education. Both stimulated positive and realistic attitudes and beliefs, which enhanced effectiveness and appropriateness of practice. In writing about the shaping of social oppression, French (1993) suggested that examination of disability issues develops and deepens knowledge which enables attitudes to change – a view supported by a small study on attitudes of physiotherapy students and qualified physiotherapists towards people with disabilities (Atkinson, 1994). Since these studies were completed, there has been an increasing inclusion of disability awareness training in pre-registration courses for all health-care professionals.

The social construction of disability theory (Berger and Luckman, 1987) assumes that people discover their identity through interactions with others. It highlights influences in society that affect the experience of disability. These influences have generally led to negative attitudes towards people with learning disabilities and to their social alienation. It is, therefore, important to define disability correctly, acknowledging that it has a social dimension (Oliver, 1993). Gates (1997) suggested that professionals working with people who have learning disabilities should stop and reflect on the meaning of such definitions as learning disability, profound handicap and complex needs. This social approach (French, 1994) sees the problem located in the minds of non-disabled people. It implies that, if the attitude of non-disabled people changed, some of the problems of disability would be resolved. On the other hand, Morris (1991) stated:

> . . . we can insist that society disables us by its prejudice and by its failure to meet the needs created by disability, but to deny the personal experience is in the end to collude to our oppression.

There is much debate about the social model and the personal tragedy model. The experience of institutional practices has led to prejudices by society which are perpetuated in many aspects of life (see Chapter 1). The experience of disability, therefore, is affected profoundly by social practice. Why do people with learning disabilities travel on vehicles marked 'ambulance'? Why are they segregated? Who segregates them? Why are so many buildings difficult to access? Who designs them?

Barriers to getting to know a person with learning disabilities

Getting to know another person is a two-way process. A more greatly developed and deeper understanding of the perspective of the experience and history of people who have a learning disability will produce a more positive attitude towards them.

People with learning disabilities face many barriers in getting to know other people. The experience of being disabled is one of social restriction, prejudice and oppression (Swain, 1993). They may be out of reach of relationships with people without disabilities because they live or work in segregated environments. They may lack the opportunity to frequent places where others meet and interact because they cannot afford the entrance fee or price of food and drink, they are physically impaired, access to buildings is poor or transport costs are prohibitive. They may have additional communication difficulties and sensory impairments. They may lack confidence as a result of past experiences of rejection by others.

Without both aspects of this two-way process, relationships cannot be established. Relationships help to define who we are. By helping us to build and reinforce our self-esteem, they can in turn allow us to choose to be either the same as or different from other people. Without them, we cannot know what we are like, or what kind of people we would like to be. Relationships allow us to learn about others, from others, through others and about ourselves (Firth and Rapley, 1990).

One of the key factors in getting to know a person with a learning disability is to give time to that person. Research their background, abilities, style of communication and behaviours. Do not take their reactions on face value. Remember that each person is unique and responds differently in different situations. Investigate their problem thoroughly.

Case study 1

Client A has cerebral palsy with no verbal communication. He recently moved to a new home. The carers note that he grimaces and develops spasms, especially around his hips. On movement he seems to show signs of discomfort. On examination and gentle moving of his hip joints, the client is able to relax. It is noted that, during the move, some of the supports and the foot rests of his armchair were mislaid. Having located these, the client sits more happily in his chair. But the grimacing and spasms continue. Further examination of his hips and back is made and a referral to the orthopaedic consultant arranged. On the radiograph, a dislocation of the hip is found. Conservative management with daily posture control is established. It appears that the grimacing and spasms increase after eating. He undergoes an investigation into his bowel and abdomen. A friend of the client visits and in discussion discloses that the client has often displayed these actions, especially when frustrated and unable to make himself understood!

Communication skills of adults with learning disabilities

Communication is one the most basic needs and functions of human life. The range of methods used to communicate is vast, as are the reasons for using them. Everybody, regardless of their cognitive ability, has methods of communication that are both verbal and non-verbal. These are used as part of their normal communicative repertoire.

Most adults use spoken language as their primary verbal mode of communication and a range of non-verbal communication methods to complement speech. For example, if someone is telling a story, they will convey the basic contents of the story using spoken words, but will convey a range of other aspects using non-verbal communication skills. The emotion of the story may come across through the speaker's intonation, their facial expression and body language. Descriptive information may be expressed through gesture and mime. Emotions of the characters may be portrayed through the volume of speech used by the storyteller. For many adults with a learning disability, speech may not be their strongest modality, and the range and importance of non-verbal skills in conveying the basic contents of their message can become far more significant. It is important to note that any behaviour is potentially communicative (Coupe and Goldbart, 1988) and adults with learning disability will have a very wide range of behaviours that could be potential communicative messages to those around them.

Adults with a learning disability may also use some non-verbal methods of communication at a more sophisticated level than their non-learning-disabled counterparts. Many will have had experience of some kind of signing system such as the Makaton vocabulary (Walker, 1970). However, not all people with learning disabilities will be able to use such a system. Some may more recently have been taught to use a basic object-based system known as 'objects of reference' (Ockleford, 1994). Other people will use pictorial systems of communication of varying levels of sophistication depending on their cognitive skills.

A person may have an excellent toolbox of methods of communication but have absolutely no reason to use them.

> An adult with learning disabilities is only going to learn to communicate if they have a reason, a purpose for that communication
>
> Coupe and Goldbart (1988)

East (1991) identified a range of what she terms 'functions' of communication. The following were the most fundamental.

Needs satisfaction

A person has some kind of need that requires another person to satisfy it. Examples could be a hungry person requiring food, an unhappy person requiring a hug, or a bored person requiring stimulation. This need provides the reason and motivation to communicate with another person.

Attention to self/other or an action

This is a complex and absolutely fundamental function of communication. Before beginning any communication, if it is to be successful, the attention of the listener must be gained. Frequently, attention is discussed in a negative sense, for example, 'He is only doing it to gain attention'. There are, however, a number of very positive scenarios in which gaining attention is a very valid reason to communicate.

A person may want to gain attention in order to communicate 'look at me, I want to tell you something' or so that he can focus his communication partner on something of joint interest – 'look at that thing with me' – or to focus his communication partner on himself: 'look what I'm doing'.

If that initial attention cannot be successfully gained, any further attempts at communication become redundant. To give a practical example, a client may be able to sign 'drink' perfectly but, if he cannot gain attention, he won't get his drink.

Protest

A person has the desire to express unhappiness with a situation – to get it stopped or changed. Some clients with learning disabilities use such a dramatic method of protesting – for example, kicking, throwing, smearing – that it distracts their communication partner from their original message. This may particularly be the case if the client is poor at gaining attention and as a result is forced to protest. At the opposite end of the scale, some clients present with such a high level of passivity that it is difficult to establish when they are unhappy about anything.

Answer

Answering a question is a reason to communicate. This may be a simple 'yes' or 'no' response. It is common, particularly for people with primarily non-verbal communication, to find that they are rarely given encouragement to answer and that communication partners may answer for them.

Gain permission/clarify

Another reason to communicate is to check that it is going to be all right to do something, or to make sure that something is understood correctly.

This is a function that for people with mainly non-verbal skills could easily be mistaken for requesting or protesting.

Give information

This is a means of giving information to others, for example 'I am tired', 'You have forgotten something'.

Greeting/social

Although this may in some cases be a way of gaining attention to communicate, there are other times when communication is used simply as a way of being polite and sociable with those in the environment, most commonly 'Hello' and 'Goodbye'.

There can be a wide range within these basic categories. More often than not, more than one of these communication functions will be used at one time. For example, in order to communicate it may be necessary to gain a person's attention before a request can be made for a need to be satisfied. In another scenario, a client may be answering a question by protesting and trying to divert the communication partner's attention on to the cause of the protest.

For people with learning disabilities both the methods of communication and the functions of communication may be impaired.

Formalised communication

Formalised communication refers to any organised system of communication. This can include both spoken systems and signed systems.

Spoken language

People with learning disabilities may present with disorders in either understanding or expressing themselves using spoken language, or with both. This could be a profound problem resulting in no spoken expression or comprehension. It may present as a subtler problem, for instance, a difficulty understanding and/or expressing the language connected with language related to a specific concept. This could be time ('We *will be* going out'), negatives ('The bus *isn't* coming') or position ('The pen is *under* the table').

These difficulties may be part of an overall syndrome/condition from which the person suffers or may be linked to brain damage that has resulted in their learning disability. In some instances, these difficulties may be related to traumas such as head injury or stroke which have no link to their learning disability. It is also possible that a lack of experience may relate to subtler problems, for example, very limited mobility may cause difficulty in understanding positional language such as 'in', 'on', 'behind'.

People with learning disabilities are frequently taught signed systems of communication because of their more concrete nature. These, however, will be very specialised systems and approaches such as the Makaton (Walker, 1970). A system such as British Sign Language is a language in its own right and is therefore just as complex cognitively as spoken language.

Non-formalised communication

People may be impaired in their ability to express themselves non-verbally. For example, they may lack or have very unusual patterns of eye contact; they may have an abnormally flat or extreme intonation pattern; they may lack the ability to use facial expression. These difficulties are frequently those that have the biggest social implications for people, because they will frequently be judged by communication partners as 'odd' or possibly even dangerous because they give the wrong non-verbal messages.

People may present with difficulties of formalised communication or informal communication or, very commonly, with difficulties of both.

Why does communication present a problem for people with learning disabilities?

Primary difficulties for people with learning disabilities involve generalising learnt skills and dealing with more abstract concepts and information. Language in itself is symbolic. This means that it involves something, in this case a spoken word or formalised sign, being used to represent something else, in this case an object, action or concept. Take, for example, the word 'tree' or formalised sign for tree. This is used to represent a living object and when the word or sign is used it instantly brings to mind a picture of an actual tree. This is an example of the way in which spoken or signed language is symbolic of real objects.

For people with learning disabilities, speech is frequently the most difficult level of communication for them to acquire and they often need other systems in place to support this. This is because spoken language is the most abstract way in which we can represent a concept in communication.

As Figure 6.1 demonstrates, the spoken word represents the most abstract way in which the concept of 'tree' can be represented communicatively. The most concrete is using the actual tree itself. It should be assumed that those communication methods that are at the most abstract end of the scale, signing and speech, are so lacking in sensory clues that their relationship to a particular object, action or concept will have to be taught. It is a common misapprehension that a system such as signing will automatically be easy for people with learning disabilities. The diagram shows that it is less abstract than speech, but it is not necessarily obviously linked to the object or concept that it represents.

MOST CONCRETE

Real Tree

(Sensory support: colour of tree, shape of tree, size of tree, sound and smell of tree,

and 3D, is situated in context)

Miniature of tree

(Sensory support: Colour of tree, Shape of tree, 3D)

Photograph of tree (actual tree)

(Sensory support: Colour of tree, shape of tree)

Photograph of tree (any tree)

(Sensory support: Some aspects of colour and shape)

Line drawing of tree/symbol

(Sensory support: Generalised shape)

Sign for tree (MAKATON)

(Sensory support: Gross link to generalised shape of a tree)

Word tree

(Sensory support: NONE)

MOST ABSTRACT

Figure 6.1 Communicating the concept of 'tree'.

It is vital, when considering communicating needs of people with learning disabilities, to consider the level of abstraction that they will be able to cope with. This is not to say that someone cannot progress to using a more abstract system. For example, it is possible that a client who related to photographs may progress to understand line drawings/symbols. However, it is necessary to start at the level that matches their cognitive skills and gradually introduce the more abstract system, i.e. the line drawing, alongside the one that they understand, the photograph.

To give a practical example, take a client who is currently able to make a choice by eye-pointing at one of two objects. That system, although effective, lacks portability and relies on other people to produce the required objects to choose between. A way to move on would be to present the objects as before, but with a photograph of the actual object alongside each object to help the client learn that they are linked and symbolic of the same thing. After a while, the objects could be gradually faded into the background to see whether the client could make a choice between the two photographs by eye-pointing instead. This would represent a more portable and adaptable communication system. It should be noted that the transition between these two types of symbols for some clients might take a considerable period of time.

For some clients because of either cognitive difficulties or visual disabilities, the most appropriate level of communication for them may remain at the level of objects. This could involve using the system known as 'objects of reference' (Ockleford, 1994). This involves teaching a client to relate to objects as symbols for communication, for example, learning that a spoon represents food or a piece of flannel represents 'toilet'. This system has the advantage of being both concrete and tactile, and can be very simple or become quite sophisticated. It is a system that relies heavily on consistent teaching and use by carers.

How does communication develop for a person with learning disabilities?

There are a number of models of communication development, probably the most useful in terms of practical intervention with people with learning disabilities being to look at the development of intentional communication. This is particularly helpful in terms of the communication skills of people with a profound learning disability.

Table 6.1 is a representation of the way in which intentional communication occurs in normal development. The 'focal person' can potentially represent a person of any age or level of cognitive ability. It is, however, easiest to look at the examples in terms of the early development of a baby.

When someone has grasped the concept that he can use his communication to control his environment, he is truly an intentional communicator. As this diagram shows, there are steps along the way that rely heavily on appropriate 'interpretations' and 'responses' from others to ensure that those skills develop.

This behaviour comes naturally when adults are with very small babies, and the results of this in terms of the speed of children's development of communication speak for themselves. Current thinking is that this sort of philosophy should be applied when working with adults with learning

Table 6.1 Development of normal intentional communication

Focal person's behaviour	Communicative partner's interpretation of behaviour	Communicative partner's response	Focal person's learning
Earliest stage			
Reflexive crying in response to hunger	Person has a need, may be hungry	To give food while telling the person what their interpretation of the behaviour was: 'Are you hungry?' with a soothing inflection	With repetitions of this pattern, the person begins to learn that their behaviour has a response to noise effect on those around them
Smiling in response to a friendly voice and face	Person likes individual doing the talking and wants to hear more	Says something else and smiles each time the person smiles at them	With repetition, person begins to learn about turn-taking and that their actions get reaction from others
Later stages			
Makes 'word like' noise, e.g. 'di' and points at a drink	Wants a drink and is trying to say it	Gives drink and reinforces the vocalisation saying 'you want a **drink**', with heavy emphasis on the key word	With repetition, person begins to learn that speech is a powerful tool and that particular sound combinations link to particular objects/actions
Points at ball, and looks at carer (Anne)	Wants ball and wants carer to help	Gives ball saying 'you want Anne's ball?'	Person learns to control people using communication

disability who present as 'pre-intentional' in their communication skills (Hewett, 1996).

How can carers improve communication skills for adults with learning disability?

There is no doubt that, looking at all the theory, a great deal of responsibility for the effectiveness of the communication of a person with learning disabilities lies with the individual who is communicating with them on a day-to-day basis.

The following provides a checklist of basic questions to ask and actions that could relate to the answers to these questions.

How is the client communicating?

It is important to observe the ways in which the client is communicating and to decide whether the method that he is using is effective. This may lead the carer either to try to introduce a new method or to work at reinforcing the existing ones to improve their usefulness.

Why is the client communicating?

Does the client have a reason to communicate? The carer would need to create situations in which the client was motivated to communicate. For example, this may involve setting up more choice-making situations. It may involve re-evaluating the client's environment so that he needs to use his communication methods to ensure that his needs are met.

Are carers 'speaking the same language' as the client?

If a client is non-verbal, it is important that carers also use clear non-verbal communication. This may be a system such as Makaton signing (Walker, 1970) or may involve using facial expression, touch and other non-verbal signals to communicate. It makes good sense to consider the way in which people mirror and extend the communication skills of normally developing children and consider how this could be done for the adult learning-disabled client.

How much language does a client understand?

This can be established with the assessment from a speech and language therapist and is essential in order to decide at which level to pitch an interaction. Careful observation can begin to establish this, looking particularly at the way clients respond to instructions when they are out of the normal routine and context and when clues such as facial expression and gesture are kept to a minimum.

Developing the communication skills of a client with learning disabilities is a big task and one that should be embarked on in a structured way. A key factor to bear in mind is that a very small improvement in an individual's communication skills has the potential to make a massive impact on his or her quality of life.

Working with people who have a visual problem

The Royal National Institute for the Blind (RNIB) produces informative literature and references about the experience of visual impairments. With this knowledge, an understanding can develop on how to aid communication, and get to know and develop relationships with visually impaired people. The RNIB states that the term 'blind' is not really accurate. Only a minority of blind people are totally blind or just see light and dark. The majority have some sight, which they can use in their daily lives. Unfortunately, many adults with visual and learning disabilities have not been helped to use their sight and so tend to give the impression of being more disabled than they really are.

The RNIB describes five main factors that aid a visually impaired person's environment: lighting and the use of colour contrast, sound, walls, surfaces (floors), and furniture and equipment. It is important that these are taken into consideration when assessing clients. A referral to a physiotherapist for a client who 'shuffles' and has mobility problems on the stairs may not mean that the client has a physical difficulty, but perhaps tunnel vision, and therefore can see only a very small area in front of her. Her vision is limiting her physical progress; she lacks confidence because she is unsure of where to place her feet and is reluctant to stride out into the unknown. In this instance, it would be helpful to have white edging to the stairs and tactile indicators on the wall and banister.

It is necessary for people with a visual impairment to make use of other senses, usually hearing and touch. A visually impaired person may need help to learn by discovery whereas a sighted person quickly assimilates surrounding information. For example, a blind child may not know that it is worth crawling across a room to get a sweet because his hearing cannot tell him that it is there.

Communication skills are impaired because it is difficult to observe non-verbal communication or body language. A smile to show encouragement is not noticed and signs of sadness or crying may pass without recognition, so a visually impaired person may often seem passive, withdrawn and unsociable. Such people are often dependent on others to interpret their surroundings.

People with a learning disability and visual impairment need to be offered structured activities in environments that enhance their opportunities. Good lighting and reduced background noise enable them to focus on important sounds. Tactile clues are essential. For each person with a visual impairment, the experience is unique. The therapist must take time getting to know that person and understanding his responses and behaviours.

In many small group homes and day facilities used by adults with learning disability and visual impairment, this understanding is developed to high levels by using an adapted form of 'intensive interaction' (see Table 6.1). One independently funded organisation gives the guidelines in the boxes to its care staff.

How do I 'do' intensive interaction?

There are no hard and fast rules – GO WITH THE FLOW.

The most important things you need to do are to *watch* and to *follow*.

Watch

Observe your partner for little movements, gestures, facial expressions, indications of pleasure.

Take time to notice things – little things grow into big things, but if you're too busy to notice them they don't get the chance. For example:

Gestures → Signs

Sense of control over noise → Sense of control over more important things

Fun from one small interaction → Potential fun in lots of other interactions

Wait

Be patient – give partner time.

Don't try to push things along – sometimes nothing will happen for a while.

If there is a 'lull', don't assume that this is the end – share the quiet, your partner will know you are still 'available'.

Follow

Follow the lead of your partner. Keep your focus on him and what he does, and respond to what he initiates.

Make an effort to *control* less and to *receive* more from the individual.

How do I build on what happens?

You can begin to build on things that you observe by:

- responding to actions/things observed
- interpreting them, i.e. giving them some kind of 'meaning'
- exaggerating them
- adding a variation . . .

Why have specific sessions for intensive interaction?

By setting aside specific time for intensive interaction sessions, you create a regular time when the individual knows that you are there for them. They won't necessarily take you up on the offer, but what is important is that you make yourself available to them. This is unconditional – there should be no sense of you imposing your ideas about what's acceptable/appropriate.

Also, a session is more focused than the spontaneous interactions that occur during the course of the day. This means fewer distractions, less chance of the 'flow' being interrupted, and more chance to build on things.

From Training Notes for Care Staff at 'Visualise', Fountain Hall Road, Edinburgh.

Working with people who have a hearing impairment

People with learning disabilities are prone not only to visual impairments, but also to hearing impairments. Studies consistently reveal that around 40% of people with severe learning disabilities also have hearing problems. Unfortunately, many of these people go through their lives without staff and carers recognising this loss. People who have poor hearing may not be aware that other people hear better than they do. It is important to recognise that improvements can be made if a person with learning disabilities has hearing impairments. Often a relatively simple problem, such as wax in the ears, can be the cause and can be treated. Others may have long-standing ear infections which should be treated as soon as possible. Some people may need to wear a hearing aid or even have surgery. A hearing aid may not solve all the problems and, in some cases, is not tolerated by the client, but it may assist in communication.

Case study 2

Client B was admitted to a long-stay hospital aged 8, and described as profoundly handicapped. Her deafness was not identified until she left the long-stay hospital 25 years later. Staff felt that her inability to hear and communicate contributed to her challenging behaviour. Her deafness isolated and frustrated her, but she has gained considerable self-confidence and new skills since she learnt sign language.

Working with people who have visual and hearing impairments

People with learning disabilities can have both visual and hearing impairments along with, or without, other physical or behavioural problems. The organisation SENSE provides useful literature and courses to train therapists, teachers and carers. If a therapist is working with this type of person, it is important that all the relevant information is found out about this individual so that his or her needs can, if possible, be adequately met. This process will involve time spent watching and listening, identifying clues that will produce regular and reliable responses, and working through the barriers to enable progress to develop.

Case study 3

Client C is a 45-year-old woman with Down's syndrome. She has a hearing impairment and has very deformed eye sockets, causing visual impairment. She has lived in a long-stay hospital for the last 27 years. It is understood that at one time she walked. She has now moved into a small community home where she will stand to be washed and changed. The staff have requested advice on how to encourage her to walk again.

It seems that, in certain situational activities, client C will weight-bear but very quickly just sinks to the ground without warning. She is a heavy woman and there is risk of damage to herself and her carers. To achieve the goal required, the client has to want or to enjoy the experience and has to have the opportunity to practise safely. In this case, a regular routine of standing in a standing frame, with knee gaiters to prevent sudden 'sinking' to the ground, was established. Client C would stand initially for 10 minutes twice a day. To achieve this staff put her into the frame, giving her a vibrating pad to hold which she was known to enjoy.

The client was also known to enjoy water activities. A weekly visit to the pool was established where she was encouraged to walk several widths in waist-high water before venturing to the deep end where she loved to float.

This regimen has continued for the last 6 months, increasing the period in the standing frame, and the number of widths of the pool walked. The staff continue to encourage standing for functional activities. It has been noted that the client's standing time has increased and is much more reliable during functional activities. On occasions, the client has taken steps between two people. The staff are willing to continue with this regimen with regular monitoring and advice from the therapist.

Conclusion

A high standard of treatment and management of the physical disabilities of an individual with learning disabilities can be achieved only if the client and health-care professional can communicate with each other. This requires health-care professionals to examine their own attitudes towards people with learning and physical disabilities. It is essential that health-care professionals liaise with each other and with the carers to discover the client's method of communication. Finally, it is essential that all the carers and professionals take time to communicate with the client by use of his or her particular method of communication.

CHAPTER 7

Assessment

ANNELIESE BARRELL

This chapter relates primarily to physiotherapy assessment but much of it could be used by anyone undertaking an assessment with people who have learning disabilities.

In general, assessments can take anything from one hour to one week. When working with clients with learning disabilities, however, a month or longer may be required to establish a realistic pattern of ability and need. It is not unusual to gain the wrong impression of a client's ability even after several attempts at an initial assessment. Therapists must not give up at the first hurdle.

All assessments should be recorded, signed and dated according to the standards of professional practice, for example: Standards of Physiotherapy Practice (Chartered Society of Physiotherapy, 1996a, revised standards June and September 2000), Communicating Quality (Royal College of Speech and Language Therapists: Gaag, 1996), Standards, Policies and Procedures Guidelines for Occupational Therapy Services for Clients with Learning Disabilities (College of Occupational Therapists, 1995), and the Guidelines for Mental Health and Learning Disabilities Nursing (United Kingdom Central Council for Nursing, Midwifery and Health Visiting [UKCC], 1998b).

Assessment

An assessment is a systematic method of establishing a baseline for intervention, i.e. treatment and management. It involves an audit of the client's skills, abilities and pathology, and the resources available to undertake any intervention. Without an effective assessment, outcome of intervention cannot be measured. It should be holistic and needs to be valid, responsive, appropriate and sensitive to the needs of the client. It comprises markers to judge change as a result of:

- Developmental status: is the client maturing neurologically after the chronological time span?
- Pathological deterioration
- The impact of intervention: this is difficult to measure because so many influences and factors impinge on the client's life
- Habituation: the repetitious bombarding of pathways in the brain
- Compliance (carer and client)
- Mood

It can be:

- Multiprofessional: for example, community team assessments (see Chapter 5) or dysphagia team assessments
- Uniprofessional
- Condition specific, for example: musculoskeletal, including McKenzie (1981), Maitland (1986) and Cyriax (1982); neurological, including Parkinson's disease (Wade, 1992); Gross Motor Function Measure or GMFM (Russell et al., 1989); general health profile, including Rivermead (Collen et al., 1991)

It should also encompass the needs of the carers.

Evaluation

An evaluation is the analysis of the outcomes of the goals set, based on the findings of the assessment. This is described in Chapter 8.

Reasons for assessment

Physiotherapy assessments for people with learning disabilities are carried out for a variety of reasons which include the following:

- To establish health status, diagnosis and prognosis, and the effect of disease.
- To determine position and posture for effective and functional seating and the provision of the most suitable wheelchair (in some multiprofessional teams, this may be the role of the occupational therapist or it may be a combined role).
- To determine the suitability of a client for, and to aid the physiotherapist's decision on, the most effective use of treatment modalities, such as those described in Chapters 9–16.
- To identify the requirements for orthoses, e.g. spinal jackets and specialised footwear, and for specialised equipment to aid mobility.

- To ensure that assumptions are not made that may lead to inappropriate goal setting, which could lead to a reduction in quality of life and/or deterioration of health status.
- To indicate clients' problems and needs, including level of support, improvement, maintenance, skills level and functional ability.
- To highlight resource and service deficit, and indicate service effectiveness and efficiency for service developments and contracts.

They are used as a baseline of health, social and/or educational status. They are also used to determine disability and handicap and the level of function and ability, which assists the physiotherapist in selecting the form of intervention to use and in measuring the outcome of that intervention, be it improvement, maintenance or deterioration. (Maintenance should be viewed as improvement if deterioration is slowed down or halted.) The assessment will highlight any necessity for further intervention by another profession or agency and will form the basis of a referral on to the most appropriate person according to the client's needs.

Multiprofessional team assessment

As part of its initial screening process, a multiprofessional team may complete a non-therapy-specific assessment before determining which profession(s) will need to be involved with the client. One example is a social service core assessment carried out by care managers such as the OK Health Check (Mathews and Hegarty, 1997) and the *Face* Profile Learning Disability Walnut Assessment (see Appendix II). These assessments should be considered as part of the holistic assessment, thus enabling efficient and effective care programming (see Chapter 8).

Factors that can affect the assessment process

Time of day

It is important that the physiotherapist familiarises him- or herself with the client's likes, dislikes and daily routine.

Time of day can severely disrupt and/or prevent the assessment process from taking place. Times to be avoided are: immediately before or after a meal; after a long journey to a day centre, sports centre or swimming/hydrotherapy pool when the more disabled clients have had much preparation handling; and at the end of the day. Conversely, some clients react well to handling and travelling and have a very positive outcome to an assessment undertaken then.

Fear of the unknown

Initial contact with the client may provoke an out-of-character response such as: unusual quietness, over-confidence, verbosity, aggressiveness, abusiveness or non-compliance. Time is required to get to know and establish a rapport with the client and the carers before an attempt is made to start a formal assessment (see Chapter 6). It is good practice, if time and geography allow, for the therapist to make contact with the client, home, family and other carers, in order to establish a rapport with all concerned before embarking on a formal assessment. It is possible at this point to gain valuable and often more accurate information on the following:

- The client's communication methods
- The client's concentration span
- Relationships between client and carers
- Reaction of the client to new situations and people
- The client's mobilisation methods when unobserved
- The client's preferred posture and seating
- The client's use of leisure time
- Does the client prefer to be alone or with others, and if others are these carers or peers?

All this information is important to the physiotherapist when deciding in which form and at what venue intervention should take place to achieve the best outcome, and what advice and training are necessary for the family and carers.

This period of building a relationship becomes part of the informal assessment process which is equally as important as the structured assessment:

- A rushed session giving insufficient time to establish a rapport between the physiotherapist and the client can produce nothing except a frustrated physiotherapist and a non-compliant client, not to mention the negative compliance of the carer who feels angry because the client is not being valued.
- The presence of the parent or carer may help or hinder the assessment process and affect the outcome. Major problems can be caused by clients who react to their parents or carers being present, and so prevent an accurate assessment of skills or function taking place. On the other hand, the parents or carers know the client well and can offer assistance and information which can enhance the assessment

outcome. The physiotherapist has to involve all those concerned in the care of that client and if possible the client him- or herself.

- Consultation with all other members of the education, health and social care teams who are familiar with the client before assessment is very valuable. Previous knowledge of difficulties, needs, and successful or failed interventions can shorten and/or enhance an assessment process. In some teams, all clients are discussed at team referral meetings before any intervention takes place, so the most appropriate people are involved at the outset of any assessment process. It is very easy for a physiotherapist to embark on a first-time home visit, armed only with the referral information, to find later, by chance remark from another member of the team, that there is some reason for not following that chosen route of assessment or that it has been tried before unsuccessfully.

When should assessment take place and how often?

Following referral

The assessment takes place before any treatment intervention. Referrals come in a variety of ways.

Open referral

Where anyone, e.g. a client, carer, teacher or health professional, can refer to a team or to any one of the individual professions within the team. Teams operating an open referral system often have distinct referral and admission criteria, stating the terms of reference of referral to the learning disabilities service. The teams can have a common referral source and allocation to physiotherapy will come following a multiprofessional referral discussion and screening for previous known contacts. Information given with open referrals may state only a non-specific problem or need, e.g. problems with feeding.

Specific referrals

The service admission criteria still apply. These referrals may come from general practitioners, hospital consultants and other professionals in all agencies involved with the client, usually for a defined problem or because they need help in determining the problem. Some generic therapists and health professionals routinely refer clients on to the specialist service, although this practice is becoming less frequent as access to appropriate generic hospital facilities and health-care services is being encouraged and fostered for clients with a learning disability (Lindsey, 1998).

Informal assessment

This takes place at every therapeutic intervention; change is recorded and adjustments are made to the client's therapy programme. This may be a 'one-off' change because client condition and compliance can change for a variety of reasons including: mood, time of day, who brings them for therapy, or where therapy occurs. The therapist has to be prepared to be very flexible and to have infinite patience. Many physiotherapy departments use:

- S (subjective)
- O (objective)
- A (assessment)
- P (planning)

notes to record each physiotherapy intervention.

Before the client's individual programme planning review

This is done as an indication of change in the client's condition and to assist in the setting of team goals.

Placement assessment

The therapist may be asked by social services or other providers to assess the client for a specific need, e.g. the type of housing accommodation required, or for the most suitable day care provision. Such assessments are frequently carried out jointly with an occupational therapist or another member of the multiprofessional team.

Regularly

This is done with clients whose therapeutic intervention is on-going over a lengthy period; assessments should be undertaken at intervals decided on at the time of the initial assessment.

Before change in the client's condition or circumstances

This is done when there is, for example, a move to another area or a change in residential or day care accommodation.

On request

This is on the request of carers or the care manager.

On discharge

This may accompany a discharge letter/plan to the client's medical practitioner.

Legal assessments

Experienced specialist physiotherapists may be asked to carry out assessments in cases of compensation, for a disciplinary process or complaint. These would be initiated by lawyers, health or service managers or the individual professional body.

Where do assessments take place?

Assessments can take place in a variety of settings:

- In a community day care centre: it is usually possible to arrange for a quiet area in which to carry out the assessment, but this is not always possible and the physiotherapist then has to be creative and flexible. Many day care establishments have designated and equipped therapy areas.
- In the client's family home.
- In a private, voluntary or statutory residential home.
- In the physiotherapy department of a hospital for people with a learning disability.

Assessments should be carried out in the place and at the time of day that are most appropriate for the client, as described in the ACPPLD (Association of Chartered Physiotherapists for People with Learning Disabilities) Standards for Good Practice (Barnes et al., 1993). Assessing for a feeding problem, for example, is usually best carried out during a meal time, not in a simulated session. There are of course exceptions. If a client's behaviour at meal times with other clients around exacerbates the problem, a simulation would be desirable.

Wherever the setting the physiotherapist must ensure that:

- Enough time is allowed for the physiotherapist to carry out the assessment.
- The client is comfortable and feels at ease.
- There is a minimum of disruption and disturbance, for example, by telephone calls, the presence of other clients, interruptions by or conversations with other staff, or the presence of unnecessary distracting equipment.

- The client and/or carer is aware of where the toilets are situated and also, if available, refreshments.
- The therapist has all the equipment and assessment tools to hand, e.g. charts and measuring instruments.
- All involved in the assessment understand what is happening or about to happen.
- In cases of suspected disruptive clients an alarm/panic system/process is in place. This is usually part of a team policy for all staff working in hospital or community settings. Team policy could be: a panic button in a treatment area; having another staff member present either in hospital or community residential or day care settings; leaving information in a team diary before embarking on a home visit; being accompanied on a home visit; and having a code on known client files to alert all therapists of potential difficulties before arranging an assessment session. In some general hospitals, codes are also used on client files to denote that the client has a learning disability. These are to ensure that the client is valued and given time and understanding by all the staff, especially in a busy outpatient/accident and emergency department.

Which assessment?

This will depend on the reason for referral, the desired outcome, the level of disability, and a multiprofessional or uniprofessional approach to assessment.

Assessments vary in format and could be one of the following.

Developmental and systematic checklist and test format

- McKenzie (1981)
- Bereweeke (Jenkins et al., 1983)
- Gross Motor Function Measure (GMFM) (Russell et al., 1989)
- MOVE (Mobility Opportunities Via Education) (Kern County Superintendent of Schools, 1990 – see Appendix II)
- The Caring Persons Guide to Handling the Severely Multiple Handicapped (Golding and Goldsmith, 1986)
- Mary Marlborough Disability Centre (1997) – see Appendix II
- The Functional Independence Measure (FIM) (State University of New York, 1994)
- Barthel Index (Mahoney and Barthel, 1965)
- Goal Attainment Scaling (GAS) (Kiresuk et al., 1994; Reid and Chesson, 1998; Young and Chesson, 1998)

These highlight ability and deficiency, degrees of disability and handicap, problems and need. Results are easy to read and to evaluate. Intervention plans follow a logical pattern.

Video assessment

This gives the only accurate record of movement.

- It can be used in situations where deterioration or maintenance is the expected outcome.
- Video assessment can highlight improvement that is so small and imperceptible that it cannot always be seen during day-to-day contact. The effect of this visual change is of benefit to the morale of carers, who find it difficult to believe that all is being done to assist their client.
- Behaviour, concentration and compliance are also recorded.
- Gait, mobility and functional ability are recorded in a visual way which enhances the checklist or test results.

Case study 1: Jane

Jane, aged 45 years, lives with eight other clients in a voluntary organisation's residential home. She has myotonic dystrophy and was referred because of problems with gait and falling. A checklist assessment was not able to give an accurate assessment of gait because, although she wishes for help, she will not comply with any requests to demonstrate her problem. She did walk around the home using furniture to assist her and, when not being watched, was able to walk unaided with an exaggerated lordosis and pelvic rotation. She would not walk outside or leave the car if taken out. It was impossible to assess stamina, pain and gait, and the need for assistance. The physiotherapist thought around the problem; Jane loves animals, so a trip to the local wildlife park was arranged. Jane left the car to explore and was able to walk around the park using a frame for half an hour before resting.

The trip was videoed. Jane's walking and gait were analysed and a programme of activity was devised with Jane's agreement which aimed at increasing motivation, ambulation and stamina.

Still photography

Photographs make a permanent current record of:

- Position
- Posture
- Deformity size
- Seating
- Wheelchairs

(Note that permission must be obtained from the client or advocate before undertaking a video assessment or taking photographs.)

Most physiotherapy services working with people with a learning disability have devised their own form of assessment, a mixture of all the above, based on a plethora of validated assessment forms available, for example: Golding and Goldsmith (1986), Mary Marlborough Lodge (1997). This is because, at present (1998), there are few validated assessments that cover all the aspects of a holistic assessment or are able to record minimal change.

Assessments should include, for example:

- Client's personal details: name and preferred name, address, contact telephone number, date of birth, next of kin
- Names and addresses of the GP and care manager
- Name and address of day-care provider
- Reason for referral, client's/carer's expected outcome
- Previous medical history
- Diagnosis (if available)
- Weight and height
- Colour/texture/temperature of the skin and the Waterlow scale reading
- Presence of epilepsy, type and degree
- Medication
- Method of communication (see Chapter 6)
- Sensory ability
- Current wheelchair/seating, date of provision and name of provider
- Current orthotic appliances, date of provision and name of provider
- Client's behaviours and tolerance to handling
- Functional ability
- Range of movement and muscle tone
- Posture and deformity
- Mobility and gait
- A problem/needs list
- A checklist following referral (ACPPLD Standards for Good Practice: Barnes et al., 1993)

Example

Physiotherapy Assessment Forms are shown in Figures 7.1–7.7. One client may have a number of assessments carried out by the physiotherapist, for example:

- Standard physiotherapy assessment, as used in the local service
- Assessment for a specific modality, e.g. riding for the disabled, rebound therapy

- Wheelchair assessment, as determined by local wheelchair provider, e.g. Disabled Services Centres
- Seating assessment, as determined above
- Orthotic assessment, in conjunction with orthotic providers
- Mobility equipment assessment, often jointly with social service occupational therapists
- Manual handling risk assessment (Chartered Society of Physiotherapy, 1998)
- Team assessments, e.g. dysphagia (eating) teams, fitness screening

These assessments may not all be part of the standard assessment package, but are 'add ons', as and when required, and are kept as part of the client's complete assessment record.

As most referrals are based on requests for a maintenance or improvement in function, a clinical assessment is not always the physiotherapist's first priority, although clinical knowledge and assessment underpin all actions by the physiotherapist who uses all the core skills and basic general assessment procedures.

Referrals for specific clinical conditions are assessed in the prescribed way for that condition, e.g. low back pain, when a validated musculoskeletal assessment would be used. The following categories may be used with people with learning disabilities (Hoffer et al., 1973):

1. Community ambulators: walks indoors and outdoors, may need crutches or braces or both; wheelchair for long trips.
2. Household ambulators: walks only indoors with apparatus, good transfers, may use wheelchair indoors and for all community activities.
3. Non-functional ambulators: walking as a therapy session at home or centre; uses wheelchair for all other activities.
4. Non-ambulators: wheelchair bound but can transfer from chair to bed.

It is advisable to add two further categories:

- Before (1): Independent walkers: walking independently under all conditions.
- After (4): Entirely dependent: unable to transfer without assistance.

Within those categories, there will be a wide variation of condition and ability demanding different outcomes and expectation. It is therefore essential that the physiotherapist assesses the relevant needs of the client in terms of function, quality of life and health gain. A large number of clients present with a multiplicity of needs and often it is necessary to

PHYSIOTHERAPY ASSESSMENT

Page 1

Name:	
Address:	Sex
	D.O.B
Tel. No.:	Ethnic Origin:

G.P. Name:	Date of Initial Assessment:
G.P. Address:	Diagnosis:
G.P. Tel. No.:	Physiotherapist:
Medical Personnel:	

History of Present Condition:

Past Medical History (including Birth History):	Medication:

Figure 7.1 Physiotherapy assessment, sociodemographic information form 1.

PHYSIOTHERAPY ASSESSMENT   Page 2

Client Name: **Physiotherapist:**
Date:

Method of Communication, including communication aids:	Method of Feeding, e.g. self/assisted
Vision ☐ Normal ☐ Total blindness ☐ Partially sighted ☐ Double vision (etc.) ☐ Glasses (reading/day wear) ☐ Other	**Hearing** ☐ Normal ☐ Complete deafness ☐ Partial deafness ☐ Hearing aid Date of last hearing test:
Behaviour/Concentration Levels:	
Activities of Daily Living (e.g. washing and dressing):	

Social History

Home Environment (e.g. family members, own home, residential…):
Adaptations (e.g. stair lift, rails, extension…):

Figure 7.2 Physiotherapy assessment, sociodemographic information form 2.

PHYSIOTHERAPY ASSESSMENT

Client Name: **Physiotherapist:**
Date:
Main Carer   **Day Centre**

Name:	Name:
Address:	Address:
Tel No:	Tel No:

Other Carer   **Respite**
Facility

Name:	Name:
Address:	Address:
Tel No:	Tel No:

Equipment

Wheelchair (including make/model, adaptation): **Supplied by:**   **Date:**   **Review Date:**
Orthotics (e.g. footwear, ankle–foot orthosis): **Supplied by:**   **Date:**   **Review Date:**
Summary:

Figure 7.3 Physiotherapy assessment, sociodemographic information form 3.

Client Name: **Physiotherapist:**
        Date:

If an activity is performed independently, please mark the corresponding **Yes** box. If
assistance is needed or the client is unable to perform the activity, mark the **No** box.
Activities performed using a mobility aid (e.g. stick) are independent.

		Yes	No	Comments
In Bed	Turn prone to supine			
	Turn supine to prone			
	Move up/down bed			
	Sit over edge of bed			
	Transfer from bed to chair			
Chair	Move to edge of seat			
	Balanced sitting			
	Transfer from chair to bed			
	Stand up			
	Sit down			
Floor	Get on to floor			
	Get up off floor			
Walking	On level ground			
	On rough ground			
	Slopes			
Stairs	Up			
	Down			
Wheelchair	Adjust sitting position			
	Apply/release brake			
	Propel – forward			
	– backward			
	– to turn			
	Negotiate – doorway			
	– slope			
	– kerb			
	– transfer to chair			
Fine Motor	Hold a spoon			
	Hold a cup			
	Turn pages of a book			

Figure 7.4 Functional ability.

Client Name ....
Physiotherapist ....

PROBLEM/NEEDS LIST

Date identified and signature		Date resolved and signature

Figure 7.5 Problem list.

Date	INITIAL PLAN	Signature
	GOALS	

Figure 7.6 Initial plan and goals.

Assessment of Deformities,
Range of Movement & Muscle Tone

Client Name: **Physiotherapist:**   **Date:**

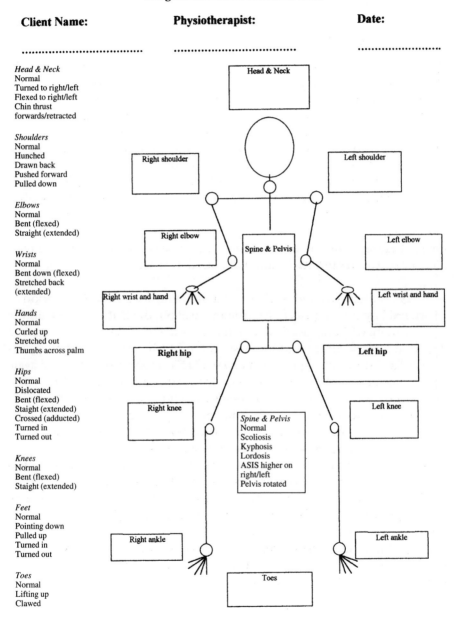

Head & Neck
Normal
Turned to right/left
Flexed to right/left
Chin thrust
forwards/retracted

Shoulders
Normal
Hunched
Drawn back
Pushed forward
Pulled down

Elbows
Normal
Bent (flexed)
Straight (extended)

Wrists
Normal
Bent down (flexed)
Stretched back
(extended)

Hands
Normal
Curled up
Stretched out
Thumbs across palm

Hips
Normal
Dislocated
Bent (flexed)
Staight (extended)
Crossed (adducted)
Turned in
Turned out

Knees
Normal
Bent (flexed)
Staight (extended)

Feet
Normal
Pointing down
Pulled up
Turned in
Turned out

Toes
Normal
Lifting up
Clawed

Figure 7.7 Assessment of deformities, range of movement and muscle tone.

make priorities of what can be addressed only by the physiotherapist. The client can then be referred back to the carers to extend this treatment as part of his or her social and leisure education.

Case study 2: David

David, aged 43 years, is an independent walker referred by his care manager for deteriorating mobility as a result of painful arthritic hips. He is not very motivated but, after being assessed for level of pain, gait, range of lower limb movement, exercise tolerance, muscle strength, adequate footwear and concentration span, he recognised the need for exercise to relieve hip pain. He cannot sustain a programme of exercise because he lives alone. He loves the water and benefits from exercise in a pool. After a few sessions of treatment in the hydrotherapy pool, with the physiotherapist who taught exercises to a volunteer carer and David, he was soon joining in a session in a local swimming pool as part of the day centre's leisure programme. He is regularly reassessed in the leisure pool by the physiotherapist with the carer. His motivation and exercise tolerance have increased, gait has improved and pain has decreased.

In 1997, the Chartered Society of Physiotherapy with the Association of Chartered Physiotherapists in Neurology (ACPIN), the British Association of Bobath Trained Therapists (BABTT), the Association of Paediatric Chartered Physiotherapists (APCP) and the Association of Chartered Physiotherapists for People with Learning Disabilities (ACPPLD) undertook a study of available assessment and evaluation procedures currently in general use. The brief was to find a method that was sensitive enough to show change in the most profoundly disabled client following physiotherapy treatment. The outcome of the study indicated that the method devised by A Le Roux (TELER: Le Roux, 1993) was the most flexible and sensitive.

The TELER method is designed to be a systematic method of clinical note-keeping, not a stand-alone assessment tool. The use of the TELER method relies on the physiotherapist's underpinning knowledge of pathology, disease, disability and handicap, and the ability to carry out an informed assessment as a basis for developing a programme of intervention, goal planning and evaluation. The TELER method is about setting goals, creating indicators for measurement and enabling outcomes to be clearly identified. Examples can be found in Chapter 8.

Conclusion

For physiotherapists working with clients with a learning disability, there is currently no single assessment method that will satisfy all the needs of the client, primarily because learning disability is not a single medical condition with identifiable boundaries. Physiotherapists need, therefore, to be flexible in approach and aware of available resources, so that they can undertake accurate assessments on which to base physiotherapy intervention and measure its outcome. The intervention may in turn be part of a multiprofessional programme.

CHAPTER 8

Interpretation of assessment results as a basis for intervention and outcome measures

ANNELIESE BARRELL

Assessments, as mentioned in Chapter 7, can be undertaken for a variety of reasons and in a variety of ways. The underlying purpose of any assessment is to establish a baseline for further action or intervention.

The assessment report

The assessment report should contain the following:

- The client's name, address and date of birth
- The client's day care establishment
- Name and status of the referrer
- Initial reason for the referral
- Date and result of the assessment
- Problems and needs identified
- Goals and aims of the intervention
- The intervention plan to include: times, dates, venues, who is involved, an exercise programme (if appropriate) and plans for staff and carer training
- Monitoring and review dates, times and venues

Aims of assessment

The aims fall into different categories dependent on the reason for the assessment.

The identified needs of the client

This could include the following:

- Improvement/maintenance of function and ability levels
- Development of new skills
- Improvement in quality of life
- Reduction in pain
- Reduction of spasticity
- Improvement in muscle tone
- Improvement in muscle strength
- Improvement in health status
- Increased range of joint movement
- Increased concentration
- Increased exercise tolerance
- Improved motivation

The client's assessed therapeutic needs do not always coincide with the client's wishes, so the choice of goals will need to take that into consideration. For example, a client may express a wish to walk without pain and without the use of a walking aid, but is not happy to undertake a regular exercise programme aimed at reducing the pain, thereby increasing mobility and improving the gait. The therapist then has to consider all the alternative options to encourage the client's participation, e.g. JABADAO, hydrotherapy or a suitable leisure activity adapted to meet the client's needs (see Part III).

Needs of the carer/parents

These cannot be ignored, especially for semi-dependent and totally dependent clients. To achieve any goals or carry out the intervention plan, dependence on their cooperation is essential. If a parent is not the main carer, there may be differing opinions between carers concerning perceived needs. To address this, there needs to be good communication between the therapist and all concerned with delivering the care to the client. Assessment results and intervention plans need to be very clearly identified, discussed and communicated in order to avoid non-compliance and increased carer stress. The needs of the carer and parents can be identified as the following:

- Being able to maintain and/or improve their abilities to undertake all that is required to manage the client on a day-to-day basis
- To improve their own and their client's quality of life

- To improve the client's functional abilities
- To relieve and reduce stress on the carer
- To improve the client's health

Service needs

The provision of any services, assessed as being needed by the client, is dependent on accurate information in order to do the following:

- Decide how to maximise effective and efficiently delivered treatment, based on the best available knowledge, research evidence and current practice.
- Manage resources efficiently. This will include management of staffing levels, provision of modalities such as hydrotherapy and rebound therapy, and the provision of therapeutic equipment and treatment bases.
- Plan strategically for future service delivery.
- Develop service and treatment protocols and policies.
- Undertake audit.
- Improve health care.
- Improve outcome measurement.
- Ensure client satisfaction.
- Comply with the rights and choices of the individual as laid down in the statute and patient's charters.
- Fulfil health and safety requirements.

Interpretation of assessment results

Interpreting the assessment results will depend on the following:

- The reason for the assessment
- The type of assessment
- The problems and needs identified
- The resources available

A therapist may have been asked to assess a client's position while eating. During the assessment for seating and positioning, further problems and needs may be identified, for example:

- a medical problem
- a problem of diet
- a problem with the client's swallowing mechanism

These problems will then be referred to the appropriate professions or, if available, to a dysphagia team for further intervention and possible team goal setting.

Assessment results vary considerably and are often completely unexpected. The Bereweeke Assessment (Jenkins et al., 1983) suggests that the client has to be *seen* to perform an action, and not to rely on the opinion of a carer. Clients with a learning disability constantly surprise therapists by their ability to do something that had previously been thought impossible from historical and anecdotal data. It is very easy to disable a client further by not being accurate and specific in assessment and by the interpretation of assessment data. However, what is *seen* is not always the *problem* or the *need.* Clients with a learning disability have an uncanny ability to mask symptoms and problems and their pain threshold can be high, very low or non-existent.

The therapist then has to enquire further by visiting the day centre or home and consulting the medical file (if it is available and accessible):

- It is not uncommon for the client who has always lived in the family home not to have a medical file that is easily accessible to community-based therapists.
- Clients in the community are usually referred by non-medical personnel (see Chapter 7).
- Clients resettled from long-stay hospitals into the community may have their medical files lodged within the community team base or with the team physician/psychiatrist.

Action plan

Once the assessment result has been interpreted, e.g. a worsening scoliosis, a plan of action is decided on. This plan must be discussed and decided on by all concerned with the client's care and, if possible, with the client. Intervention for a scoliosis could involve any or all of the following:

- Exercise programme
- Positioning advice to carers
- Special seating, assessment, reassessment or provision
- Hydrotherapy
- Rebound therapy
- Orthotics, provision of a spinal jacket
- Staff/carer training
- Surgery

The aim of the therapist's intervention would be the following:

- To prevent further deterioration
- To maintain/improve upper limb function and trunk mobility
- To maintain an acceptable posture in sitting and lying (and standing if possible)
- To maintain and improve quality of life
- To increase the range of choices available to the client
- To maintain/improve respiratory function

(For more detailed management of scoliosis, see positioning in Chapter 10.)

Results from the assessment, which are embodied in the action plan, can create real problems for carers and therapists when planning appropriate interventions. These involve time, venue and resources.

Time

The time taken to enable any intervention to happen can cause the following:

- Staffing and staff rota problems
- Problems for busy parents
- The time of day can create problems for busy community therapists trying to fit in with everyone else's timetable and their own large case- and workload

Venue

The venue for the intervention can create problems with the following:

- Transport from home or day centre to physiotherapy department, hydrotherapy pool or rebound therapy
- Staff available to accompany the client

Resources

The availability of required resources to carry out the intervention plan can be a problem. If not available, these should be recorded as unmet need. For example, the unavailability of a hoist or manual handling aids at the pool side or for rebound therapy could restrict their use by the more physically disabled client.

Treatment plan

Therapeutic intervention requires a treatment plan. Once this has been written, further practical questions are raised, including the following:

- Who is going to be responsible for overseeing the treatment plan in a multiprofessional/multiagency situation? Is there a key worker?
- To whom should the treatment plan be sent?
- Who needs to be taught how to implement the plan?

In a uniprofessional situation, the therapist responsible for the client's treatment will be responsible for setting reassessment, review and evaluation dates and times, and informing all concerned. In team situations, the need for a key or link worker is agreed and a decision is made as to who should assume that responsibility.

Most learning disabilities teams have a strategic policy, which gives guidelines to its staff for time scales, e.g. from referral to first contact with the client, from assessment to assessment report being written and sent, and to whom. If this is not in place, a fair time would be 5 working days from receipt of referral to first contact and 21 working days after the assessment to the report being written and sent to the client, carers, care manager, medical practitioner and the day care centre.

Goal planning

The plan of therapeutic intervention – the goal plan – is decided after assessment and discussion between the client, the carers, relevant therapists and members of the multiprofessional and multiagency team, the care manager and, if relevant, the client's general practitioner, who should always be informed of any proposed action. It should be a part of the client's care plan. The advent of the Care Programming Approach to client care takes all of this into consideration, making it part of assessment and screening protocols.

Goals are set which will be based on a combination of desired outcomes, decided by the client, the carers, the health care team, the therapist and the service. Plans for the teaching and training of carers and support staff skills are necessary to enable clients to achieve these goals. They should be decided on and communicated to the relevant people.

The long-term goal may take a considerable time to achieve. It can, therefore, be broken down into a series of short-term goals. Short-term goals are smaller targets which should be:

- measurable, achievable, timed and realistic, and able to lead towards achieving the long-term goal
- written in a language easily understood by all those involved in implementing them
- recorded, monitored and reviewed at regular and stated intervals

Example

Household ambulator 2: Hoffer et al. (1973); see Chapter 7.

Long-term goal: to walk independently.

Short-term goals:

- To stand independently for a timed period at an agreed frequency.
- To walk a short measured distance indoors without apparatus; frequency to be agreed.
- To walk a short measured distance outdoors with apparatus at agreed frequency.
- To walk a short measured distance outdoors without apparatus at agreed frequency.
- To walk independently at all times.

The method of intervention and monitoring will be decided on after discussion with the client and carers.

Monitoring the intervention

In Chapter 7, a recent study of assessment and evaluation methods was mentioned which found that the Le Roux method (TELER Information Pack; Le Roux, 1993 – see Appendix II) was sensitive enough for people with profound learning and physical disabilities.

The Le Roux method

Goals are written with specific indicators on an ordinal scale of 0–5. They can:

- be constantly monitored
- show change
- show the factors influencing change, whether client/carer compliance, change in client health status, change in venue, therapist, weather, time, staffing levels, level of skills of the key staff assisting the client
- indicate the training needs of the key personnel

In addition, the unique method of TELER recording gives an accurate, at-a-glance indication of the client's current situation/state.

The TELER method is sufficiently sensitive to indicate minute change or no change, which is very relevant when the desired outcome is maintenance of the health-care status in cases where there is profound and multiple disability (Chartered Society of Physiotherapy pilot study on the 'measurement of outcome of profound disability', 1997, unpublished data, see Chapter 7). This and all other methods are very dependent on an accurate and informed assessment of need and on a sound underpinning of clinical knowledge.

Example: moving from supported standing to taking independent steps forward

0   Unable to take steps forward unsupported by therapist or carer
1   Able to stand supported by apparatus
2   Able to stand unsupported but cannot shift balance
3   Able to stand unsupported and shift balance for a timed period
4   Able to stand unsupported and shift balance all the time
5   Able to move independently forward

For each goal, the treatment plan would include specific exercises or activities to enable the client to progress.

Goals that are not achieved within the specified conditions should be evaluated for:

- appropriateness
- achievability
- other factors

New goals should be considered taking all the above into account.

It is always possible that some goals may never be achieved for a variety of reasons. The therapist then has to decide if it is time to give up. The decision may be influenced by any of the following:

- health-care service requirements/policies
- staffing resources
- time
- availability of carer support
- transport

The MOVE curriculum

The MOVE (Mobility Opportunities Via Education) curriculum, which incorporates an as yet unvalidated method of measurement for functional movement is beginning to be used with adults in the UK. This educational philosophy was originally used with children in schools in the USA. It involves testing, setting goals, task analysis, identifying equipment and measuring prompts required to achieve a task, identifying where a reduction of prompts could be achieved in an agreed duration, and identifying how to teach the skills for everyday life. It is highly dependent on commitment to the plan by all carers and staff who work with the client.

Both the Le Roux and MOVE systems require expenditure before they can be fully used.

Measurement of outcome

This should reflect:

- changes in health status of the clients
- changes in knowledge or behaviour pertinent to any future health status
- client satisfaction

It can be as simple as:

- non-achievement
- partial achievement
- full achievement

There are many forms of research-based outcome measurements now available to the therapist, as shown by the following example.

Therapy outcome measures

Therapy outcome measures (TOMs: Enderby, 1997) are described as 'a multiprofessional approach to outcome measurement incorporating the International Classification of Impairment, Disability and Handicap (ICIDH) and based on a 0–5 core scale'. Enderby noted that 'A need for an extra classification of "distress and well-being" was identified by Rosser and Associates (1976) following observations that many therapists frequently work to reduce: anxiety, depression, anger, fear and improve emotional control.'

WHO (World Health Organization ICIDH revision, commenced 1993) defined impairment, disability and handicap as follows:

- Impairment: dysfunction resulting from pathological changes in the system.
- Disability: consequences of impairment in terms of functional performance (disturbance at the level of the person).
- Handicap: disadvantages experienced by the individual as a result of impairment and disabilities; it reflects interaction with and adaptation to the individual's surroundings.

Example: disability

0   Totally dependent/unable to function.
1   Assists/cooperates, but the burden of the task/achievement falls on the professional or the caregiver.
2   Can undertake some part of the task but needs a high level of support to complete.
3   Can undertake task/function in a familiar situation but requires some verbal/physical assistance.
4   Requires some minor assistance occasionally or extra time to complete the task.
5   Independent/able to function.

Further examples of outcome measures that have been adapted for specific modalities and activities can be found in Chapters 11, 12 and 14.

Conclusion

Interpretation of assessment results, writing of goals and care plans, and the training and teaching of carers, parents and other professionals are dependent on a variety of circumstances and events, which alter from client to client. The whole process has to be individual to the client's needs but it is also essential that the needs of the carers are included.

The most effective level of service to the client is achieved when good communication between all those involved with delivering the service is accepted as a priority.

Treatment must be monitored and the outcomes of the goals set must be measured to ensure that the intervention is effective and is seen to be effective. To this end, methods of measuring outcomes are constantly being developed, tested and peer validated.

PART III

PRACTICAL TREATMENT AND MANAGEMENT

CHAPTER 9

Developing a service to provide postural care at night

JOHN AND LIZ GOLDSMITH

People who are unable to move well may be at risk of developing distortions of body shape over a period of time. In 1976, Fulford and Brown identified destructive positions as a cause and called for therapeutic intervention. The development of a postural care service will seek to allow individuals to enjoy life while providing them with supported symmetrical postures in sitting and lying, with standing being included if appropriate, over most of the 24 hours a day to protect body structures.

Over the past 20 years, therapists and manufacturers have worked together to develop symmetrical support in sitting and standing. Seating systems to control upright functional sitting feature stabilisation of the upright posture, which can be tolerated for limited periods (Mulcahy, 1986), whereas multi-adjustable armchairs with facilities to tilt in space cater for the need to provide symmetrical supported postures during the hours that must be spent relaxing (Medical Devices Agency, 1995). In one variety, the facility to use the chair for side and prone lying, and postural drainage offers the individual changes of position and function with one piece of equipment. Moulded seating interfaced with a wheelchair offers support for mobility for people whose body shape cannot be accommodated in more conventional wheelchairs (Nelham, 1984). Pressure relief is provided by a variety of foams, gels and flotation cushions (Young, 1992; Lowthian, 1997). Standing frames offer the opportunity to bear weight progressively from prone to upright for those who are able to do so (Green et al., 1993).

The routine application of support and protection of a growing body in the lying posture is a concept that is acknowledged (Bell and Watson, 1985), but that has not been generalised within community services. The distorting effect of gravity on the body shape of young babies has long been recognised and their need for supported positioning to counteract abnormal tone has been developed (Fulford and Brown, 1976;

147

Bellefeuille-Reid and Jakubek, 1989; Turrill, 1992; Hallsworth, 1995). These principles logically extend to the motor-impaired child and adult, and it is suggested that abnormality of tone and movement with the critical factor of resultant loss of joint range at the hips and knees causes individuals to lie in destructive postures for long periods at night from a very young age; these habitual lying positions very often become recognisable as the pattern of fixed distortion of body shape as the person grows. Therapeutic skill lies in recognition and correction of seemingly innocuous deviations from symmetry before damage to skeletal structures occurs. Evidence on which to base clinical practice is plentiful and readily available by investigating habitual lying postures and analysing the consequent body shapes in adults.

Recently, equipment has been developed that allows for comfortable, versatile adjustment of support and control in any lying posture, for any shape or size of user. Short-term results of use indicate significant benefits, even for those with established problems, and it is considered that accurate therapeutic positioning at night offers an important opportunity to influence body shape for the following reasons:

- The time available for application of corrective forces is in the region of 10 hours per night, offering periods of stretch in excess of the 6 hours frequently accepted as being necessary to maintain muscle length (Tardieu et al., 1988).
- During sleep, with the comfort of supported positioning, the perverse influences of abnormal tone are reduced, allowing more correction than is available during the day.
- At night, there are no other demands being made on the individual, so that therapy can be carried out without inconvenience.
- Associated improvements in sleep patterns and well-being ensure that parents are continuously motivated to carry out the therapy consistently in the long term.

This chapter reflects the experience of provision of this care by therapy services in Mansfield, Nottinghamshire. Feedback has been extracted from a study involving 31 families who have been offered Symmetrisleep night-positioning equipment.

Identification of those in need of postural care

'The Mansfield checklist of need for postural care'

Provision of a postural care service requires acknowledgement of the need for and cooperation from all those involved in the individual's care, including management and hands-on carers, and these factors have therefore been expressed in non-medical terms to increase accessibility:

- Does the individual tend to stay in a limited number of positions?
- Do the knees seem to be drawn to one side, or outwards, or inwards?
- Does the head seem to turn mainly to one side, to the right, or to the left?
- Does the body tend to flex forwards, or to extend backwards?
- Does the trunk tend to bend to the right, or to the left?
- Is the body shape already asymmetrical?

Developing a register of people in need of postural care

It is suggested that minimum data collection for each individual on the register would include the following:

- An estimation of the dominant distorting tendencies within the body using the Mansfield checklist.
- Photographic evidence of the individual's unsupported and supported postures in lying. (It has been found that photographs taken from the end of the bed tend to give a useful perspective.)
- An estimate of lying, sitting and standing ability using the Chailey scales (Mulcahy et al., 1988; Pountney et al., 1990).
- Measurement of body symmetry (Goldsmith et al., 1992).
- X-ray analysis.

This register and minimum data collection would form the basis of educational material to alert clinical and financial management to the need for postural care within a community, and also to work with individual parents, carers and clients.

Providing training and support for carers

Analysis of time spent in day-time occupation and with parents and carers reveals that most time is spent at home (Table 9.1).

Table 9.1 Breakdown of time spent during a year

Hours in the year	8760
Day-time occupation, e.g. 9.00 am until 3.00 pm × 5 days a week × 48 weeks	1440
Hours at home	7320
Hours in bed, e.g. 10.00 pm until 8.00 am × 365 days	3650

Providing good postural care as a routine domestic habit may require behavioural change within the family. To initiate that behavioural change, a high level of training, support and efficient equipment provision is needed in the early stages. The younger the individual is when carers are introduced to the principles of postural care, the easier it is.

Support for carers is provided in the following ways:

- Good training and preparation
- Regular phone calls during the first weeks
- Individual practical sessions
- Follow-up clinics in which carers set up the positioning so that effectiveness can be checked and changes made if necessary
- Home visits.

The aims of training are that the carer will understand the destructive effect of static asymmetrical postures, be able to identify joints at risk, and correct the individual's posture effectively. The following strategies are used in this programme:

- Individual teaching
- Demonstration
- Diagrams
- Photographs
- Keeping a postural care diary
- Group family workshops.

'Postural care: family workshop'

These formal workshops provide a theoretical basis for the carer's developing skills. The text of the Families Workshop contained in a slide show and booklets (Goldsmith and Goldsmith, 1996; Goldsmith et al., 1998) contains the following concepts.

The postural care slide show

> Therapy has two halves: (1) postural care and (2) development and maintenance of function.

Development and maintenance of function have tended to be a high-profile aspect of therapy, perhaps because it offers the possibility of short-term rewards. Unfortunately, without systematic provision of supported postures in sitting, standing and lying, short-term gains can be lost in the long term by developing distortion of body shape. Postural care, offering long-term protection of body shape, should become the foundation of therapy. On this foundation, the individual can be encouraged to function according to their natural condition.

> What is postural care?
>
> Protection of body shape by supporting the body in a straight and comfortable position both in the day and at night.

Carers are empowered by the assurance that providing postural care is a common-sense, practical skill, akin to packaging any vulnerable object.

> Does the person I look after need postural care?

The Mansfield checklist is used to allow carers to identify for themselves that they may need to provide postural care.

> Working together

It is stressed that there is a need to work together with therapists in an ongoing relationship, constantly changing strategies as the individual grows and changes.

Once the carer is skilled in positioning, they are able to continue providing postural care despite changes in therapy personnel and service provision.

> The following three terms are used when talking about postural care: (1) destructive postures, (2) supported postures, (3) postural moulding.

A basic vocabulary needs to be established, which is often simplified to such terms as 'bad postures' and 'good postures' once they have been identified and photographed in individuals.

> What are destructive postures?
>
> Postures in which the body may be damaged by being left unsupported. While in these postures, some of the joints may be stressed.

Carers need to be aware of the damage that can occur when individuals are left in destructive postures. To date, some therapists may be unaware of these destructive postures, often occurring at home and in the night, negating hands-on therapeutic effort, when traditionally the therapist's remit has been to provide input during the day. When parents are uninformed and without the necessary equipment, these postures can act as an unacknowledged threat to the body shape and abilities of the individual. The prospect of their child not growing into a conventional human shape is a notoriously hard concept for parents of young children to accept, but it needs to be stressed that early intervention is necessary because it is easier to maintain symmetry than to correct damage and distortion. This effect is illustrated by a series of slides, below, of Sarah. They show how her body shape adapted over the years, to suit her habitual position.

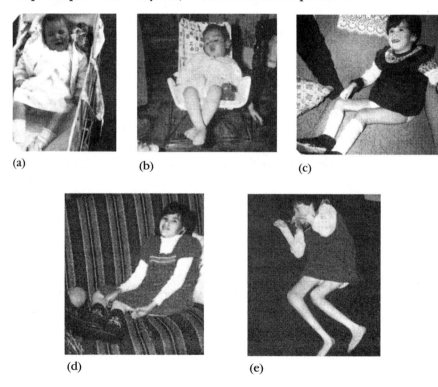

(a)   (b)   (c)

(d)   (e)

Figure 9.1 (a) at 10 months old her shape was still symmetrical although she could not move from one position; (b) at 18 months old she used to sit in a baby chair, because the seat fitted she was able to sit in a conventional position; (c) at 4.5 yrs old she was being placed in the corner of the settee and began to adopt a destructive asymmetric posture; (d) by 11yrs old she received physiotherapy and symmetrical positioning at school but continued to sit in the corner of the settee at home; (e) by 13 yrs old her body shape had flattened and twisted. Sarah's story is reproduced with kind permission of the English National Board for Nursing, Midwifery and Health Visiting (ENB).

What are supported postures?

Postures in which the natural shape of the body is protected and all joints are supported in a neutral, comfortable position.

The key to provision of a postural care service is that individual work is done to devise, equip and photograph supported postures for each person. The implications of informing parents of this need is that a service must be integrated to provide the equipment necessary. To date, service provision is not integrated, resulting in a haphazard and all-too-often unsuccessful aspect of care.

Symmetrical support is needed in sitting, standing and lying

Very often the possibilities of providing supported standing reduce as the individual grows larger and handling becomes more difficult. However, support in symmetrical sitting and lying should continue throughout adult life. For many adults who have not had the benefit of postural care, the aims are to increase comfort levels, reduce tone and gradually to coax the body into a less destructive position. Slides illustrate this effect.

What is postural moulding?

The use of posture to allow the force of gravity, as it presses down, to mould the body to the shape you want.

This can be explained with particular reference to the chest; it is demonstrated that, if the chest is positioned in lying with the sternum directly above the spine, gravity will flatten the chest in a symmetrical manner as it presses down. Lateral support will reduce the flattening spread of the chest. If the chest is positioned with the sternum to one side, the flattening effect will tend to distort the chest and spine asymmetrically.

Night time is the best time to provide postural moulding because:

1 Muscle spasms are reduced when the individual is asleep
2 The individual is lying down flat so that gravity can be used to straighten the body
3 At night there are long periods of time during which no other demands are made of the individual

---

The benefits of successful postural care

1 Protection of body shape
2 Improved function
3 Reduced long-term need for surgery
4 Reduced need for expensive, complex equipment to cater for future problems in body shape
5 Health gain for the individual, improved quality of life, improved sleeping patterns and reduced pain
6 Resultant health and emotional gain for all the family

Postural care leaflets

To explain the concept that habitual static night positions will have an influence on the individual's shape and ability to develop and maintain function in the day, the following lighthearted illustrations and simple text are used (Figure 9.2).

The assessment procedure

Sleep and the family

All assessments must be carried out with hands-on participation by the carers. Before assessing the physical support that is needed, it is important to have an understanding of sleep processes (Ferber, 1986) and to gain an insight into the established sleep behaviours of the individual.

It has been acknowledged that individuals with multiple neurological disabilities associated with distortion of body shape often have disturbed sleep, which does not respond easily to treatment. Polysomnographic evidence reveals increased apnoea of central and obstructive origin, decreased ability to change body position and epileptiform discharges in the sleep of people with severe cerebral palsy (Kotagel et al., 1994). Circadian rhythms may be disturbed (Okawa et al., 1986), and the behavioural approach, sedation and analgesics may have been tried but found to be ineffective with this group (Jan et al., 1994). In these circumstances, the physician may be presented with an exhausted individual, who is unable to communicate adequately, possibly suffering from chronic pain of uncertain origin, and accompanied by a desperate family with no simple answer to their problems. Careful consideration should therefore be given to any potential solutions that may offer some help to this small minority of people who find themselves providing care in the community under almost intolerable circumstances. It has been suggested that melatonin

Lying squint can cause problems

Lying with legs to one side makes it difficult to sit straight

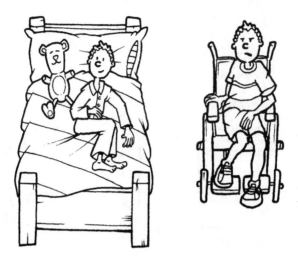

Lying with knees out to the side makes it a problem to bend in the morning

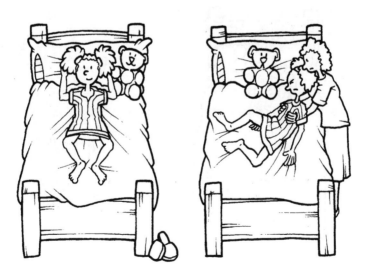

Figure 9.2a

Lying with knees together makes it hard to sit and stand

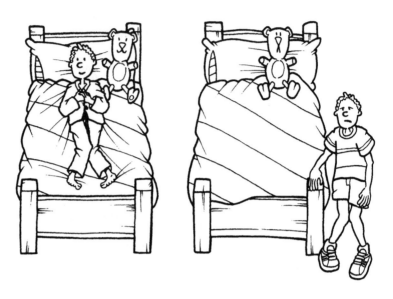

Lying with backs bent makes it hard to sit straight in the day

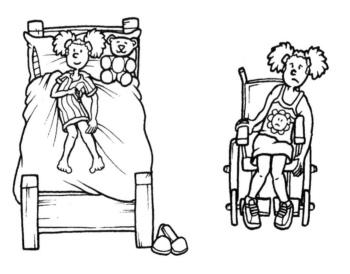

Figure 9.2b

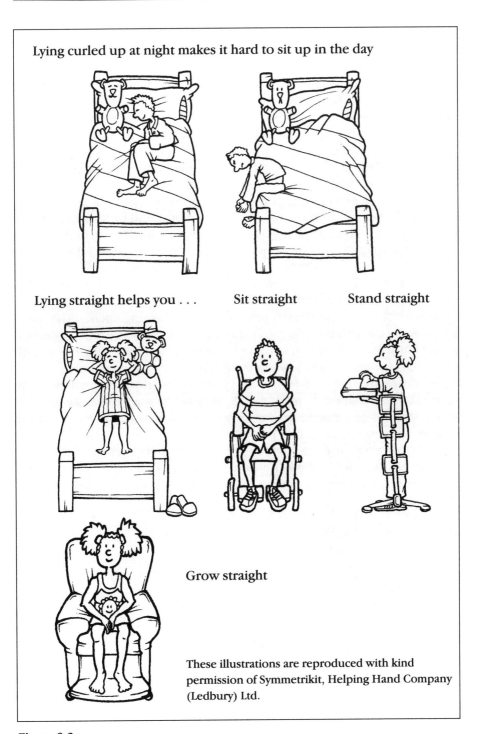

Lying curled up at night makes it hard to sit up in the day

Lying straight helps you . . .   Sit straight   Stand straight

Grow straight

These illustrations are reproduced with kind permission of Symmetrikit, Helping Hand Company (Ledbury) Ltd.

Figure 9.2c

may be helpful in the management of individuals whose main presenting problem is interruption of circadian rhythms and who are unable to respond to other interventions (Jan et al., 1994).

As sleep behaviour will have a profound effect on the family, it is a subject that must be addressed in a tolerant, sensitive and generous manner. Therapists who do not enjoy working closely with all kinds of families will not find this area of therapy rewarding.

Physical assessment will be carried out over a period of time, with some individuals adapting immediately to the intervention and some requiring a period during which both the position and the equipment used are adjusted. There may also be a need for time spent 'getting used' to the equipment and a willingness to 'give up' for a time and to 'try again' when the family feel ready. The 'aches and pains' experienced in the initial stages of even slight alterations to sleeping positions must be allowed for. Many people find that positioning is best applied after the individual has settled into bed and has become drowsy; there is no need to apply positioning the moment the individual goes to bed. In general, simple solutions are more likely to be accepted by families than complicated arrangements. The long-term benefits of 10 hours' therapy a day are worth every effort to establish a successful habit, although most mistakes are made in the introduction of too much change, too soon, with insufficient training and support.

Feedback from the 31 Mansfield families illustrates the variations in time taken to establish a night-positioning habit, with some taking to it 'instantly' and one needing 12 months to establish the correct position and become used to it.

Detailed results of the study have been written up (Hewitt et al., 1998) and are encouraging, with benefits described in reduction of high tone, improvements in sleeping patterns and with users described as sleeping as shown in Table 9.2.

Table 9.2 Benefits from the study

In a much straighter position	19
In a straighter position	5
About the same	5
In a less straight position	0
In a much less straight position	0
Could not answer	2

From Hewitt et al. (1998).

Positioning at night

It has been recognised that individuals with severe movement problems do not move from one position to another during the night as able-bodied people do. Kotagel et al. (1994) observed that, in a group of nine disabled people, there were only three significant changes of position during a night, compared with 59 changes in position in an able-bodied control group. Assessment will start from the habitual position and seek to reduce the destructive tendencies of the position. The equipment, patented as Symmetrisleep, allows for infinite variations of support and control for these habitual static positions. It comprises a Velcro sheet (Figure 9.3a) attached to the mattress to fix the positioning components, which are a variety of brackets, pads and cushions. An 'overmantel' of foam or sheepskin may be used to cover the supporting structures and this in turn is covered by a stretch sheet.

A Symmetrisleep Knee Cosy (Figure 9.3b) is used for those individuals who need control to maintain a particular hip posture in association with total body control. Temperature-sensitive foams of various consistencies are adjusted within zipped compartments to offer the support and control that is needed.

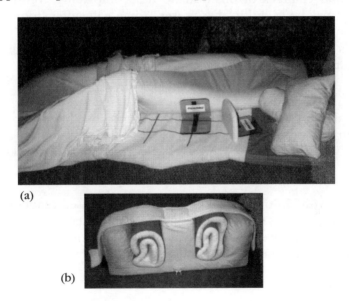

(a)

(b)

Figure 9.3 (a) Velcro sheet with grid marking, brackets, pads, cushions, overmantel and elasticated sheet. (b) Knee Cosy.

Positioning exercises

Therapists and carers can experience the sensation of changes in body position by using the equipment themselves, although they will probably be habitually too mobile to tolerate restriction overnight. Use of strapping to simulate loss of hip and knee extension will enable them to experience the obligation to lie in typical windswept, adducted or abducted postures when prone or supine.

Safety considerations

Considering the vulnerability of this group, care should be taken when assessing risk. The following factors need to be considered when thinking about introducing subtle change to night-positioning habits:

- Breathing
- Reflux
- Epileptic seizures
- Temperature control.

Breathing

Individuals with fixed distortion of body shape may have a very limited repertoire of breathing patterns, so extreme care should be taken to ensure that changes of position do not compromise ventilation; an oximeter may be useful in these cases. Some will suffer from apnoea of obstructive or central origin as a result of their condition, resulting in use of alarms and positive-pressure breathing equipment. In these individuals, positioning of the head and neck must be carefully monitored.

Reflux

Individuals who suffer from reflux must be positioned in such a way as to ensure that airways are not compromised should this occur during the night. Position with regard to how it affects tube feeding should be considered.

Epileptic seizures

As people with multiple disabilities have an increased tendency to have epilepsy and seizures may occur during the night (Kotagel et al., 1994), care must be taken to investigate the type and severity of seizures and advice should be sought about the implications of control of posture at night.

Temperature control

A variety of equipment can be selected to ensure that temperature can be regulated to suit the individual. With use of an overmantel, the moulded shape created will decrease the amount of air circulating over the skin surface and will therefore tend to increase body heat beneficially for those who tend to be cold. For those with a high body temperature, brackets and pads, sometimes combined with the use of sheepskins and gel pads, allow for efficient positioning without an increase in body temperature. These strategies, along with alterations in the quilt, blankets and sheets used over the top, will allow for temperature to be regulated in association with protection of body shape.

Analysis of destructive and supported postures

The following section, illustrated using an individual with normal movement, is included to sensitise therapists to the innocuous early stages of deviation from symmetry. In each position, destructive and supported postures are identified, and the need to control the whole body must be recognised because control of one segment will often result in abnormality of tone transferring to another part. There are typical destructive postures that are often adopted, with typical, easily identifiable results. Observation of the body shape of adults will often betray the habitual lying posture, which will vary in detail according to the individual but may be the result of the downward force of gravity working in combination with four main factors:

1. Lack of physical support
2. Abnormality of tone associated with loss of joint range at hips and knees
3. Habit
4. The flattening effect of the weight of bedclothes.

Side lying position

Although often identified as a functional position for during the day, particularly for people who tend to extend, unsupported side lying is potentially an extremely destructive position to sleep in. When an individual is asleep, extensor tone is reduced and function is not so relevant, so the factors influencing the choice of side lying at night should therefore be recognised as very different from those influencing the individual during the day. The choice of side lying will be influenced by an established positional habit, often with an associated limited repertoire of breathing patterns and the need to protect the airway for individuals who suffer from reflux or seizures.

Destructive postures in side lying

When side lying, the shoulder underneath will inevitably be moved either forwards or back, introducing rotational distortion into the chest; combined with the weight of the top arm, this will effectively flatten and twist the thorax. Typically, the shoulders will be pushed upwards and inwards with the scapulae migrating around to the sides. The pelvis will be pulled either forwards or back by the weight of the top leg compounding rotational destruction, stressing the hip joints and establishing gross asymmetry of the leg posture. It is very difficult to balance the chest and pelvis in a true side lying position. As illustrated in Figure 9.4, and described in Fulford and Brown (1976), as soon as an individual becomes asymmetrical the moulding effect of gravity quickly distorts both the chest and pelvis. This pattern often becomes recognisable as the pattern of fixed distortion as the individual gets older and attempts are made to seat the rotated pelvis and support the scoliotic chest.

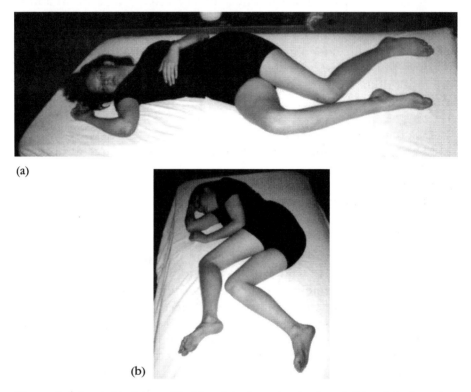

(a)

(b)

Figure 9.4 Semi-side lying with (a) pelvis dropping back and (b) pelvis dropping forwards.

Supported postures in side lying

Supporting side lying symmetrically is difficult; attempts must be made to shape the supporting surface to accept the shoulder underneath; taking the weight of the top arm will reduce its flattening effect on the chest. The head, neck and waist need shaped support in order to keep them in line. The weight of the top leg needs to be completely supported to prevent it from tilting or rotating the pelvis (Figure 9.5).

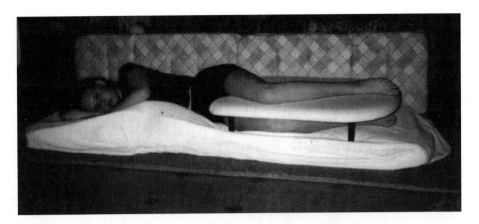

Figure 9.5 Side lying with trunk and weight of top leg supported.

Prone position

For those who like to sleep in a prone position, it is often a strong and comforting habit, and it can be difficult for a person who habitually sleeps prone to be able to adapt to an alternative position, although the destructive patterns can be extremely perverse.

Destructive postures in prone

When lying unsupported in prone, the head will be turned to one side to breathe, introducing rotation to the chest. An asymmetrical lordosis is typical in this group.

There are three main categories of destructive posture affecting the legs and pelvis in the prone position.

Windswept prone

To accommodate hip flexion contractures, evident in many subjects, the body is often moved into a semi-side lying position with the legs rotated to one side and the knees drawn up. Typically, a 'windswept' body shape results in severe internal rotation of the leg underneath (Figure 9.6).

Prone with legs turned out

This group are those who lie with the knees out to each side. Frequently, anterior dislocation of the hips leads to associated severe difficulties with sitting and subsequent spinal problems (Figure 9.7a).

Figure 9.6 Prone with 'windswept' legs.

Prone with legs turned in

This group will often start with a seemingly innocuous internal rotation at the hips but as loss of extension increases at the hips and knees an extremely perverse pattern emerges, with leverage of the lower leg creating severe internal rotation at the hips (Figure 9.7b).

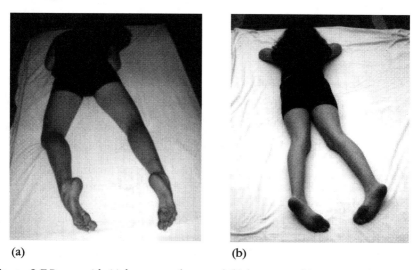

(a)   (b)

Figure 9.7 Prone with (a) legs turned out and (b) legs turned in.

Supported postures in prone (Figure 9.8)

If the chest is raised with a small wedge the individual may be able to turn the head with less rotation travelling into the chest.

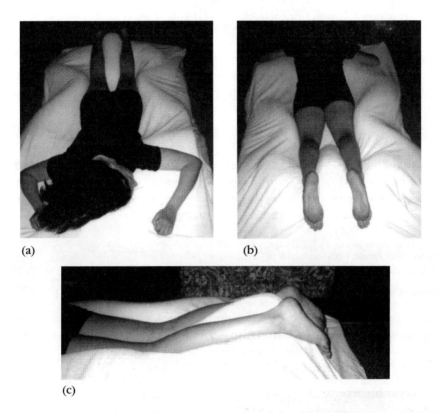

(a)   (b)

(c)

Figure 9.8 Supported prone lying with (a) minimal shoulder girdle rotation and (b) legs in neutral rotation. (c) Minimal knee flexion to allow feet to remain neutral.

For those who are 'windswept', packing under the hips to accommodate hip flexion enables the pelvis and legs to be moved to a more neutral position. Lateral support combined with a pommel shape will help to support the legs.

For those whose legs turn out, hip flexion combined with lateral support may reduce the severity of external rotation combined with extension at the hips.

For those who internally rotate, correction is relatively easy in the early stages with a pommel and lateral supports, becoming more difficult once the lower leg is raised from the supporting surface when the hip is in a more neutral position.

For all categories, packing to support as small an amount of knee flexion as possible will help to allow the feet to remain plantargrade.

Supine position

This is the easiest position in which to reduce destructive tendencies in the body and to provide symmetrical support. Persuading an individual to sleep in supine may be introduced very gradually, perhaps introducing the position for periods in the day to start with and then for short periods at night. Achieving a symmetrical supine sleeping position will have significant beneficial impact in the long term.

Destructive postures in supine

Although the chest will often rest relatively symmetrically in supine, lateral trunk flexion may occur and the chest will tend to flatten. There are three main categories of destructive posture of the legs and pelvis in supine, resulting from loss of joint range, as in prone.

Windswept supine (Figure 9.9)

In this posture the legs are frequently drawn or fall to one side with the result that the knees flatten to the ground and the pelvis drops backwards on the opposite side.

Supine with legs turned out (Figure 9.10a)

In this posture the extreme external rotation at the hips may cause anterior dislocation and create problems with hip flexion and resultant spinal problems.

Supine with internal rotation at the hips (Figure 9.10b)

The natural tendency of some individuals to adduct at the hips combines with hip and knee flexion to lever the hips into increased internal rotation.

Supported postures in supine (Figure 9.11)

Minimal support to provide enough knee flexion to give comfort, combined with lateral boundaries, will maintain the hips, knees and pelvis symmetrically without increasing hip and knee flexion contractures. Any device that introduces more hip flexion than necessary will merely increase the disability of the individual.

Lateral boundaries at the hips and sides of the chest can be used to maintain trunk symmetry. Support for the feet can be provided with cushioning or soft ankle–foot orthoses.

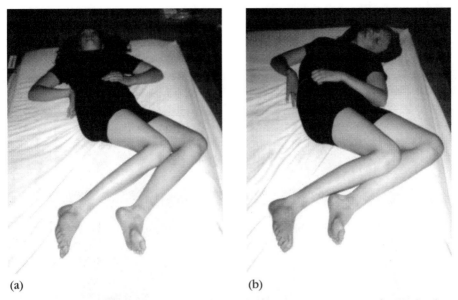

(a)   (b)

Figure 9.9 Supine 'windswept' with (a) knees dropping to supporting surface and pelvis falling back on the contralateral side and (b) additional trunk and neck side flexion.

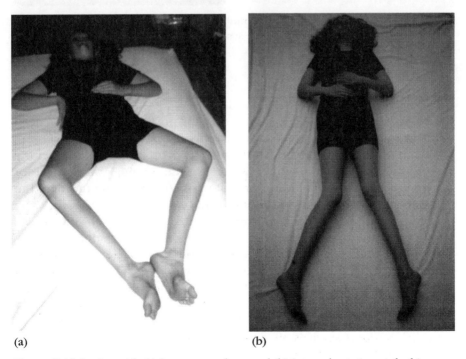

(a)   (b)

Figure 9.10 Supine with (a) knees turned out and (b) internal rotation at the hips.

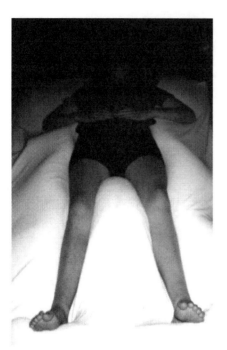 

Figure 9.11 Supported supine with (a) minimal knee flexion to allow neutral rotation and (b) lateral trunk support to maintain symmetry.

Conclusion

Controlled and comfortable symmetrical lying postures at night have been demonstrated to have significant benefits for people with movement problems. This provision should be seen as complementary to postural care in the day. An integrated service to provide training and support for all hands-on carers and efficient provision of equipment is considered to be essential for the success of this intervention.

The present expensive but haphazard system, in which individuals attempt to fit in to the different agendas of service providers and seek equipment from a variety of uncoordinated sources including health, social services, education and charities, represents a waste of resources with inevitably unsuccessful results. Although pioneering therapists are encouraged by results within individual services, they are discouraged by lack of uniformity of provision across areas and the difficulties in providing support services after the individual leaves school (Thomas et al., 1987). Until a consistent service is provided, it must be recognised that therapists cannot fully investigate the efficacy of this treatment.

It is felt that it would be cost-effective for a single authority, however resourced, to be responsible for provision of a reliable, integrated, postural care service which covers sitting, lying and standing, over the age ranges, in the day-care and home setting. Once reliable, long-term, postural care has been established, longitudinal studies in this context will be needed to monitor the long-term effects of this therapy.

CHAPTER **10**

An approach to individual treatment and management of learning disability and severe physical disability

ANN FINDLAY

A significant number of learning-disabled clients referred for physiotherapy have congenital neurological deficit. Others have one of a variety of 'syndromes' or chromosomal disorders. The vast majority of clients with a neurological deficit present with abnormal tone, movement and posture, which are the primary cause of contractures and deformity. Central brain damage is compounded by resultant muscle and bone growth disparity and change of muscle properties (O'Dwyer et al., 1989; Gage, 1991; Croal, 1999).

When working with clients who have learning disability, therefore, the approach must be holistic in nature. Therapy intervention is also likely to be extended to include parents/carers or staff, ensuring a consistent approach to the physical management and care of these clients.

Along with the learning disability comes a variety of levels of handicap and impairment, but all have multiple problems. This needs to be fully understood by all clinicians, because awareness of all physical, sensory and communication problems as well as any challenging behaviour is necessary to ensure effectiveness of treatment.

It is not that therapists working with clients who have learning disability differ significantly from others, and they do not perform magic with clients. It is the broad base of previously learned knowledge and a change in approach to the client that prove important when working within this field. A desire to work in the field is also vital, together with an understanding that change may not be dramatic, and a variety of methods for measuring change may be required for one individual client

170

(see Chapters 7 and 8). Many of the skills used when working with learning disabilities are identical to those used in neurology, general medicine, orthopaedics, etc., but with a totally different approach.

General overview

When working with clients who have learning disability, the broad aims of physiotherapy management and intervention are as follows:

- To assess the needs of the client and carers
- To maintain the good general health of the client
- To prevent or minimise contractures and prevent fixed positional deformity
- To maximise the client's functional movement, ability and independence
- To share specialist knowledge and skills with the client, carers and relatives.

Achieving these aims of good physical management can assist clients in maintaining and improving their quality of life.

In general terms, an eclectic approach to treatment will be used, with therapists considering more than one specific method of treatment to achieve even the smallest change. However, as a result of the neurological nature of the deformity and impairment, the Bobath approach is often used as a basis for treatment, and will be considered later in this chapter.

Brief mention should be given to electrical equipment and electrotherapy techniques. Although occasionally used with clients with learning disabilities, usage is not common. This results primarily from the fact that many clients cannot give a reliable response. Physiotherapists may decide that their client would benefit substantially from certain modalities, and on occasions choose to use modalities such as Flowtron, ultrasound, transcutaneous electrical nerve stimulation (TENS) and laser. All of these would need to be supervised by the physiotherapist. Commonly, Flowtron is used for treatment of oedematous limbs. Some physiotherapists have found that it can be used for clients with a limb contracture to maximise extension with good effect. Laser is not available in all areas, but has been used successfully in the treatment of varicose ulcers, diabetic sores, infected wounds and various pressure areas. This is usually carried out in association with a clinical nurse specialist, to enable the best use to be made of dressings. Laser therapy and the correct effective dressing can undoubtedly speed up the healing rate of wounds, but must be used in conjunction with the dressings that are most effective, and not simply the cheapest. Neuromuscular electrical stimulation (NMES) has not been tried with clients with learning disability. Research has so far tended to be undertaken with patients who can respond reliably. Clients with 'moderate to severe cognitive impairment' or 'severe, frequent epilepsy' fall into the excluded category (Croal, 1999).

When using TENS, Flowtron and ultrasound, the exclusions applicable to clients without a learning disability would also apply.

Individual treatment

Individual treatment can be broadly subdivided into the categories of 'hands-on' treatment, education, seating and equipment, and acute treatment. An individual may dip into any or all of these sections when receiving physiotherapy intervention. What is vital is that it is a client-centred, needs-led approach, respecting the individual's needs and opinions and including their participation, where possible, in any intervention and decision-making.

'Hands-on' treatment

Hands-on treatment incorporates all physiotherapy techniques and exercise, either passive, active or active assisted. Depending on the setting, hands-on physiotherapy may be undertaken on a therapy ball, floor or plinth. This involves the facilitation of normal movement. As long ago as 1943, the Bobaths observed that muscle tone was an alterable state and they have shown that muscle tone is influenced by handling and positioning. The Bobath concept aims to change/influence postural tone, and then to enable the client to experience normal movement. The concept looks at groups of muscles and the patterns of movement that their activity creates. It looks at the contractures and deformity often seen in cerebral palsy as secondary to the condition, and aims to make patterns of normal movement possible.

No standard treatment is available; each client has his or her own treatment regimen. Again, as Karel and Berta Bobath wrote in 1984 of their treatment:

> It is not a 'method' as it is neither rigid nor standardised. It takes into account that CP and allied conditions comprise a group of symptoms in which there is great variety, therefore treatment has to be flexible and adapted to the many and varied needs of the individual child. No standard set of exercises will be adequate to the needs of all children.

An in-depth knowledge of normal movement and the process of normal development is essential when working with adults with a congenital neurological deficit.

Water-based activities also fall into this category. Again, decreasing tone and facilitation of normal patterns of movement in hydrotherapy would be common when working with this client group. All other benefits of hydrotherapy are also evident. For the more able or mobile client, the Halliwick method may be used (see Chapter 11).

Education

Education in the use of equipment, orthoses, seating and 24-hour physical management for each individual is essential. This may involve a number of people, including parents, carers, hospital staff, social work staff and private providers, to name but a few.

Good communication is vital in the field of learning disability, and involves a broad spectrum of people. If treatment for the clients is to move forward, close liaison with other professionals is paramount. Clients with learning disabilities must not be denied access to services, such as medical consultants, surgeons, orthotists and bioengineers, for financial or other reasons. However, it is important that any such professionals are aware of the complex needs of the client, and the difficulties that may arise from their handling or care. Physiotherapy can play a lead role in education and management of other staff should the need arise. Uniprofessional support should also be given to colleagues not so familiar with the learning disability client group. This is particularly important with relatively newly qualified staff who may find the varied and challenging work in learning disability difficult initially, and offputting if appropriate support is not available. Many staff from the Social Services and independent sectors, such as resource centres, adult training centres and small group homes, will look to physiotherapists to lead them in aspects of an individual's physical management.

Seating and equipment

Postural care/management

Postural care/management is a term used to describe the use of specialist equipment to achieve good positioning, known as a physical management programme, and worked over a 24-hour period. This programme must be designed to meet individual needs, maximising strengths and personality. Regular change of body position is essential for everyone, for both comfort and prevention of deformity. Good basic positioning is also the foundation of all useful movement. This is discussed further in Chapter 9.

Seating

Assessment, provision and maintenance of specialised and adapted wheel-chair seating and indoor seating are required to provide an appropriate degree of comfort and postural control. This involves a lengthy process from assessment to delivery. Wheelchair and seating systems have become some of the most important positioning devices available, on which the client is very dependent. Positioning within a seating system is the foundation on which an effective therapy or physical management programme can be built. This complex area is shared by many professionals, and the lead role varies from area to area. It is usually taken by either a physiotherapist or an occupational therapist, and both must liaise closely to achieve the best outcome for each individual.

Each area also has different financial restraints, and therefore seating is not consistent between different areas of the country. This can be a source of great frustration for all concerned, and therefore clear boundaries should be clarified before assessment is carried out, particularly if parents are involved, in an effort to prevent disappointment. Often carers may have seen a chair that they deem to be suitable at an exhibition or demonstration, which may not be within the financial boundaries of the providers. It is easier if this is clarified at an early stage to enable alternatives to be sought.

Equipment

This includes provision, maintenance, renewal and ongoing assessment of equipment used in the physical management programme. Orthoses, such as ankle–foot orthoses, footwear, splints, epileptic helmets and spinal jackets, also require provision and maintenance, as well as equipment such as mobility aids of various types. This equipment will not always be used when the physiotherapist is present, but it will remain the physiotherapist's remit to oversee and monitor the use of all equipment and orthotics, and to ensure its safety and suitability for its purpose. Many physiotherapists within the learning disability service refer clients to the local orthotics or podiatry department but also have access to an orthotics clinic specifically for clients with learning disabilities. This is useful because it gives the time necessary to assess fully and discuss the very individual needs of the client. Where clients are part of a generic clinic, adequate time must be provided, and allowance made for more noisy or disruptive clients. Some system for running trials of new equipment should also be in place, because often a client may not be able to tolerate the orthotic device provided, or may take a longer period to adjust to it than is anticipated by the orthotist.

Acute treatment

Acute conditions are usually classified as problems that need to be responded to within a period of 24 hours. They may be associated with seating, orthotics or more medical problems such as chest infections, pneumonia, asthmatic attacks, fractures or inability to weight-bear, to name but a few. Acute conditions may also arise as a result of a psychiatric problem. If the client is already on the caseload of a physiotherapist, and remains in his or her own home, treatment is often undertaken by that physiotherapist. If it is a problem requiring specific techniques (such as mobilisations), liaison with the generic services is advisable. On occasions this may result in a joint visit. Learning-disabled clients must not be denied their right to access generic services, but often a physiotherapist from the learning disability service can respond more quickly, or can achieve the best result because of the clients' and carers' recognition of them and of their knowledge of the client.

Physiotherapists working in learning disability can often be used as a screen by carers looking for advice in an acute situation. They may be the first line of call for carers (barring 999 situations) and their ability to respond quickly may prevent precautionary hospital admission. The skills gained before specialisation are never forgotten, and frequently used. Mobility problems, gait problems and chest problems often result in a telephone call for assistance from a general hospital or generic physio-therapy service to the learning disability physiotherapy service. In turn, physiotherapists working in learning disability need to know clearly their limits, and when to call on the skills of the generic services. Physiotherapy staff discharging clients from hospital wards should also ensure that an adequate hand-over has been undertaken and sufficient information has been supplied to facilitate ongoing treatment of the client.

Ensuring continuity of management

The clients described in this chapter have complex needs, and can be very vulnerable. The requirement for 24-hour postural management continues in various settings. This may include respite care, holiday accommodation, hospital admissions and clinic appointments, or a transition in life, such as moving from child health to adult services, or moving into a residential unit. If contractures are to be contained, pressure care maintained and lifelong deformity prevented, postural management must be continued in all of these settings. Complications also arise between staff in group homes and those in nursing homes, where not all staff are in regular contact with the physiotherapist or, as a result of staff changes common in such establishments, there is liable to be a delay before new staff can be individually trained by a physiotherapist.

A 'communication passport' produced for each individual is one example of a way to alleviate these problems:

- It is tailored to meet the individual needs of each client.
- It is user friendly for all staff, family members, carers and other professionals.
- It can be multiprofessional.
- It provides accurate information and photographs which allow continuation of care in any setting, and in any area of the country.
- It provides immediate information on admittance to a general hospital, which often makes a considerable difference to the management of a client admitted, preventing deterioration in condition, either medical or physical, while appropriate information is sought.

It may also be used to show the ideal positions that can be incorporated into daily living tasks. This may be of particular importance for a client showing a challenging behaviour, where therapeutic intervention may not be tolerated or be very limited. The same movements built into daily tasks may pass unnoticed by these clients, but carers have a constant reminder of the necessary movements, and can compare various tasks and positions with the 'wanted' and 'unwanted' positions.

Communication passports are best in a small format, such as A5, allowing the information to be easily carried in a handbag or bag on the back of a wheelchair. Ring binders have proved successful, allowing sections of the passport to be removed if necessary, depending on which appointment or visit is being undertaken. This may be particularly important if confidential information such as drug history is contained within this passport. It is *not* intended that this passport replace vital letters such as hospital discharge letters and full therapy assessment reports, and it must be remembered that information contained within the passport will be freely available to a variety of people.

Each passport will be personal, reflecting the lifestyle and personality of the individual. Their needs must also be reflected in this document, and the amount of help required if the passport is to work effectively.

The case study at the end of the chapter is presented as a modified version of a communication passport (page 177–183). It shows the postural management (Figures 10.1–10.11) and describes the physiotherapy needs of a client written in the first person. This amount of information from a single profession would not generally be required in the passport, but this example was used as an aide memoir by the care staff in the small group home where this young man lives. Information not required can be removed when visiting hospitals or holiday locations, where all the equipment would not be used.

Please note that this is an example only, and various versions, formats and ideas can be incorporated (McEwen and Millar, 1993).

Communication passport

Page 1

HELLO

My name is Alan. I have cerebral palsy which affects my trunk and all four limbs. This means that although I have some movement, which should be encouraged, my movements are limited and I have difficulty controlling my limbs for doing purposeful activities. This means that I require a lot of help with most aspects of my daily life.

One way of maximising what I do is through physiotherapy treatment and postural management. This communication passport is designed to briefly explain what these physiotherapy sessions involve, and how YOU can help me out with physiotherapy. It will also mention some of the equipment that I need to use. I hope it will give you an idea of what I can do for myself, and in what ways you can help me.

Page 2

Unfortunately I am unable to speak, although I can answer yes and no. I have a good understanding of what people are saying, so I am able to let you know how I feel or what I need. My non-verbal communication is also good.

So, PLEASE give me the chance to communicate with you. Just give me plenty of time to answer, and keep your questions simple! I'd be happy for you to communicate with me all day – I hate being ignored.

In general I am a very sociable person, but I do get a bit cross if no-one is giving me any attention. Well, would YOU like to sit in one position for hours on end without any stimulation or conversation? I particularly enjoy music

and people singing and I am a Jambo! (Oh, sorry – this means a Hearts FC fan if you don't follow football!)

Page 3

This jacket has been specifically designed and made for me to keep my trunk in a good position and to prevent my spine from twisting further. It also helps me to maintain good posture, as without it I would not be able to sit up straight. Although the jacket looks hot and uncomfortable, it is important that I wear it almost all the time during the day. A close-fitting T-shirt underneath the jacket makes it more comfortable. Getting the jacket on properly may take practice, so please ask my key worker or physiotherapist to show you the first time.

[**Figure 10.1** I'm wearing my jacket.]

The trainers that I wear are also specially made and help keep my feet and toes well positioned.

Page 4

The chair I sit in is my own 'Symmetrikit' chair. I should always use this chair when sitting as it gives my whole body support and keeps it in the best position. To benefit I must be correctly positioned in the chair. Firstly get my bottom as far back in the chair as possible. The back cushion should be puffed up, so that I'm not slouching. An 'Edinburgh harness' is in place to stop me from sliding down. The straps should always be kept at the same length, and should not be adjusted or I am not safe and secure. My feet then need to be strapped in place and a pommel is placed between my knees to keep my legs well positioned. This method of positioning is also followed when I am in my wheelchair.

[**Figure 10.2** Sitting in my Symmetrikit chair.]

Page 5

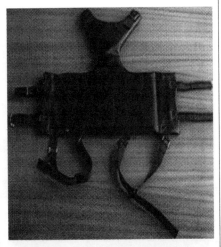

[**Figure 10.3** This is my Edinburgh harness.]

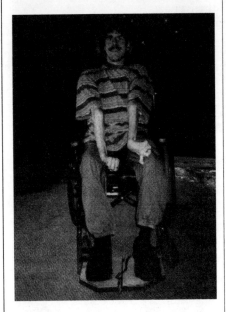

[**Figure 10.4** Here I am sitting in my wheelchair.]

Page 6

During my physiotherapy sessions I spend some time lying on the mat without wearing my spinal jacket. The physiotherapist is trained to do stretching exercises to help maintain the range of movement in my arms and legs. I also do bridging and rolling exercises to maintain the flexibility of my trunk. These exercises should only be done by the physiotherapist, as there is a risk of damage to my bones and tendons. However, this does not mean that I cannot enjoy lying on the mat out-side physiotherapy sessions – there are lots of other things we can do!

Lying on the mat gives me freedom to move myself safely without my spinal jacket. You can't imagine how good that feels! My legs can be positioned in an 'E-Block'. If music is playing I am encouraged to move independently and I enjoy this very much.

It is also a good position for relaxing. I need two people to help me from my chair to the mat and back again, and if I'm not too tired I can manage to take a few steps.

Page 7

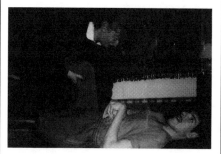

[**Figure 10.5** Doing my physiotherapy exercises.]

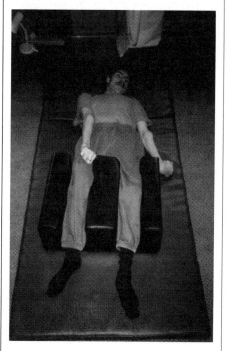

[**Figure 10.6** Lying quietly on the mat.]

Page 8

The next photographs show me lying on my front on what is known as the 'prone lyer'. This is my least favourite position, but it is a good way of straightening my body, especially my hips and knees, preventing them from fixing in a chair-shaped position. It also gives my spine a stretch and relieves pressure from areas I've been sitting on. I normally stay on the prone lyer for about half an hour, and it is much more enjoyable if you stay and keep me company. For example, I enjoy drawing with help while in the lyer.

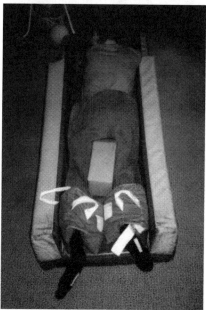

[**Figure 10.7** My prone lyer.]

Page 9

[**Figure 10.8** I do smile in this position!]

Positioning is a big part of my care plan and it makes a huge difference to my long-term quality of life. Remember I need to be positioned 24 hours a day, 52 weeks of the year! It is better if my own equipment is used as it has been set to suit my individual needs. At night I sleep in a special system called a 'Symmetrisleep'. This keeps me in a good position but allows me to be turned during the night by my carers. They will show you how this system works so please ask.

Page 10

Another useful piece of equipment for me is the Bayreuth standing frame. As I am unable to stand unsupported, this frame allows me to experience weight-bearing which has many benefits. It stimulates sensation in my feet and legs and helps prevent osteoporosis (a bone disease) from occurring. Standing is good for other parts of the body including bladder and bowel function and circulation, and it stretches the leg muscles which may become tight from frequent sitting. It also allows me to be the same height as other people, and in this position there are more activities I can do, such as throwing a ball, drawing or painting. Frequent standing in the frame will also help maximise my ability to stay upright when transferring, e.g. from my chair to bed, bed to chair, etc., which hopefully in turn will help YOU, my carers!

To position me in the standing frame first make sure that the frame height and knee pads are set correctly for my height, then bring my chair as close between the bars as possible. Place my feet, using the straps provided. A wooden block goes under my right foot, as my right leg is shorter than the left. Two people can assist me forwards (don't lift) and once I am leaning against the frame the back

Page 11

support can be positioned and tight-
ened, to keep me upright. My elbows
can rest on the table, with a pillow for
comfort if I'm not involved in an
activity. I stand in the frame for half
an hour each day, but must be
wearing my spinal jacket to keep me
upright.

[**Figure 10.9** Me standing in my
Bayreuth standing frame – from behind.]

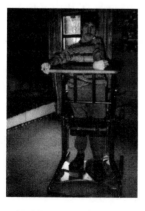

[**Figure 10.10** Me standing in my
Bayreuth standing frame – from the
front.]

Page 12

The following diagram shows the
ARROW walker. It is a gait trainer
which allows me to take a few steps
by myself. Its wheels have locks which
can limit the movement of the wheels
in different directions. Again, two
people are required to get me onto
the seat, and the walker is set just for
me. Leaning on the front pad and
holding the rail, I can use my legs to
propel myself but need help steering.
The walker is best used outside where
I have more room to move about
without knocking something flying.

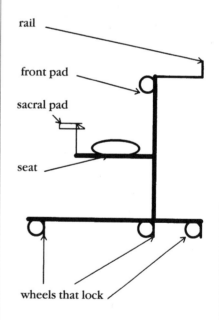

rail

front pad

sacral pad

seat

wheels that lock

[**Figure 10.11** This is just a diagram
of my ARROW walker.]

Page 13	Page 14
My weekly physiotherapy session also includes a hydrotherapy session. The physiotherapist does similar stretching exercises to those on dry land, and the warm water is excellent for relaxing my tight muscles, allowing my arms and legs to move more easily. I am even able to take a few steps with support from the physiotherapist. Floating mats are sometimes used, giving me the security to relax while my exercises are done. Hydrotherapy is something I LOVE – it gives me freedom to move without my jacket. Please don't take me swimming in colder water – I can't cope with that.	I hope you have found this booklet useful in giving a brief overview of my physiotherapy management. All of the things mentioned have been designed to maximise my abilities and help with the things I'm not so good at. They are necessary to give me the best quality of life both now and in the future. This booklet is not long enough to detail everything, but my carers and physio-therapist, who know me well, will be happy to demonstrate anything you would like to know more about. Thank you for taking the time to read about me and for helping me to help myself to get the very best out of life. CHEERS!

Conclusion

As a result of the ongoing, life-long problems associated with a neurological deficit, treatment will also be life long. There is very little benefit from a physiotherapy session lasting half an hour once or twice weekly, without the consistent associated management from *all* other people involved in the life of the client. Although this is generally more prevalent in the child health services, there is no reason why this should not also be the case with adults. It is only through a dedicated multiprofessional and multiagency approach that deterioration in condition and worsening of contractures resulting in deformities and diminished quality of life can be slowed or prevented.

The problems associated with abnormal muscle tone, posture and movement are always present, and it is only through a combined effort by all that normal movement can be encouraged. This does not mean, however, that physiotherapists expect all this work to be carried out by others; they must remain the link between all parties if success is to be achieved. It should not be the intention of the physiotherapy service to 'medicalise' the problem of a learning disability. The aim must be to maximise the physical potential and facilitate function so that disabilities do not become handicaps and people can live their lives in the way they find most fulfilling.

CHAPTER 11

Hydrotherapy

PATRICIA ODUNMBAKU AUTY

Hydrotherapy is the treatment of disease or disability in heated water, using its properties of buoyancy and thermal assets to relieve pain, promote relaxation and foster confidence and independence. It is recognised as an effective treatment method for rehabilitation of physical injury and can provide an aquatic recreational activity for those whose physical musculature could not tolerate cold water.

This chapter does not cover the whole subject of hydrotherapy. Its objective is to combine the knowledge of pool therapy with learning disability to demonstrate expansion of the properties of water to allow for risk-taking, experiential learning, tactile and body awareness training, and guidance of behaviour before use of public pools.

Care must be taken to distinguish between the therapeutic/rehabilitation aspects of hydrotherapy and recreational activities in water: each require different skills. Both water-based activities are beneficial, but the physiotherapist's role is predominantly in therapeutic aspects of hydrotherapy. The role of training support staff in water safety and the introduction of clients to community pools is a smaller, but valuable, part of the service. Where resources and skills allow, therapists can be the instigators of water-based sports. Participation in activity holidays could be one consequence of using the hydrotherapy pool to build confidence in water and instil an understanding of risk and safety in the client.

Factors influencing provision of hydrotherapy

Clients

- The number of children or adults requiring hydrotherapy
- The complexity of the clients. Their physical disability, sensation loss, pain factor, cognitive ability, behaviour that challenges

- The clients who have minimal dysfunction and require pre-public pool experience

Staff

- The staff resources available and their level of skill

The pool
- Its shape, size and depth
- Its surrounding/environment
- Its accessibility
- The equipment available.

When acting as a consultant to introduce clients to public pools, prior visits to these pools are important to discover and, where possible, to reduce the areas of risk. Clients should be encouraged to familiarise themselves with the pool and its facilities to enable a smooth and successful introduction. This may not be necessary for children.

Clients

More children and adults with multiple complex disabilities than ever are entering the paediatric and adult services (see Chapters 1–3 and 7). Added to this, their expectations have grown so that hydrotherapy is seen as an essential part of their intervention. Most clients with complex needs have some degree of cerebral palsy, treatment of which is described in many books (Reid Campion, 1991; Cogher et al., 1992). One condition that requires special consideration is, however, epilepsy (see Chapter 2 and Chadwick, 1997).

It was not unusual some time ago to see epilepsy listed as one of the contraindications to hydrotherapy. If such a group were to be excluded, 90% of complex clients with learning disability would be affected – the very people who benefit from this modality. Epilepsy has to be accepted as one of the risk factors to be accommodated and planned for.

Safe guidelines can be provided only if the type and duration of seizures, the recovery period of the individual and any medication required are known. The carer/support worker will be responsible for providing the medication and its administration. It also helps to know if there are any precipitants and warnings. These must be noted and taken into consideration when writing up risk assessments and emergency procedures for both inside and outside the pool.

Further problems are encountered with clients who have eating and drinking difficulties and who are known to aspirate. Some may have a percutaneous endoscopic gastrostomy (PEG) inserted. How do we manage a hydrotherapy programme for them and should we? This is a difficult decision for some services because the risk is high. It will depend on the medical advice, the skill of the individual therapist and the outcome of the risk-taking meeting around the client. Once the decision is taken that the hydrotherapy outcomes would outweigh the risk factors, protocols are then developed to suit this need. Rules of conduct are required for the staff team and support staff/parents so that, should the client go into stasis, everyone knows and follows the action plan. It was easier to deal with such incidents when a pool was on a hospital site; community placements require an ambulance to be called in case of an emergency. An established protocol must be written and all staff trained in whatever procedures are established by that service. As long as these procedures are established and followed, there is no need to exclude such clients from hydrotherapy.

It is not only the clients with complex needs who require hydrotherapy. There are many clients with minimal physical dysfunction who have a need for confidence, esteem building and assistance with any aspect of their inappropriate sexual behaviour, in preparation for introduction to public pools.

Many clients may be tactile defensive and the close proximity of the therapist may increase their tension or fear. Their resultant behaviour could interfere with support provided, the programme plan or even their safety, thus knowledge of the client is essential. Each service will establish its own basic information requirements and these must be within reach at the session (Figure 11.1).

Contraindications

- Infections
- Cardiac conditions
- Extreme high or low blood pressure.

Care must be taken regarding:

- Sensation level
- Urinary and bowel incontinence – there is no solution, but it is important to be aware of the local pool procedures in case of an accident – see an example of a letter to be sent to GP to ensure that there are no unknown contraindications (Figure 11.2).

Staff

In many areas, clients live in community houses with support staff. It is important that staff are aware of their clients' strengths and requirements

HYDROTHERAPY INFORMATION

NAME:	**D.O.B.**
Address:	
	Tel.

Tel. No. for contact ....

REASON FOR REFERRAL:

RELEVANT CLIENT INFORMATION e.g. disability, specific requirements,

GP NAME & ADDRESS

HAS GP BEEN INFORMED?   **YES/NO**   **DATE**

ANY AREAS OF CONCERN?/RISK ASSESSMENT (Movement & Handling Equipment e.g. hoist, sliding board)

CARER INVOLVEMENT

SIGNED: **DATE:**

Figure 11.1 Example of Hydrotherapy Information Sheet developed by Lewisham and Southwark ALD Physiotherapy Services.

when they bring them to a hydrotherapy session. Parents must also feel involved in their offspring's therapy.

In sessions provided by some services, support staff are expected to work alongside therapists in the pool. If possible, training could be

Dear Dr

Your patient ...... is being seen by the physiotherapy service for people with learning disability.

We feel that a course of hydrotherapy would be greatly beneficial to this patient. I should be grateful if you would let me know if there is any reason why your patient would not benefit from this form of treatment.

Yours sincerely,

Physiotherapist

NB: *The word patient and not client is used deliberately in this context.*

There are legal implications in ensuring that the correct information about the clients' ability to receive hydrotherapy intervention is given. It is therefore important to ensure that the GP receives this letter.

Figure 11.2 Example of letter to GP developed by Lewisham and Southwark ALD Physiotherapy Services.

arranged to acquaint them with the purpose of the intervention and the most appropriate holds for their client. This enables them to position, facilitate and support clients correctly in the water. Parents should also be encouraged to participate, but there is a need to be sensitive as to how much one can expect from over-stressed parents. There are many older parents who have never been in a pool and it would not be right to expect this type of involvement. Cultural issues must also be considered for the client's staff and parents. Some cultures would not wear European swim wear for modesty and religious reasons and other dress must be accepted.

If we want this type of involvement, it is incumbent upon us to provide training for them. Everyone must know what we aim for, and what objectives we want to achieve both short term and long term. The illustration in Figure 11.3 shows team work in action.

The movement and handling directives must be complied with. When clients arrive for their session, the information pertaining to their individual requirements should be recorded on the hydrotherapy infor-

Figure 11.3 Working together in the pool: client involved, mother leaning over pool, participating, support worker watching, student holding client, physiotherapist guiding hand.

mation sheet and must be followed. Support staff should also understand the movement and handling regulations. Advice around this may be necessary. It is sometimes difficult to get parents to comply with these procedures. This must be recorded. However, they should be shown a safe method of movement and handling for their offspring.

It is essential that, whoever is present at the pool side, he or she understands and is aware of the safety and emergency procedures. It is helpful if resources allow the presence of a colleague on the pool side who can observe and offer advice.

The pool

Most people with learning disabilities now live in the community and receive services that they require within their locality.

Many councils now provide public pool facilities that have been heated to correct temperatures so that clients can receive a hydrotherapy service within this public environment. However, this excellent trend increases physiotherapists' responsibilities because they may no longer have the added protection of a hospital site or institution. They have to learn different pool protocols or influence the establishment of them. The equipment may not always be suitable and risk assessments can be problematic. However, every opportunity should be taken to influence any building of pools to gain the best facilities for those who have a disability.

The physiotherapy service for learning disability in Southwark cooperated in the design of a new community hydrotherapy pool. It was designed with a hydraulic variable-depth facility. This allows increased opportunities for freedom and independence and less touching/handling from the therapist. As part of a community facility, with enabling equipment, it allows complex clients to access the pool and assists in community integration.

Pool equipment

The responsibility for supply and maintenance of essential equipment to allow clients access to the facilities lies with the provider of the hydrotherapy pool, for example, height-adjustable beds, hoists and rails.

However, it is the responsibility of the therapists using the pool to check the date of service on this equipment, so that it conforms to the movement and handling directives on equipment. Anomalies should be reported immediately to the managers of the pool.

Information required before commencing sessions

Client

- Essential information (see Figure 11.1)
- Aims and objectives for 6-week period of hydrotherapy (Figure 11.4)
- At each session: an achievable goal should be set that is integral to the 6-week programme plan
- At end of period: evaluation outcomes (Figure 11.5).

Environment

- The local pool and service-specific protocols
- Risk assessment of pool facilities
- Available equipment which complies with EC Directives
- The water condition and temperature.

A 6-week period is selected for the hydrotherapy after the results from a project undertaken to evaluate and cost the effectiveness of hydrotherapy in the Lewisham Disability Service (Odumnbaku Auty, 1990). Part of the project aimed to establish the optimum number of sessions required to do the following:

- Maintain range of movement
- Maintain the client's learning curve
- Improve and maintain function
- Maintain carer/support worker involvement and enthusiasm.

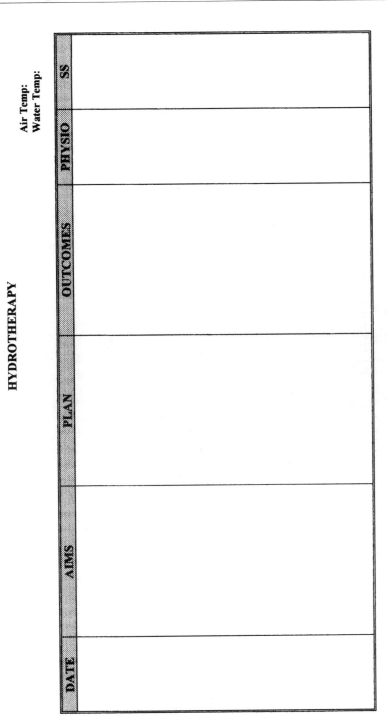

Figure 11.4 Example of Hydrotherapy Aims, Plan and Outcome developed by Lewisham and Southwark ALD Physiotherapy Services.

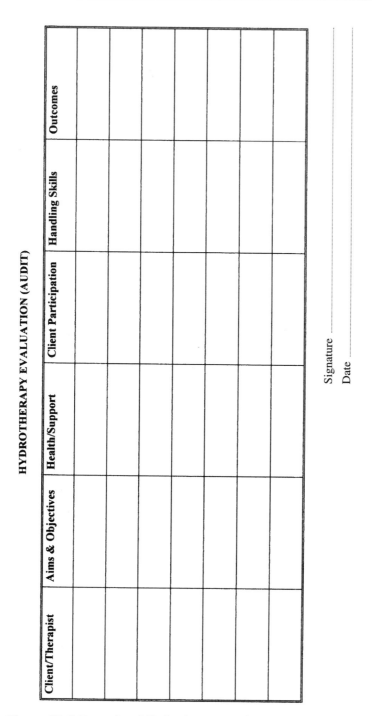

Figure 11.5 Example of Hydrotherapy Evaluation developed by Lewisham and Southwark ALD Physiotherapy Services.

The results showed that the optimum number of sessions was 6 weeks, with the option of starting another 6 weeks following a rest period of 6 weeks.

For clients with pain, burns or recent injuries, session times would need to be revised. Many such clients are treated in the acute sector, but it is often in their best interest to be treated by the specialist therapists who understand their specialist needs.

Therapy in the pool

Adjustment to water

Children may find this easier than older clients. Previous experience of hydrotherapy will have been recorded in the client's notes. However, time must be taken to allow for both mental and physical adjustment to the medium. It is important to allow for adjustment because clients may fear water or even experience dizziness. As verbal communication for most of the clients is difficult or non-existent, the reaction to this may be to push the therapist away or become aggressive. This may be interpreted as challenging behaviour, a difficult label to lose. Time is therefore well spent in allowing adjustment to occur and confidence to grow.

Effect of water

The physical properties of water, its weight, specific gravity, density, buoyancy, refraction, hydrostatic pressure and viscosity must be taken into consideration when planning a programme.

People with musculoskeletal fragility will react to the pressure of water and may experience breathlessness.

The density of the body changes with age; children and young people on the whole carry less adipose tissue than those in their middle years. It is more difficult for clients who have little muscle bulk or fat to float. Many clients with a complex disability have difficulty in eating or drinking and are often underweight, and subsequently may be undernourished and therefore carry very little muscle bulk or fat. The energy expenditure of these clients must be monitored.

It is difficult to find the point of balance in water with clients who have severe deformities and asymmetrical body lines. Observation must be acute to detect the moment of balance so that only the required minimal support is given.

Refraction of the water can cause extra difficulties to those who already have perceptual difficulties, poor body image and visual impairment. The intervention should be modified to take this into consideration.

Turbulence can be made use of to assist and resist movement in the pool. Care must be taken not to allow unintentional turbulence emanating from a therapist's movement to interfere and prevent the client performing an activity: this is a particular problem when trying to teach clients cause and effect.

Client motivation

Learning disabilities services offer a range of interventions to clients from birth to elder care, adjusting the modality to suit individual needs. It requires knowledge, training in the therapeutic aspects of pool therapy, skills in assessment and handling, ability to pass on those skills to support staff and carers, and the ability to motivate clients to achieve success.

None of the above can be obtained without the cooperation and participation of the client. This cooperation requires staff to have the ability to motivate, empower and modify a client's behaviour.

Expectations of children and adults must always be realistic but high, otherwise there will be no achievement. It is especially important in learning disability where a client's motivation is frequently low and little has been expected of them.

It is essential that the learning curve of individuals is understood so that teaching is adjusted to allow them to achieve their aim. An appropriate way should be selected which gives them the ability to comprehend, respond, attempt or initiate the desired activity, enjoy it and succeed. To be successful, the following areas require attention:

- Communication
- Task analysis of activity
- Aims and objectives of assessment or intervention
- Pre-set outcome measures
- Evaluation of outcomes.

Programme

There are different approaches and methods of treatment, each of which have merit. The therapist should select the appropriate treatment technique for each client, be it Bad Regaz, Halliwick techniques (Martin, 1981) or an individualised method for that client, based on the principles and properties of water.

Support staff and carers should be encouraged where possible to participate within the pool.

The aims and objectives of hydrotherapy may be the same for a child as for an adult, these being closely related to the disability or disease. The differences will be the way in which the physiotherapist communicates and conducts the session. Children learn best through play. Age-appropriate music and singing can be of assistance to facilitate smooth gentle motion or more rapid excitable movement. It is often at this stage where cultural differences, though not insurmountable, are difficult to overcome as a result of lack of knowledge of other cultures' music and songs.

Programmes for clients are individualised and the client receives one-to-one attention in the water. This may be from the therapist for only part of the programme; the parent or support worker will also be involved. Traditional rehabilitation programmes can be adjusted to suit the individual's cognitive development. Assumptions cannot always be made about the client's understanding of body or spatial awareness. This must be taken into account as part of the assessment in the pool.

Development of body awareness is promoted by supporting clients supine with minimal effort in the water and encouraging them to move. If they lift their head, their feet will go down. If they put their head back into the water, their feet will rise. These movements can be encouraged by the therapist until the client realises that *he* or *she* can initiate these movements purposely. It takes patience and skill to hold the client as he moves his head in different directions. If the client is in a floating position and makes a movement with hand, arm, foot or knee, the therapist assists the action by moving the client through the water for a proportional distance. Once the client ceases to move, the therapist stops. This assists the client to learn cause and effect. It is difficult to stand still in the pool waiting for the next tiny movement, but it is essential to do so.

The following may be incorporated within the programme:

- Body/spatial awareness
- Cause and effect learning
- Stretching of spine or limbs (Figure 11.6)
- Relaxation
- Beginnings of independent floating (Figure 11.6)
- Non-weight-bearing walking or weight-bearing walking
- What the client wants to do and achieve (Figure 11.7)
- Fun

Each part of the programme must be interchangeable to adapt to the client's initiative. Observational concentration is an essential part of the therapist's skills so that no part of the learning curve initiative of the client is missed. A client floating on his back may turn his head to follow a sound or person. The therapist can then facilitate the body to follow the turn. It would be frustrating for the client and wrong to miss their first attempt of

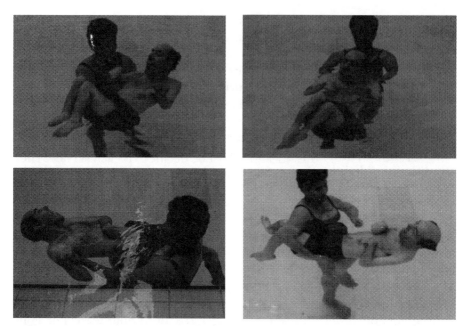

Figure 11.6 Disengaging support from the client aiming to decrease flexion, and gaining more independence by floating.

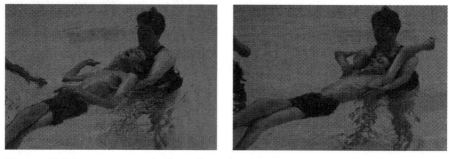

Figure 11.7 A young man who has athetoid movements aiming to achieve stillness in water, fixation, and control to improve upper limb and hand function.

initiating movement for swimming. At times it is necessary to judge when to interrupt the learning curve for the sake of safety, e.g. how do you learn not to put your head into the water and breathe if you do not know it is an unpleasant experience?

It is important to note that one of the effects of hydrotherapy is that clients vocalise more in the pool, not only with increased volume but with changes of sound. This interesting outcome should be encouraged.

The sessions may last 20–30 minutes depending on the client's condition and the temperature of the pool (Skinner and Thomson, 1983). Therapists must be aware of their own energy expenditure and time their input appropriately. Davis and Harrison (1988) accepted that 2 hours was possible but this depends on the complexity of the clients within each session.

Pool floats and equipment

'To use or not to use?' This question must be decided by each service. They can be used to support the client completely to allow him or her to experience non-personal support and freedom – an unusual experience for complex disabled clients.

Floats can be used:

- To assist buoyancy
- To resist buoyancy to strengthen muscle
- To support one area of the body while the therapist concentrates on another
- For recreation

The hydrotherapy programme for adults in Lewisham and Southwark does not use floats. The rationale is that people who already have difficulty learning would have to learn all the sensations of pool therapy using floats and relearn them when they are removed. The aim is to foster as much independence as possible and to disengage from the client as soon as feasible. This can be achieved if physical support is given, which can be instantly monitored by touch and finely controlled. When the aquatic programme is recreational, all pool equipment can be used to increase enjoyment.

Outcomes and evaluation

Each session should have a pre-set outcome, which will be part of the overall 6-week plan. Notes of each session are written. Photographs or videos provide a helpful record. Permission for these must be obtained from the client if they are to be used beyond their private file.

At the completion of the interventions, the outcomes are evaluated and a rating may be given. Each service may have its own outcome rating, be it TELER (see Chapter 8) or the Goal Attainment Scale (GAS) (Brown et al., 1998). Table 11.1 is an example of a simplified outcome rating system.

Table 11.1 A simplified rating system

Rating	Outcome
−1	The presenting difficulty has increased, skills have been lost, opportunities narrowed since the start of intervention
0	The presenting difficulty or skill level has remained the same. No or minimal change
+1	Objectives are partly achieved, some progress has been made, there has been a moderate reduction in difficulty, and skills have increased somewhat, although not as much as was aimed for
+2	Objectives have been almost or totally achieved. There is the aimed-for reduction in difficulty, increase in skill

Recording

Clear, concise, accurate records must be kept so that, should there be a changeover of staff, continuity of programmes can be promoted.

The personality of the therapist, parents and staff will also influence the outcomes. This is an undisputed dimension and must be understood and noted in the outcomes.

Discharge

If the original referral was for an introduction to water with the intention of using public pools, discharge can be completed once that has been achieved. However, with more complex clients, they can continue with hydrotherapy for many years with the required break in between sessions. On their return, new programmes will be devised building on previous outcomes, progress and new objectives for further achievement (Figure 11.8).

For the best results, continuity of the therapists and carer in the pool is preferable so that the understanding of the individual's learning and achievements is continued and allowed to flourish.

Conclusion

Hydrotherapy is seen to be an expensive modality and has high resource implications for staffing. However, the project on the evaluation and costing of hydrotherapy showed it to be cost effective. The survey of the clients and the carers showed that they appreciated and understood its benefits and limitations but all agreed that it was effective and successful. It is therefore important to keep in mind that in these days of scarce resources, hydrotherapy is a clinical and resource-effective intervention.

CONFIDENTIAL

PHYSIOTHERAPY SERVICE FOR ADULTS
WITH LEARNING DISABILITIES

DISCHARGE SUMMARY

NAME:

D.O.B.:

ADDRESS:

DATE OF REFERRAL:

REASON FOR REFERRAL:

SUMMARY OF INTERVENTION:

FURTHER ACTION TO BE TAKEN:

Signed .... Date ....

Figure 11.8 Example of Discharge Summary developed by Lewisham and Southwark ALD Physiotherapy Services.

Case studies

Case study 1: Molly

Molly is a woman in her mid-30s with a right hemiparesis as a result of the Sturge–Weber syndrome. She has extensive haemangiomas. She uses a wheelchair but can stand and transfer herself. She wears a calliper on one leg. She was referred to hydrotherapy as a safe environment in which to work towards swimming for leisure and to be encouraged to use and mobilise her right side.

She challenges the service because she is noisy, bites her left hand, and has been known to hit out at people when frustrated or distressed, especially over unfamiliar activities. If cut she bleeds profusely. She also has seizures.

Molly is self-conscious about her appearance, which requires a sensitive approach. It was decided to overcome this problem by suggesting that she, and all the staff who work with her, wear a T-shirt over their swim wear.

An understanding of her needs and how to work through her challenging behaviour was obtained from her physiotherapist, challenging needs worker and staff. A consistent approach to her behaviour was undertaken and guidelines written in her hydrotherapy notes.

She was given a 6-week course of hydrotherapy. The short-term aim was to encourage activity in the pool and to work towards swimming. The long-term goal is to enable use of a public swimming pool. The same care worker and therapist always worked with Molly in the pool.

A risk-taking assessment was undertaken and followed throughout her sessions; contingency plans were set in motion should she have a seizure or bleed in the pool.

The first session was used as an introduction to the pool environment and water. This proved, in the beginning, to be difficult and ground rules of acceptable behaviour were set. Molly was supported in the pool so that it was difficult for her to bite her hand. She was encouraged to experience and enjoy the sensation of water. The therapist and carer were careful in positioning themselves so as not to encourage poor behaviour. The first session was short and ended when the client was enjoying the session. It was important never to take her out of the pool when she was not enjoying it.

Over the 6-week period, Molly became accustomed to the consistent routine and began to enjoy the session. By the end of 6 weeks, she was lying on her back supported by the therapist and beginning to have confidence in the floating position. She had begun to lie on her front and glide towards the wall bar. Her confidence had grown to being able to hold on to the bar on her own and beginning to let go while needing only minimal support.

Action

1. The outcomes were evaluated and it was decided that another session was required to build on the confidence, and to introduce more people into the pool to allow Molly to adjust to public pools after this session.
2. To assess the public pool near her home and to set a date for a swimming pool session with Molly and her carer.

Case study 2: Adam

Adam is a man in his 40s, wheelchair dependent, who has spastic quadriplegia. He is able to express his needs and participate verbally in his programme planning.

He was referred for hydrotherapy because of acute pain in his right hip and very limited mobility. He was very anxious and fearful of pain increasing movement. He was awaiting hospitalisation for surgery to his hip.

He presented almost lying in his chair in extension as a result of spasticity and limited hip movement.

The reason for hydrotherapy was explained to Adam, his support staff and worried family. A 6-week course of hydrotherapy was agreed upon. His GP was notified and the date set.

Transfer from the wheelchair to the changing table and pool trolley was stressful and painful, and required careful movement and handling. A hoist was used. Adam was introduced to the water carefully, allowing time for adjustment while reassuring him verbally. He was supported under his shoulders while the plinth was lowered, and buoyancy assisted him to float off the plinth. He was rigid and fearful so he was also supported around his hips.

Gentle side-to-side movements (weaving) were used and the thermal aspects of the water given time to work. Movements were smooth and gliding, and no other turbulence was allowed. Gradually, Adam relaxed and, as the experience became pleasant, some reduction of pain was achieved.

The main area of concern was how to get Adam out of the pool, dressed and seated, with as little pain as possible so as not to negate the relaxation achieved.

The support staff had been very well prepared before the session so that they would be aware of the necessity to hold and move him gently and smoothly. They therefore understood the difficulties and had realistic expectations of the session.

The aims of the session were to achieve relaxation of the muscles, relieve pain and increase joint movement.

Over the 6-week period, the outcomes achieved were relaxation of muscles, which led to pain reduction and greater willingness on Adam's part to move and experiment a little in the pool. By the end of his session he was looking forward to further hydrotherapy.

The carers learnt to move and handle Adam in a more appropriate way so as not to exacerbate pain. They enjoyed the hydrotherapy and were pleased with the pain reduction and Adam's ability to sleep after these sessions.

Action

To continue hydrotherapy until Adam was admitted to hospital.

CHAPTER 12

Riding for disabled people

ALYS WATSON

Riding for the disabled in the UK could be said to date from the initiative of a physiotherapist, Olive Sands, who took her horses to the hospital where she worked during the 1914–18 war for men wounded in France to ride as part of their rehabilitation.

By the 1950s and 1960s, a handful of pioneers was exploring the possibility of riding for all types of disability. These pioneers included occupational therapists and physiotherapists. By 1969, the Riding for the Disabled Association (RDA) was founded. It developed more as a recreational and group activity than one with any specific therapeutic aims. Unlike the German and Swiss models, it lacked the structured educational standards and a clearly defined treatment approach necessary to attract health-care professionals, other than in an advisory capacity.

Now, physiotherapists through their clinical interest group, the Association of Chartered Physiotherapists in Therapeutic Riding (ACPTR), formerly the Association of Chartered Physiotherapists in Riding for the Disabled, have developed a three-part accredited course: 'The Horse in Rehabilitation'. This provides a nationally and internationally recognised qualification, encouraging systematic study and research, and emphasising treatment. Successful completion of the course requires the physiotherapist to have demonstrated appropriate riding and horse-handling skills, a knowledge of equine anatomy and psychology, and an awareness of the risks inherent in a riding situation. The most significant requirement is the ability to analyse the horse's movement, assess each rider and select an appropriate horse to obtain the maximum therapeutic advantage.

This chapter offers an introduction to horse riding and the use of the horse as a part of a treatment programme for people who have learning disabilities and associated physical disabilities. It includes RDA classifications, criteria for selecting riding as a treatment method, and contraindications and special precautions of which to be aware. This chapter is illustrated by four case studies.

Classifications within the RDA

Hippotherapy

This is treatment using the movement of the horse, based on the principles of neuromotor function and sensory processing. It is carried out by an appropriately qualified physiotherapist working with a horsemaster.

Back-riding, a highly skilled technique, is included under hippotherapy. Here a suitably qualified physiotherapist either sits behind the client on the horse, or supervises another back-rider, to achieve therapeutic aims not possible from the ground. Baker (1993) emphasises the careful selection of clients for back-riding.

Therapeutic riding

Riding is taught, the physiotherapist assesses the rider, and with the instructor plans a riding programme and monitors progress.

Recreational riding

Although this chapter deals primarily with treatment and is more concerned with the first two classifications, recreation using the horse has an acknowledged therapeutic input.

Every rider is encouraged to progress through these classifications as far as their disability allows, gaining the maximum stimulation and enjoyment from the experience.

Treatment on the horse is dependent on the horse's ability to move the rider's pelvis and trunk through three dimensions: laterally, anteroposteriorly and rotationally. The response is automatic, with no cortical input, demanding balance and sensory integration to remain centred and upright on this moving base, a base that at the same time is being carried forwards through space.

There are striking similarities between a human pelvis when walking and when being moved by a walking horse. Fleck (1992) has shown that linear displacements of a rider's pelvis walking and riding differed only in magnitude, not in timing or sequence.

An average human walk is 110–120 steps per minute and that of the average horse 100–120 steps per minute; this stride length provides a rate of movement at which the rider's pelvis and trunk can learn to accommodate. In 10 minutes, at 100 steps per minute, the rider experiences 1000 displacements to which she must respond.

Riede (1988) maintains that the overall treatment goal of hippotherapy is automatic postural stability in alignment with the centre of gravity. To see how this occurs, Table 12.1 analyses the horse's walking pattern and rider response. The horse's walk is a 4-beat sequence. Rider response comes mainly from the hind limb movement. Table 12.2 gives the rider response to variations of stride and direction.

Table 12.1 Rider response to walking horse[a]

Horse	Rider
Left hind leg pushes off ⟶ (acceleration)	Pelvis – tilts posteriorly Trunk – flexes
Left hind leg swings forward ⟶	Pelvis – rotates forward on left Trunk – counter-rotates to left
Left hind leg directly underneath ⟶ and takes weight (deceleration)	Pelvis – lifts on left Trunk – flexes laterally to left Pelvis – tilts anteriorly Trunk – extends

This sequence repeats for the right hind leg.

The rider's pelvis and thighs form an interface with the horse. Proprioceptive receptors from here signal disturbance of this sitting base when the horse walks and require a response from the rider for balance to be maintained. Having correctly identified the disturbance, there is a need for an adaptive response in the rider's trunk to realign his body in answer to his pelvic movement, keeping it upright and facing forwards.

Table 12.2 Variations in stride and direction

Walking horse	Rider's response
Work in straight lines	Flexion and extension of pelvis and trunk
Stride lengthening and shortening	Greater demand to follow movement
Halt to walk to halt transitions	Biggest challenge to flexion/extension control
Upward transitions (halt to walk)	Flexor truncal response
Downward transitions (walk to halt)	Extensor truncal response
Work on circles	Weight shift to outside, with trunk elongation to that side (Citterio, 1985)

Mandel (1984) states that 'Without doubt, the best sitting posture is obtained on horseback'. It encourages a position optimally aligned for balance. Where correct alignment is achieved, a plumb-line dropped from the rider's ear passes through shoulder, hip and heel (Figure 12.1a). The small degree of hip flexion encourages an upright pelvis. This is posturally important, but also allows maximum transference of movement from horse to rider. A familiar deviation from this, sacral sitting, with a posteriorly tilted pelvis and increased hip flexion, blocks movement and reduces the horse's therapeutic input (Figure 12.1b).

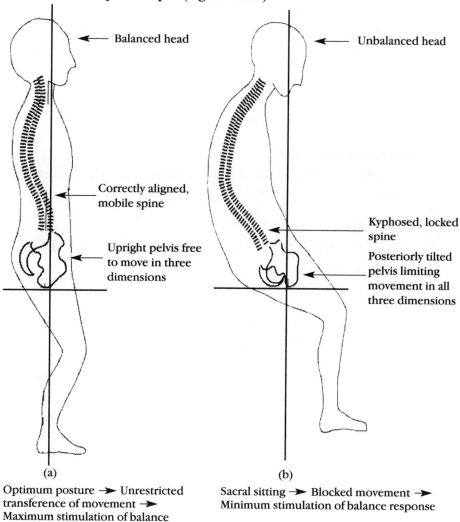

← Balanced head	← Unbalanced head
Correctly aligned, mobile spine	Kyphosed, locked spine
Upright pelvis free to move in three dimensions	Posteriorly tilted pelvis limiting movement in all three dimensions
(a)	(b)
Optimum posture ➤ Unrestricted transference of movement ➤ Maximum stimulation of balance responses	Sacral sitting ➤ Blocked movement ➤ Minimum stimulation of balance response

Figure 12.1 (a) Optimum posture; (b) sacral sitting.

In planning a therapy programme the most important consideration is the horse's movement. The stride should be rhythmic and regular, but variations such as stride length, smooth gait with little rider disturbance or 'big' movement requiring maximum rider response will be considered by the physiotherapist in selecting an appropriate horse.

Other factors to be considered in planning a therapy programme are the following.

Height of horse

The average horse provides the optimum movement but, in selection, the amount of assistance needed from the side helpers, who must be able to reach their riders, must be considered.

Width of horse

This should be narrow for clients with tight adductors, although broad may give a better base for balance.

Psychosocial/social factors

This includes the relationship of horse and rider and the integration of horse and rider within a group.

Special equipment

This is usually advised by the physiotherapist, and used to enhance the therapeutic input.

The team

This consists of a leader competent in horse handling and side helpers specially trained in mounting and handling riders.

Criteria for selecting riding as a treatment method

The most significant factor in using the horse in rehabilitation is the influence of his movement on improving neuromotor function and sensory processing. This being so, the following disabilities should benefit the most:

- Neurological motor dysfunctions
- Problems of sensory integration
- Difficulties with perception and coordination.

Contraindications

- Uncontrolled epilepsy: although clients with controlled epilepsy are welcomed, those in whom it is uncontrolled could be a hazard to themselves and others in the riding situation.
- Arthritis in the acute phase, including Still's disease.
- Multiple sclerosis in the acute phase.
- Unhealed pressure sores.
- Behavioural problems that cause a safety hazard to the client, horse or staff.
- Severe allergies or asthma exacerbated by the horse or his environment.
- Clients who are too heavy, either for the horse or to be safely mounted and dismounted.
- Clients who, after a suitable trial period, clearly do not wish to ride.

Special precautions

- Monitoring of clients with sensory loss for pressure sores, not only over the ischial tuberosities, but over the inner surface of lower limbs.
- Careful fitting of riding helmets where a shunt is situated behind the ear.
- Regular information exchange between clinical, care and riding teams on relevant medical and general management.
- Ongoing re-assessment of clients by the riding team to allow for the considerable changes that may occur with riding therapy.
- RDA Health and Safety Guidelines relating to assisting with mounting recommends:
  - assessment of the task (risk assessment); where the rider's weight exceeds the recommended limits, it may be necessary to refuse to allow that rider to ride
  - full use of mounting blocks and wheelchair ramps
  - instruction in correct lifting of those involved in mounting.
- Education, health and social work staff assisting at riding sessions should seek insurance from their employing authorities. At present a disclaimer form is not required from volunteers, but will be in the near future.

The following four case histories illustrate the practical application of using the horse as part of a rehabilitation programme.

Case studies

Case study 1: Peter

Peter was a 14-year-old boy with spastic quadriplegia and profound learning difficulties. He had bilateral cataracts, leading to the loss of sight in his right eye, and eventually to total blindness. He had no speech, but showed recognition of familiar voices and sounds, responding to simple commands. He indicated pleasure by smiling.

Until then, physiotherapy and good management at school and at home had maintained his functional ability, movement range and posture, but the onset of total blindness had resulted in a steady deterioration. He stopped rolling independently and moving around in his walker. He was less ready to turn to sound or explore with his hands. The school staff reported increasing difficulty in positioning him upright in his chair and standing frame, because he slumped to the left, with increasing reluctance to raise his head or respond to stimuli. This limited his involvement in and benefit from all classroom activities. Over 6 months, hip abduction decreased by 20° (bilaterally) and he developed a scoliosis concave to the left, a flattened lumbar curve and increased thoracic kyphosis. He stopped using body tilt reactions to maintain sitting balance, substituting excessive, disruptive, parachute responses.

The concern over this deterioration led to consideration of alternative therapy and hippotherapy was proposed.

The following assessments were made at the start of the programme:

- Posture and balance on the horse
- Body tilt reactions in sitting, off the horse
- Mobility, using a standard functional mobility chart
- Range of hip movement
- Reports from mother and school staff on general alertness and well-being.

Peter rode on a sheepskin, giving a soft, warm, sitting surface, allowing an unimpeded transference of movement from horse to rider that is not possible with a saddle.

In spite of tactile and verbal prompting, Peter remained in sacral sitting throughout the 20-minute session. It was therefore decided to use back-riding at the next session. The aim was to correct Peter's pelvic position sufficiently to allow the movement from the horse to stimulate his balance responses.

A bigger, specially trained horse was used to accommodate the two riders. The back-rider's hands over Peter's pelvis facilitated anteroposterior pelvic movement in rhythm with the movement of the horse's hind legs. As Peter's pelvis became more upright, he started to straighten his spine, lifted his head – and smiled.

By the fourth week, Peter's pelvis was following the movement input from the horse with minimal facilitation from the back-rider. He was also responding to verbal cues to 'sit tall' and of 'head up'. During the next two sessions, accelerations and decelerations at the walk were introduced to facilitate anteroposterior trunk control.

By the seventh week, Peter rode without a back-rider. Initially he relapsed into a degree of sacral sitting. This time, tapping his lumbar spine and repeating 'sit tall and head up' produced a positive response. If the horse maintained an active walk, pelvic and adaptive trunk responses occurred, and Peter laughed and clapped his hands. If the walk slowed, he relapsed into posterior pelvic tilt. Re-establishing the active walk again produced an upright pelvis, correctly aligned spine and head, and pleasure from Peter.

From the start, the commands 'walk on' and 'halt' were used to the horse to allow Peter to anticipate, prepare and make the appropriate response to these movements. As DeLubersac (1985) has pointed out: 'The rider is able to anticipate an action that is already familiar'. Peter now started to show a feed-forward response, a mechanism for postural control discussed by Carr and Shepherd (1987), anticipating and staying with accelerations and decelerations without loss of balance.

After 12 weeks, Peter had made good progress. Figures 12.2 and 12.3 record his posture and balance and he showed an increase in hip abduction of 10° (bilaterally). A report from his school reads:

> Peter returns from riding animated and happy. At first, his improved response level only continued into the afternoon, but we now recognise an overall improvement throughout the week. We have noticed real progress in his posture since he started riding both in the classroom and going out in his wheelchair. If he slumps to the left, he will now usually correct his position on request and he has again started to move around in his walker. He is turning to sound and reaching out to locate various objects placed on his table. We feel that he is now adapting to his loss of sight and starting to use his other senses to compensate for his lack of vision.

The innovative element of using the horse and the powerful impact that he has on his rider may, as in Peter's case, provide the catalyst to move the whole rehabilitation process forward again.

Case study 2: David

Wade et al. (1986), among others, now recognise stroke patients as having disturbances of concentration and learning. While acknowledging that stroke patients are not usually included in the caseload of those working

Name: Peter   **Assessor:** AW

Horse: Eddie   **Equipment:** Sheepskin

	Date: 1st Week	Date: 2nd Week	Date: 6th Week	Date: 12th Week	Date: 24th Week
Maintain Position					
At Halt	C1	A3	B5	D4	E6
At Walk	C1	A6	B6	D6	E6
Acceleration/Deceleration at Walk	C0	A0	B2	D4	E6
Halt to Walk to Halt Transitions	C0	A0	B1	D3	E4
Comments	Uncorrected sacral sitting blocking movement and balance responses	Head lifted and smiled	Good posture stimulated by walk	Showed pleasure at response to active walk	Greater response to verbal cueing

Poor Posture (PP)   means sacral sitting, flexed spine, head not erect OR uneven
                                       pelvic weight-bearing with spinal and/or head asymmetry

Good Posture (GP)   means upright, level pelvis with centred head and spine

Coding:

A = Back-rider – maximum facilitation
B = Back-rider – minimum facilitation
C = Side helpers only, stabilisation at knee
    and ankle
D = Side helpers only, stabilisation at
    ankle only
E = No stabilisation

0 = Unable to perform
1 = PP 30 seconds, unreliable performance
2 = GP 30 seconds, unreliable performance
3 = PP 1 minute, variable reliability
4 = GP 1 minute, variable reliability
5 = PP 5 minutes, greater reliability
6 = GP 5 minutes, greater reliability
7 = PP indefinitely, complete reliability
8 = GP indefinitely, complete reliability

Ideal score = E8

Figure 12.2 Hippotherapy assessment.

Patient's Name: Peter   **Assessor:** AW

		1 Week pre-riding	After 12 weeks riding
Angle	10°	No response	No response
of Lateral	20°	No response	Delayed response
Tilt	30°	Loss of balance with lateral parachute	Some body tilt response preceding lateral parachute
Angle	10°	No response	Minimal response
of A/P	20°	Increased flexion	Correct body tilt
Tilt	30°	Loss of balance	Correct body tilt

Patient in cross-legged sitting

Figure 12.3 Assessment of body tilt reactions using vestibular board and tiltmeter.

entirely in the field of learning disability, it is hoped that the following case history will be of value. Readers will recognise familiar problems and be able to relate them, and the problem solving, to some of their own clients.

David was a 64-year-old ex-army officer who suffered a right-sided stroke 2 years before coming to the RDA. Before his stroke, he had been very active and enjoyed physical challenge. With such a temperament, his physical and learning disabilities were a shattering blow to his morale. He was very depressed and was looking for a suitably demanding and stimulating physical activity. Riding appeared a possibility to fulfil this need, at the same time helping with his therapy requirements.

At his pre-riding assessment, he walked with a circumduction gait using a tripod stick and wearing a right ankle–foot orthosis (AFO). He had limited right shoulder movement, and could grasp and release an object if placed in his right hand, but had a tactile astereognosis.

He had problems of right–left discrimination, concentration and memory, and his expressive aphasia led to frustration and tension. Physiotherapy was no longer available, but he had regular speech therapy.

A prime aim of riding was to promote midline symmetry with prospective carry-over into standing.

Riding Eddie, David sat as he did at home, with a left lateral pelvic shift, weight-bearing predominantly on the left with a compensatory right trunk and head side flexion, and retraction of his right pelvic and shoulder girdles. Johnstone (1987) emphasises the need in stroke rehabilitation for meticulous positioning of the base in weight-bearing and for lateral transference of weight over the affected side to achieve this. The principles of riding therapy agree with this – that the first requirement, where asymmetry exists, is correction to midline.

Initially David was not expected to hold the reins and Eddie was led. We used a sheepskin rather than a saddle, allowing David to focus his attention on attaining a symmetrical sitting base. By keeping his hands on his thighs, he facilitated right shoulder girdle protraction.

Leading Eddie on a 20-metre circle to the left gave the centrifugal effect of transference of weight to the outside (right) seat bone, with trunk lengthening on the right (Citterio, 1985).

Using the riding school mirror, we asked David to correct his position at halt, and then asked him to make the same corrections with Eddie walking towards the mirror. Berquet (1977) found using a mirror essential in correcting postural dysfunction.

David was encouraged to give verbal commands to Eddie, and we liaised with his speech therapist, listing the words relating to the horse, his equipment and the riding lesson.

Exercises were introduced, all performed at the walk, giving the unique benefit of an underlying continuum of three-dimensional movement throughout. These encouraged the postural responses to external perturbations, in this instance the walking horse, as well as the postural adjustments preceding voluntary limb movements and centre-of-mass displacements described by Horak (1987). Reaching across with his left hand to touch successively his right hand, knee and then slide down towards his right foot served the double purpose of weight transference to the right and cross facilitation. Right rotation transferred weight to David's right seat bone, whereas left rotation gave right pelvic and shoulder girdle protraction, so rotations in both directions were practised. By introducing variations in the horse's stride length and direction, use was being made of the theory that motor learning requires repetition in a variety of settings to assist learning.

David was now starting to appreciate the greater freedom with which Eddie moved when the rider's weight was centred and used this as a feedback to check for his correct position. With midline symmetry now established, a saddle was introduced. David's posture remained symmetrical and he was given adapted reins, allowing him to place both hands on the reins. By doing this, symmetry and visual and tactile awareness of the right side were encouraged.

David could now start controlling his horse and steering around a course, following demonstrated instructions to turn left or right.

A year after starting to ride, David was riding independently in the school, as part of an adult class, following right/left commands. He could trot and achieved an unscheduled but successful canter, which he described as 'marvellous!'

His confidence had returned and his horizons widened. He had taken up swimming again, was dinghy sailing and was no longer reluctant to go out and meet people.

Functional progress was assessed using a timed walking test with an ABAB design. This simple test has been shown to have both validity and reliability. It provides multiple information, as Goldfarb and Simon (1984) have shown that gait speed relates strongly to cadence and stride length, and Bohannon (1989) that it also relates to balance (Figure 12.4).

Riding, for David, had helped his motor and cognitive learning, but perhaps the greatest benefit for him had been psychological.

Name: David   **Assessor:** AW

Test	**Time in seconds**			
	A	**B**	**C**	**D**
Walking 5m and return (total 10m)	24.16	18.07	19.53	16.30

A = 1 week pre-riding   Using tripod
B = After 8 weeks riding   Using stick
C = After 8 weeks no riding   Using stick
D = After 8 weeks resumed riding   Using stick

Figure 12.4 Timed walking test.

Case study 3: George

George, aged 32 years, lived at home with his parents and attended a day centre. He had learning difficulties and a moderate ataxia, but walked independently both indoors and out. His understanding was good, but speech was limited. He lacked motivation and confidence, had difficulties with sequencing and had spatial problems.

His typical posture was sacral sitting with flexed spine and head, making eye contact difficult and interaction with his associates at the day centre very limited.

With his history of being withdrawn, with little interest in his environment, it was encouraging to note his positive reaction when introduced to his horse, Dandy, patting him, talking to him and examining his saddle and bridle.

George's saddle had a cover with adjustable sacral pad and anterior thigh rolls to correct his sacral sitting. With his good understanding, it was possible to ask George to sit tall and look at the rider ahead, at the same time asking him to check if this rider was himself sitting tall. This produced a postural response in George of a correctly aligned spine over his now more upright pelvis, and at the same time encouraging him to raise his head and relate to the other rider.

As his sitting balance and manipulative skills were reasonably good, he started by holding the reins, but with a leader in attendance.

Although getting individual attention where necessary, George rode in a group lesson. The advantages for him were that it provided a more interesting social environment, gave him an opportunity to copy and learn from the other riders, and later provided the possibility of developing social skills of one rider helping the other.

Initially, George had difficulty in judging distances and adjusting Dandy's pace before he either bumped into the leading pony or left a yawning gap, with the rest of the ride bunched up behind. The safety reasons for keeping a correct distance were explained, and the problems caused for the other riders when this didn't occur. George had already demonstrated his ability to control Dandy's pace and was now given the responsibility of showing how well he could do this to get his spacing right. To help him, it was decided to vary the approach, turning the activity into a game and providing more group interaction. The ponies were halted at intervals round the school. George on Dandy walked forward and, on reaching the correct distance from the pony in front, George called 'Walk on' to that rider, both riders and ponies then walking on towards the next pony where the sequence was repeated until the whole ride was moving, correctly spaced. George's anticipation and judgement of distance started to improve and he even reproved a rider for not walking on immediately!

Another of George's problems, poor sequencing, gave rise to difficulties with mounting and dismounting. To dismount, George would drop the reins and try to dismount with both feet still in the stirrups, often before Dandy had stopped moving. Asking George to verbalise his intention as he performed the task proved helpful. Thus:

'Halt. Reins in left hand.' (Assistant touching his hand.)
'Both feet out of stirrups.' (Assistant checks.)
'Right [indicated by touch] leg back and over. Dismount.'

Unvarying repetition improved his performance, which over 8 weeks became increasingly reliable.

Praise for success in this task, as recognised by McGibbon (1994), was invaluable in building George's self-esteem and confidence.

Correct sequencing during games brought the reward of successful completion of the activity and, to everyone's surprise, George started to prove himself quite competitive.

Taking a coloured ring, selecting a matching coloured bucket in the arena, riding to it, halting and dropping the ring in the bucket required colour matching, judgement of distance, steering and controlling the pace of the pony and sequencing, e.g. halting the pony before releasing the ring. Performed as a team game, this called for awareness of the team members and of other competitors. Taken together, these activities demanded a combination of motor, cognitive and social skills.

There was no doubt about George's progress in the riding class, but it was important to his quality of life that there should be carry-over into his daily living activities. After 12 weeks of riding, there was the following response to questions relating to his everyday life, noted and recorded both at the day centre and at home.

- Improved interaction with his peers
- Increased verbal communication
- A marked change in his general interest and confidence
- Improvement in activities involving correct sequencing

George had been able to demonstrate the transfer of learning skills acquired during riding to his everyday life and we were assured by this that his learning had become more secure.

His father felt that it was the motivation of the whole riding situation that had produced results so far not achieved by other means.

Case study 4: Wai Kwan

Wai Kwan, a small Asian girl aged 7 years, came with her special school to ride with the Hong Kong RDA.

Horses are seldom seen in Hong Kong, except on the racecourse, and Wai Kwan's mother was very doubtful about allowing her to come to ride.

Although able to walk indoors, Wai Kwan did not use this as a purposeful activity and staff used a wheelchair for all community outings because she had a tendency to fall and objected to having her hand held. She had periods of hyperactivity, alternating with total passivity, and body rocked and bit her hands when distressed. She had very poor sensory discrimination, tactile defensiveness and an aversion to handling. She had no speech and her understanding was difficult to assess.

Our aims for Wai Kwan were to use the constant sensory input provided by the rhythmic, repetitive movement of the pony to facilitate sensory discrimination. So far she had not developed the ability to sift through and suppress irrelevant sensory information and produced inappropriate responses to incoming information.

Although a small pony made it easier for the side helpers to reach the child, its shorter, choppier gait in this case provided too much stimulation, so a larger pony with a longer stride and smoother movement was chosen.

Wai Kwan's tactile defensiveness gave her an aversion to touching fur, so a smooth cotton fitted rug was used to cover the pony. She would not tolerate a riding helmet but, as the session was to be conducted by a physiotherapist, we were able to start without.

Her teacher walked on one side and acted as interpreter for the English-speaking physiotherapist.

Wai Kwan body rocked violently, closing her eyes and biting her hands. She resisted any attempts to steady her balance, so a rather nerve-racking policy of 'hands off but eyes on' was pursued. After 10 minutes, she tried to throw herself off the pony, but her teacher reassured her and the session continued. After 20 minutes, she had opened her eyes, but continued to body rock and bite her hands at intervals. We agreed to continue for a further two sessions to see if there was any improvement.

The second session started as the first but, half-way through, she lay back spontaneously on the pony and we continued to walk with her lying quietly in supine with her head in midline and her arms relaxed by the pony's sides, and this pattern was repeated at the next session.

This amount of progress justified a continuation of the riding programme. With subsequent sessions, we allowed her to continue to choose her position, following the principle of Ayres (1972) of allowing the child to direct her own actions. She moved between supine and sitting with eyes open and hands relaxed, without body rocking or hand biting, as long as we remained in attendance only, without touching her

By the sixth session, she spent the entire time sitting, propping forwards on open hands and getting movement from the pony's shoulders through her own upper limbs and shoulder girdle. She now tolerated a riding helmet, if it was fitted once the ride had started.

Riding had so far been in a sheltered indoor arena. To test her progress we moved into the adjoining outdoor arena. It was breezy and sunny, with some noise from the neighbouring school. Wai Kwan reverted to her body rocking and we realised that we were trying to move too fast, the smallest change in sensory input generating a disproportionately large effect with which she still could not cope. Fortunately, returning to the original arena allowed her to recover and we finished the session without noticeably having lost ground.

Eight weeks of hippotherapy produced the following results:

- She sat quietly on the pony for a 20-minute ride, tolerating a degree of handling from the side helpers to correct her balance.
- She accepted a riding helmet throughout the ride.
- Provided the ride started in the more sheltered school, she was now able to cope with the outdoor arena in calm weather.
- By folding back the front of the rug, she was able to place her hands directly onto the pony's shoulders and tolerated this as long as the pony was moving. This correlated with the findings of Fisher et al. (1993) in their treatment of tactile defensiveness. The moving pony provided the controlled vestibular–proprioceptive stimulus, facilitating the appropriate interpretation of tactile sensory input.

Her achievements to date led us to hope that progress would continue and that there would eventually be measurable carry-over into her everyday life.

Her mother's amazement, on coming to the RDA, in seeing what her daughter could achieve provided ample justification, even had there been no other, for continuing her hippotherapy.

Conclusion

Riding for disabled people has become increasingly valued throughout the world because, as Hamilton wrote in 1997:

> The traditional treatment setting has no modality to match the versatility of the horse. This alive and moving 'apparatus' provides a multitude of stimuli to treat a variety of diagnoses. The horse can assist the client in attaining motor skills that would be difficult or slow in coming in the clinic.

CHAPTER 13

Rebound therapy

SALLY SMITH AND DEBBI COOK

Rebound therapy is one of the newer treatment modalities used in the field of learning disability. Many physiotherapists working in this area use trampolines in day centres, leisure centres, schools or specialist hospitals to establish rebound therapy.

The trampoline was invented by a French neurologist who called it the 'trampolino' and used it to treat brain-injured children. In the UK, the trampoline was originally used for sports and recreation in schools and leisure facilities. By the early 1980s, its use as a therapeutic tool was becoming more obvious.

Bhattacharya et al. (1980) published results of studies undertaken for NASA, which showed that jumping on a trampoline was less stressful to the neck, back and ankle than jogging on a treadmill for an equivalent oxygen uptake. In fact, the conclusion was that 'any activity on a rebound unit is more efficient than a treadmill running at any speed'.

Peterson (1981) described studies undertaken at UCLA in California on the use of the rebounder. She quoted Frost who stated that:

> . . . it improves the performance of the heart, lungs and lymphatic system. It improves circulation and muscle tone and challenges the skeletal muscles to increase stamina without any of the jarring associated with other aerobic activities.

This study also claimed that 'children who had learning problems were found to have a 70% improvement in co-ordination and balance after some months of rebounding'. The alternating movements – such as slapping the right knee with the left hand – were the ones that most quickly improved coordination.

At the same time as these studies were being carried out in the USA, Eddie Anderson – then headmaster of Springwell Special School in

Hartlepool – started using the trampoline with children with physical and learning disabilities. His aim in introducing them to the equipment in an integrated movement programme was to give the children a full range of movement experience. This led to the regular use of the trampoline with children for specific therapeutic outcomes according to the needs of the individual child: 'rebound therapy'. Through the early to mid-1980s, these techniques developed by Anderson were adopted by physiotherapists and remedial gymnasts, and expanded and adapted for use with adults with learning disabilities. Today they have been consolidated and are now in regular use by therapists in the field of learning disability.

Rebound therapy has taken its place as an established treatment modality alongside the more familiar components of a whole movement programme such as hydrotherapy, fitness training and horse riding. It is still growing and developing as physiotherapists gradually become more skilled at assessing and formulating programmes for this equipment and other therapists, carers, teachers and day centre staff become equally skilled at working with people on the trampoline.

Use of rebound therapy

Rebound therapy can be used for people with a mild physical and learning disability, to people with profound and multiple learning disabilities. There is a wide range of starting positions, from lying to kneeling, sitting or standing. These can be graded according to the person's ability.

It is used in a strictly controlled manner by a skilled therapist or operator. The idea of using a mobile, unstable surface to activate movement is not new to physiotherapists; gymnastic balls and wobble boards have been used for many years.

Rebound therapy for adults, as for working in water, can assist in the training of movement by using the power and lift in the trampoline bed to initiate or energise movement, where on 'land' this may be very difficult or impossible. Like any other modality, rebound 'should not be used in isolation but should be integrated into weekly programmes and should be viewed not as a substitute for existing therapies but as a complement to them' (Smith and Cook, 1990).

Screening and contraindications

There are very few people who would not be suitable for rebound therapy (ACPPLD Rebound Working Party, 1997). Any person who is to participate should be screened for the following:

- Cardiac or circulatory problem
- Respiratory problems
- Vertigo, blackouts or nausea
- Epilepsy
- Spinal cord or neck problems
- Spinal rodding
- Open wounds
- Any recent medical attention
- Brittle bones
- Friction effects on the skin
- Unstable/painful joints
- Severe challenging behaviour
- Gastrostomy/colostomy bags
- Hiatus hernia
- Pregnancy after 20 weeks.

There are only two absolute contraindications for taking a person on a trampoline; these are:

- Detaching retina
- Atlantoaxial instability.

Any therapist considering starting rebound therapy should refer to the Association of Chartered Physiotherapists for People with Learning Disabilities (ACPPLD) standards of good practice which state that:

> No physiotherapist should undertake rebound therapy until they have had sufficient training and are competent in their own interpersonal trampoline skills, handling and therapeutic skills, and have knowledge of the physical properties of the trampoline and the physiological effects on the body.
>
> (ACPPLD, 1997)

Before starting treatment, the operator should have the following skills and be competent and confident about using them:

- Getting on and off safely both for operator and client
- Bouncing in a stable position
- Killing the bed, which is absorbing all energy from the bed so that it stops moving completely
- Kipping the bed, which is transferring kinetic energy from operator to client by depressing the bed beneath the client's feet as he or she bounces
- Damping the bed, which is absorbing some of the energy from the bed so that the client can maintain a controlled bounce

- Riding the bed – it is essential that the operator stays in contact with the bed to enable him or her to maintain a stable position
- Emergency stop.

The operator should also be able to perform the following manoeuvres safely:

- Half-turn
- Star jump
- Tuck jump
- Straddle jump
- Pike jump
- Seat drop.

Physiological and therapeutic effects

Rebound therapy has been found to have the following observable physiological and therapeutic effects.

Physiological effects

Cardiorespiratory system

There is a high demand on muscles to support the body against the increased gravitational effect and in the control of movement required when acceleration takes place. This causes the heart and respiratory rate to increase and as a consequence venous and lymphatic drainage increases. Constant muscle work to maintain position and balance increases the demand for oxygen.

Muscle tone

The effect on muscle tone can be observed in people with physical disabilities. Application of the right level of bounce is critical; too much can increase spasticity and too little under-stimulate.

Vigorous bouncing can cause an increase in tone by stimulating the sensory systems, e.g. the stretch receptors in muscles and proprioceptors in joints. Gentle bouncing can reduce high tone/spasticity by having a shaking effect on the muscle spindles.

Postural mechanism

By creating a dynamic movement situation that challenges balance mechanisms, observable improvement can be made. This is particularly relevant when working with adults where a dynamic balance situation can be difficult to create in lying, sitting or kneeling.

Kinaesthetic awareness

By multiple stimulation of joints, pressure stretch receptors, skin and muscles, kinaesthetic awareness is improved, leading to improved body image and spatial awareness.

Therapeutic effects

Movement

- Movement can be facilitated at different stages of the bounce. The most active movement takes place at the top of the bounce where acceleration of the body equals the down-thrust of gravity to allow a momentary 'gravity-free' zone.
- By using good positioning and gently bouncing, relaxation can be achieved easily.
- The lowering or raising of muscle tone enables active movement to take place.
- Anticipation of movement occurs because of the effects of timing and the rhythm imposed by bouncing.
- Balance and equilibrium reactions can be achieved through stimulation of postural mechanisms. Protective and saving reactions can also be developed.
- Small impoverished body movements can produce larger movements than on land, when a bounce is correctly applied, because of the ability of the trampoline springs and their recoil to amplify the movement.
- Momentum and rhythm can be used to help teach new movement skills and energise movement.

Perception

- Body image, body part awareness and positional sense are enhanced through tactile compression and joint sensation.
- Increased perception of body image and spatial awareness combined with rhythm and movement develop concentration.
- The experience of being free in space and falling is important for stimulating postural reflexes and saving reactions.
- Sensory input is increased via tactile, proprioceptive, auditory and visual channels.

Communication

- Cardiorespiratory effects and excitement may increase vocalisation, leading to exclamations and gasps.

- Eye contact tends to be increased as the client and operator are in close face-to-face contact. Establishing better eye contact leads to better concentration.

General health and social benefits

- It can be used to develop fitness.
- It improves chest condition by shaking the lungs and stimulating the cough reflex.
- It increases flatulence by creating gaseous movement in the body.

Use of the trampoline is a valued activity by the population as a whole and rebound therapy allows people with a learning disability to access this for its physical, social, emotional and recreational aspects.

Practical application of rebound therapy

Rebound therapy always starts with a full physiotherapy assessment and medical information must be gained from the appropriate source.

Following this, the client's strengths and needs are noted and documented and an individual programme is devised. A number of care factors must be taken into consideration before treatment commences. Care factors are directly related to starting positions.

The following information should not be used without the operator having undertaken formal training on a recognised rebound therapy course.

Care factors

When a client is placed in any one of the starting positions, which may range from lying through to standing, the therapist/operator must always check for safety and comfort. This must never be left to an assistant or carer.

For example, if a person is placed in prone (on the stomach) over a wedge, the operator must ensure that that person has sufficient head control to maintain a safe head position. It is also essential that the amount of bounce put into the trampoline does not cause unnecessary whiplash as a result of poor head control. The operator should also check that the client is weight-bearing correctly through shoulders and elbows. Fingers should be checked to ensure that they are not through the holes (webbing) of the trampoline and, if the client is a woman, that she has a pillow underneath her to protect her breasts.

Finally, checks must be made to toenails to ensure that they are also protected from the surface of the trampoline.

The operator must ensure that, as he moves around the trampoline, his body weight does not disturb the balance of the person on the wedge unintentionally. This is because the wedge raises the person off the bed, thus making him or her more vulnerable.

For any starting position, the therapist must run through a similar process to ensure continued comfort and safety.

The operator in charge of the session is also responsible for the training, attentiveness and positioning of the spotters. These are people placed around the trampoline whose job it is to maintain the safety of those on it. If the client is able to stand and walk the spotters need to be very alert, particularly if the person has poor balance. The operators need to move around the bed with extreme care. They must take more care with those who have tight Achilles' tendons and cannot put their heels down flat, and they must be prepared for any client to sit down unpredictably. It is dangerous to attempt to hold them up.

Therapeutic uses

Each starting position has its own different therapeutic value and use. An example of this is side lying. A client can be placed in this position for the following therapeutic effects:

- Reduction of tone: the client should be supported on pillows and gentle continual bouncing should continue until tone reduces.
- Stretching of trunk and hips – an ideal position to stretch a scoliosis.
- Relaxation: continual gentle bouncing, with client lying on a variety of textures, e.g. silk, cotton, fur. This can be accompanied by quiet music. Use different smelling oils under the bed (position these before placing person on trampoline). Place parachute/scarves/silks over person while bouncing (see Chapter 16).
- Increase sensory input: use of vibration or scratching/tapping on the bed.
- Teaching rolling or using rolling as a sensory activity.

Slow rolling

The client is approached from behind. The operator places one hand on the client's hip to prevent an uncontrolled roll. The client is placed in side lying, facing away from the operator, at one side of the bed. The head can be supported by pillows or by another operator on the bed. The operator places one foot at the client's hip level and one at shoulder level. One hand is placed on top of the hip and the other on the shoulder. Small gentle bouncing is started. The operator slides his or her feet backwards one at a time and guides the client as he rolls towards the operator down the slope created by the operator's body weight. Feet are kept apart when moving backwards. A spotter must be positioned directly behind the operator.

Fast roll

Position as for a slow roll; gentle bouncing is started, and the client is then pulled towards the operator as he runs backwards with feet still apart. The client will follow down the slope. A spotter must be positioned directly behind the operator.

Fast rolling should only ever be attempted with someone with good head control.

A more able person sitting on a soft play roll would gain therapeutically in the following ways:

* Improve balance: gentle rocking side to side, or forwards and backwards, using two operators. The closer the operator is to the client, the more the balance is stressed:
   - operator sitting in front of client on roll, each facing the other, operator's hands on client's shoulders; progress to forearm and hand holds
   - operator standing in front of roll, supporting client with shoulder, forearm or hand hold
   - operator standing in front of roll, second operator sitting behind person with hands on shoulders or hips
   - operator standing in front of roll, second operator standing behind the roll, client unsupported
   - this can be progressed further by client placing hands on head and shoulders. Further progressions include playing 'Pig in the Middle' with a ball and two operators, or throwing a ball to and from an operator.
* Improving posture: work person's abdominals by operator bouncing behind person.
* Improve weight-bearing through legs/feet by gentle bouncing.
* Stretching muscles: by sitting astride the roll and by gently bouncing to work the Achilles' tendons and hip adductors.
* Precursor for horse riding: various degrees of bouncing with client either supported or sitting free on roll.
* Improve exercise tolerance: people with very good balance can 'ride' the roll around the bed or can be kipped while 'riding' the roll.

Progression or alternatives include using a shaped roll, physio ball, or soft play block. The following are the therapeutic uses for someone who is learning or is able to stand or jump:

- To improve balance: progress from just standing on unstable surface with support of two people, to walking along or around bed, to jumping with support of two people, then one person, then independently.
- To experience being free in space: being kipped by two operators, progressing to one, then independently.
- To improve circulation: gentle jumping by client works the soleus muscles and produces a pumping action on the underlying venous system.
- To improve eye contact and concentration: operator at front uses 'look at me' commands.
- To improve fitness and exercise tolerance: gradually increase length of time a client bounces.
- To stretch Achilles' tendons: gently bounce the person in standing. The operator at the back can stand closer to the person to create slope so that the heel is lower than the toe.

In any of the starting positions a variety of equipment can be used as described in Tables 13.1–13.4.

Case study: Mr X

Mr X is a 37-year-old community ambulator (Hoffer scale 1). He has cerebral palsy and is able to walk independently, with a step through gait of the right leg and a step to gait with the left leg, around his day centre and out of doors (on flat terrain).

Table 13.1 Positioning equipment

Equipment	Use of equipment
Wedge	Positioning in prone, supine or for leg support
Roll	Sitting astride, side sitting, supported sitting together with an operator (or two), or for initiating hands and knees position over the roll
Soft play blocks	Sitting on, supporting
T rolls	Supporting legs, shoulders and head or trunk
Thin mats	To protect knees from webbing when working in hands and knees and high or half-kneeling position

Table 13.2 Sensory equipment

Equipment	Use of equipment
Parachute	Visual, auditory and tactile stimulation. Those with profound and multiple disabilities can be wrapped and supported in it and those who are ambulant can do seat drops into it
Music	To assist timing and rhythm, for relaxation or motivation and confidence giving
Bells/drums	Bells can be tied to springs to assist rhythm or in the centre of the trampoline, to help people with visual impairment locating the centre. Drums can be beaten for rhythm
Sheepskin/fur coat/ sheet/sari silk	All can be used to lie on for tactile stimulation. Sari silks can be used for visual stimulation as they float when air goes into them
Scented oils	These can be burnt for olfactory stimulation (see Chapter 16)

Table 13.3 Coordination equipment

Equipment	Use of equipment
Ball/skittles/hoops/ balloons	Throwing/catching/holding/targets, etc.
Symbols/ photographs	Provide visual reinforcement for a physical move

Table 13.4 Handling and moving equipment

Equipment	Use of equipment
Slide sheets	Transferring people into centre of trampoline
Moving and handling belt	A comfortable support for operator to use as a safety and teaching tool

This man had no concept of crawling or kneeling up and could not stand up from a long sitting position. To get up from the floor, he would have to push up on his elbows in reverse on to a low chair and then stand up. Communication was by a short vocabulary of Makaton signs and his own adapted signs. He spoke with no clear words. Rebound therapy commenced in January 1996 and continues to the present time (1998).

The following shows the progressions made in his physical ability and his communication and interaction with staff on and off the trampoline.

January 1996

- No concept of moving from long sitting to standing.
- Physiotherapy roll introduced but required maximum assistance to stand up via high kneeling while using it.
- Could only work in long sitting, bouncing forwards and backwards. He managed this independently.
- Two-handed support in standing. Maximum assistance required to stand up.
- Tried assisted rolling but very resistant.
- Willingness to cooperate on trampoline very variable.

October 1996

- Now turning in long sitting.
- Sat astride roll and initiated for the first time.
- Standing by transferring his weight forwards.
- Walking on trampoline forwards, backwards and sideways with one person's support. Occasionally independent walk but very unsure.

November 1996

- Now starting to make choices about activities on trampoline.
- Improved posture noted in standing with less flexion, working on independent standing with one operator giving gentle bounce while maintaining an upright posture.

January 1997

- Attempted hands and knees via side sitting but unable to achieve this.

February/March 1997

- Good walking forwards/backwards/sidewards with minimal assistance of one and increased confidence.
- Now progressing to jumping with two-handed support, pushing through operator's hands, knees extended; however, using arms more than legs.

April 1997

- Narrower standing base of support noted with improved standing posture.

May 1997

- Started to work in high kneeling with maximum support of two operators assisting him into this position. Used building bricks (Mr X's preferred activity) to reach for them.
- Spotter.
- High kneeling posture very poor with increased lumbar curve, wide base, flexed hips needing full physical assistance to achieve both this and side sitting.
- Precarious in both of these positions.

June 1997

- Starting to initiate movement from side sitting to high kneeling, although not achieving.
- Adopting side-sitting position by choice; reaching from this position.

July 1997

- Making choices of direction, wishing to walk around trampoline.
- Now, once in high kneeling, needs very little help to maintain.
- Improved communication noted with 'me' stated clearly.

September 1997

- Achieved hands and knees position (unable to crawl).
- Starting to attempt to stand – sit by putting hands down in front, managed halfway and fell back into side sitting.
- Maintains high kneeling independently.
- Communicating 'no' clearly and, as session was cut short because of his refusal, he demonstrated that he was sorry.

October 1997

- Good reaching in high kneeling.
- Standing and transferring to hands and knees onto crash mat.
- Crawling achieved.
- Assumed high kneeling independently with good weight transference in this position.
- Now able to stand with member of staff crouching in front and assisting him to bring his weight forward, and then Mr X stands up virtually independently.
- Also stood up from crash mat with one hand support and other hand pushing up from mat. Took several attempts but it was achieved. Makaton signs being used by Mr X for 'brick' and 'lie down'.

November 1997

- Independently moving from long sitting to side sitting to high kneeling with verbal prompt and demonstration.
- Also assuming high kneeling from four-point kneeling with same prompts.
- Good reaching in high kneeling and counterbalancing with arms.
- Stood up from hands and knees on second attempt, but with poor quality of movement.
- Standing to hands and knees to sitting before getting off trampoline.
- Now jumping with one hand support with gentle kipping – working well with less upper limb fixing.

December 1997

- Tried to improve the quality of the move sitting to standing, with work in half-high kneeling to encourage more weight transference to right side.
- Standing and jumping with two-hand support, now bending knees and joints in the jump.
- Signing attempted regularly and 'bricks' spoken.

January 1998

- Improved jumping in standing, operator almost able to release one hand support fully once initiated and in progress, and joining in well with rhythm and jump.

February 1998

- Achieved 20 independent jumps with stability.
- Independence in jumping is increasing with every session.

March 1998

- Crawling.
- Good attempt at standing to hands and knees directly onto trampoline – still needing assistance.
- Independent jumping.

April 1998

- Attempting to initiate bounce in standing.
- Able to damp bed when chooses to.
- Not scared of falling on to bed and will choose to sit if not wanting to comply.

Conclusion

The use of the trampoline is a valued activity by the population as a whole and therapists have discovered that the combination of the physical, social and emotional elements of rebound therapy has an extraordinary therapeutic value for people with learning disabilities.

CHAPTER 14

Group work

JEANETTE RENNIE, LUCY CLARK AND HELEN HOLME

In everyday life, people live and work in groups and frequently choose to spend at least part of their recreational time participating in group activities such as parties and night clubs, further education classes, team sports and exercise groups at a gym.

Chapter 6 described the necessity for people with learning disabilities to learn to build relationships and to be able to participate with non-learning-disabled people individually and in group activities.

Much of the group work undertaken by speech and language therapists, occupational therapists and learning disability nurses is specifically designed to improve relationships. Groups often need to consist of people with similar needs, such as sign groups and symbol work. Communication skills frequently need to be consolidated in a familiar environment before the speech and language therapist can transfer a group to a community setting to encourage communication in context. Nurses undertake personal development groups and assertiveness groups designed to help people with learning disabilities understand sexuality and how to express their emotions appropriately. In these groups they may liaise with psychologists or occupational therapists (Bruce, 1988). Nurses and occupational therapists frequently work with dietitians and physiotherapists, with groups that promote healthy eating and a healthy lifestyle.

This chapter looks at group work primarily as a way of improving physical ability. It describes a range of therapist-led groups that can be undertaken in homes, centres or the community. They can be used as treatment sessions or therapeutic recreation in their own right, or as a precursor to activities, sport and outdoor pursuits with the general population.

Physiotherapists have long recognised group work as a way of encouraging individuals to progress from directed individual treatment to taking more responsibility for their own exercise and for developing beyond the 'patient' attitude of being set apart because of disability (Gardiner, 1971). Gardiner also regarded peer support and mild competition and the stimulation of activities as valuable aids to recovery.

In 1970, Ester Cotton, using the term in relation to conductive education, wrote that:

> . . . it is important as it is stimulating and makes the children ambitious.

The idea of making some children, and adults, more ambitious has led to criticism of group work by people who regard it as a way of encouraging a feeling of failure in the rest of the group. (The advantages and disadvantages are explored more fully in Chapter 15.) In practice it has been found that clients who have learning disabilities enjoy encouraging each other and express delight at the feeling of achievement when they learn something new and are told that they are improving.

Clients are frequently referred to physiotherapists for a specific symptom but are subsequently found to be polysymptomatic. This reflects the trend in the general population demonstrated by results of a study undertaken with patients referred by general practitioners to primary care physiotherapists for a programme of group exercise (Crook et al., 1998).

Reasons for selecting group work to improve physical ability in people with learning disabilities

- To maintain and improve general fitness
- To monitor physical ability and transfer to individual treatment if necessary
- To encourage working together
- To improve communication
- To improve concentration
- To engender a feeling of achievement
- To have fun.

Group work involves the participants in:

- observing
- listening
- learning
- working together

- improving the skill
- appreciating the achievement.

The structure and predictability of the group build up expectations for each client. The participants can relax within this structure and learn to cope with any small changes that may be made.

Groups tend to be of long-standing duration because continuity is an important factor. If the complexity of activities in the group increases, clients may participate for several years. It is essential, therefore, to keep careful records to ensure that aims are being met and reviewed.

Figure 14.1 is an example of a weekly record sheet which is used as the basis of assessment using an individual 6-monthly report form (Figure 14.2).

Precautions

- Individual assessments should be undertaken to ascertain individual health needs and problems.
- The specific group must be appropriate for the client, for example, dancing is unacceptable to some cultures.
- Carers and day-care staff should be consulted on compatibility of group members.
- Number of group participants should be appropriate to the activity and complexity of clients' conditions.
- Numbers and experience of staff should be appropriate to size of group, complexity of clients' conditions and the activity being undertaken.
- Any group held in a home, social services or community centre will be integrated into the timetable and needs to be flexible enough to accommodate fluctuating staffing levels.

Examples of group work

Groups may consist of the following:

- Recognised exercises, which are sometimes undertaken as individual physiotherapy, but where the element of working as part of a group enhances the treatment.
- Composite groups, which include recognised exercises, but also utilise activities that cannot be undertaken individually.
- Specialist group activities used primarily with people with learning and physical disabilities.

v = participated; o = did not participate; A = did not attend; (s) = seconds   Date:

Name	Sit. Ex.	Comments, observation	Stand Ex.	Comments, observation	Slalom (s)	Comments, observation	Dance	Comments, observation	Obstacle (s)	Comments, observation	Relax
EM	v	Keen. Sustained knee ext with hip abd. adduction	v	In circle. Good balance kicking across body axis	12	Independent. Slightly breathless	v v v	All 3 dances with another client (LH, LH, SN)	37	Independent. No one near when stepping onto mat	v
ST	v	Participated in all – verbal & physical asst.	v	Poor side stepping turns in direction of movement	32	Followed staff. Lot of verbal encouragement	v v	Both dances with staff	78	1 hand support over inclines & roll. Verbal help	v
VR	o	Not in room	o	Not in room	7	Independent. Not breathless. Ran out of room	o	Not in room	11	Independent. Ran out of room	o
LG											
AM											
NM											

Signature _____

Figure 14.1 Mobility/fitness group – weekly record.

Name   Date   Physiotherapist

General health (note any change)

Individual Aims

Activity	Physical Objectives A: Reduce assistance B: Improve co-ordination C: Improve speed	Rating scale	General Objectives A: Improve participation B: Improve communication C: Improve sequencing	Rating scale
Sitting exercise				
Standing exercise	'			
Slalom course 12.5 m				
Dances				
Obstacle course 16m				

Rating scale

Rating	Outcome (Speed averaged over participating weeks)
-1	Participation in activity has decreased, or more assistance is required, or where a speed element is involved this has decreased >5%
0	No or minimal change <5%
+1	There has been some increase in participation, or less assistance is required, or where a speed element is involved this has increased a little >5%
+2	Participation has increased, or little or no assistance is required, or where a speed element is involved this has increased >10%

General comments

Figure 14.2 Physiotherapy mobility/fitness group – 6-monthly progress.

- Group activities used by the general public, but used to achieve physiotherapy goals with a group of people with learning disabilities.

It is rare for any group to be taken by a physiotherapist alone. Some groups require a contribution from different professionals and specific teaching from the physiotherapist. In all groups, participants require individual encouragement from members of staff as well as their peer group. People with challenging behaviour or special toileting needs will require the support of their own key worker (usually social services or voluntary agency staff).

Recognised exercises

Keep fit and weight reduction group

The help of a physiotherapist and dietitian was sought by a centre manager to improve the health of overweight and obese clients by running a class at the centre.

Place

A room in the centre is used for this group.

Participants

These are eight adults who are community ambulators (Hoffer scale 1) (see Chapter 7) and have mild learning disabilities. All are overweight or obese. The majority present with Down's syndrome.

Staff

This includes one physiotherapist, one dietitian and members of the social work centre staff.

Programme

The following are the aims of this class:
• To improve mobility
• To improve stamina
• To increase aerobic activity
• To reduce weight.

The keep fit (exercise) class

• Warm-up exercises in standing
• Stepping, running on the spot
• Exercises in long sitting, including pelvic rocking, pelvic lifts, touching toes
• Exercises in lying including pelvic tilting, straight leg raises and back extension
• Slow stretches in standing.

Discussion on diet

Members of the group discuss what they have eaten for breakfast and lunch and what are healthy foods. They may have a tasting session.

Dietitian

The dietitian weighs each client once a month. Weight loss ranges from 0.5 to 4 kg in one month.

Get fit group

Patients in a learning disability and forensic ward were starting to participate in walks and cycle rides at weekends with members of the nursing staff. The physiotherapist was asked to undertake a baseline fitness assessment with the patients. After the initial assessment, it became apparent that they were extremely unfit.

Discussion took place with the proposed participants about the value of becoming fitter and a regular weekly fitness group was established.

Place

The ward dining room is used for this group.

Participants

These are four men aged between 25 and 50 years. Participants have mild-to-moderate learning disability and their physical ability is level 1 on the Hoffer scale or fully independent (see Chapter 7). Individual participants present with the following: rheumatoid arthritis, cerebral palsy, genetic abnormalities, challenging behaviour, psychiatric illness.

Staff

This consists of one physiotherapist, one or two nurses and a physiotherapy student on placement.

Programme

Exercises undertaken are appropriate to the type of movement required when walking up hills and over rough ground:

- Sufficient time is allowed for participants to organise themselves and prepare mentally for participating in a group that requires physical effort and concentration.
- Warm-up exercises and stretching in standing.
- Lower limb-strengthening exercises in standing.
- Shuttle run.
- Aerobic sequence.
- Slalom course – running around cones, timed over a measured distance.
- Modified hurdle course – jumping over objects that are 15 cm high, timed over a measured distance.

- Press-ups – individually modified and counted.
- Abdominal exercises – individually modified and counted.
- Warm-down.

Fitness was monitored regularly. Over a period of 1 year the degree of difficulty and the distance run or walked, both in the exercise group and during the weekend walks and expeditions were measurably increased.

At the end of the year, three patients and three male nurses walked the West Highland Way (96 miles rough walking) over a period of 7 days. Their support vehicle carrying overnight equipment was driven by another male nurse.

The fitness group and weekend country walks have become a regular part of the ward's programme for subsequent appropriate patients. Group members are interested in seeing their progress recorded in bar chart form.

Composite groups

General mobility and fitness group

A day centre for adults with learning disabilities has a preponderance of members who require regular monitoring and encouragement from a physiotherapist to prevent rapid deterioration of mobility and to improve their general fitness. The majority do not need individual physiotherapy.

Place

A large room in the centre is used for this group.

Participants

These are 18 adults aged between 22 and 50 years. All participants have moderate-to-severe learning disability and their physical ability is level 2 or 1 on the Hoffer scale or fully independent (see Chapter 7). Individual participants present with the following: Down's syndrome, cerebral palsy, spina bifida, progressive neurological disorders, challenging behaviour, severely limited vision and poor hearing.

Staff

These include one physiotherapist, four members of the centre staff, one volunteer, and nursing, therapy and social work students on placement.

Programme

- Warm-up exercises in sitting and standing, which also increase range of

movement and improve coordination specific to individuals participating.
- Slalom course: running/walking around cones, timed over a measured
distance.
- Country dancing: three country dances, modified by Claire Dennis and
taught by her to members of the Association of Chartered
Physiotherapists for People with Learning Disabilities (ACPPLD) at their
1994 conference. The aim of these dances for this group is to:
  - improve stamina
  - improve coordination
  - improve ability to work with a peer group partner
  - improve ability to work in a team
  - improve ability to follow others
  - learn a useful activity
- Obstacle course: run/walk up and down two large wedges, over a roll,
through a roll, onto and off two mats and between two cones. Timed
over a measured distance. The aim is to:
  - improve stamina
  - improve range of movement
  - improve movement repertoire
  - improve balance and coordination
  - improve turn-taking
- Final stretch and relaxation sitting in chair.

The additional aim of this group is to encourage group participation,
interaction and peer support, spontaneous conversation between clients,
and the ability to choose a dancing partner.

Using a public leisure pool for a physiotherapy group

A number of adults with learning disabilities from two day centres and an
inclusion project have progressed beyond the need for hydrotherapy in a
specially heated pool. However, they benefit from exercising in warm
water and using its property of buoyancy to assist and resist movement,
and for the opportunity it gives for risk-taking and experiential learning
(see Chapter 11). In addition, use of a public pool fulfils the aims of the
inclusion project, which are that clients should mix with non-learning-
disabled people by using community facilities.

Place

This is a public leisure pool concurrently used by members of the general
public and with other disabled people present. It is relatively quiet during
term time and very busy during school holidays.

Participants

These are adults with moderate-to-severe learning disability; one is fully independent. The physical ability of the others is level 2 or 3 on the Hoffer scale (see Chapter 7). Individual participants present with the following: cerebral palsy, minimal cerebral palsy, progressive neurological disorder, limited vision, challenging behaviour.

Staff

These are one physiotherapist and five day-care staff.

Programme

- Physiotherapist, one day-care staff member and two participants travel together and are the first to arrive.
- Day-care staff member and one participant join in a community aquarobics group for non-learning-disabled people (usually all women), to improve client's coordination, general fitness, concentration and confidence with non-disabled women.
- Physiotherapist works one to one with each participant as they arrive, using exercises appropriate to the individual (see Chapter 11) and using the facilities of the pool for physiotherapeutic aims.
- Pool facilities appropriate for this group are:
  - variety of textures of pool surround, steps and inclines: to improve balance
  - varying depth of water: to improve balance
  - fast flow channel: to improve balance, by walking both with and against the flow and to improve coordination, walking pattern and muscle strength by using resisted walking against the flow
  - waves: to improve balance, coordination, posture and muscle strength
  - fountains: to increase balance and confidence
  - walking between other swimmers: to improve balance, coordination and confidence
  - Jacuzzi pool: for relaxation
- Day-care staff work with physiotherapist to use the pool facilities as appropriate for the participants.
- All join in a group based on the Halliwick principles (Martin, 1981) which include:
  - standing in a circle, each participant walking under a human arch made by other participants and staff (disengagement)
  - arms linked in a circle, floating supine – back-float (vertical rotation – balance restoration)

- All continue using pool facilities.
- All shower and dress, or help to dress, themselves.

Specialist group activities

JABADAO

The name JABADAO is the name of a company and charity who are a UK National Development Agency for Dance/Movement (see Appendix II). They undertake training and project work and are developing resources to establish dance/movement as an ordinary part of being human and as a medium for learning and growth.

JABADAO's work is informed by the world of dance therapy, psychology (particularly the work of Abraham Maslow in the USA), and other body therapies, e.g. the Alexander technique, Bartenieff's fundamentals, Laban movement analysis, authentic movement principles and contact improvisation and group therapy.

Basis

Their work is based on the concept that an understanding of the immediate world is learnt through movement and that this is the basis for all future learning.

The child develops emotional, conceptual and perceptual awareness of the immediate environment through using his or her hands to explore objects, and through body contact with the parents. At this time, sensory understanding of surfaces, size and weight, and perceptual concepts of distance, space and orientation of own body weight and movement of limbs into space, are established.

Understanding of self and other interactive skills, such as turn-taking, cause and effect and ranges of the primary emotions, e.g. joy to despair and fear to safety, are established through non-verbal interactions based on body movement during the first year. (For further information on development of communication, see Chapter 6.)

Group work based on the JABADAO principles provides an opportunity for participants to explore their moving selves and develop an insight into 'self' and 'other'. Participants can make connections by expressing themselves clearly and by being seen and understood. This is especially important for people with profound physical disability who are dependent on others for all aspects of self-care and mobility. As described in Chapter 6 their sensory deprivation, social isolation and inability to access ordinary experience compound difficulties with learning.

Interactive dance/movement can provide this group of people with a range of experiences to:

- stimulate
- motivate
- facilitate

natural body movement in interaction with the environment and with forces of gravity.

The direct experiences of the body help to develop recognition of:

- space
- shape
- size
- weight
- contrast

JABADAO uses the structure from 'authentic movement' principles to allow each individual to be seen or witnessed in a non-judgemental way. The individual's unique way of moving/dancing/being in the world is acknowledged in its own right and is possibly reflected in the movements of a partner or the group. Maslow (1962) outlines how growth or learning occurs only when safety is established. JABADAO seeks to provide structures that create safety in which structure and growth can occur.

Place

A room large enough to accommodate equipment and wheelchairs is used.

Participants

The number of participants is dependent on the number of facilitators and the room size. JABADAO is suitable for all levels of learning disability and participants' physical ability level can be at any level on the Hoffer scale or fully independent or entirely dependent (see Chapter 7).

Staff

Ideally there should be two therapists from a combination of physiotherapist, occupational therapist, and speech and language therapist, although more commonly only one is available, plus day centre staff and carers. One therapist or day centre staff to act as leader, the others to act as facilitators on a ratio of 1:2 or 1:3. Students and volunteers to work with participants as directed by facilitators.

Programme: structure/process (Hewett, 1994)

- Starting point for developing a movement conversation: acknowledge-

ment of each unique individual and their particular way of being in the world
- Structures may be:
  - simple games, such as individual greeting, discovering the contents of a large box, taking turns to pass under a human arch, changing places under a parachute, mirroring another person's movement
  - props such as elasticised rope, scarves, scented balls, parachute, Lycra
  - music
- Facilitators must:
  - tune in to all the non-verbal body messages being expressed, and then
  - pick up a common theme from all the participants, and then
  - facilitate an appropriate relationship to develop between the group as a whole, and finally
  - intensive interactions can be facilitated within a dance/movement group

It is through relationship that practical therapeutic aims can be fulfilled in every sphere of human potential.

Case study

- A 20-year-old man with cerebral palsy who lives with a foster family and attends a Social Services 'special care day centre' 5 days a week.
- He wears a spinal jacket to help to prevent further deterioration of his gross scoliosis and kyphosis of spine, and severe windswept deformity.
- He communicates with facial expression and whole body patterns of mass extension for fear/pain/joy.
- He has a Liberator communicator which is poorly used by the centre staff as a result of lack of time, space and sufficient training.
- He has to be hoisted for several changes in position within a 24-hour postural management programme.
- He has regular chest infections.
- He is isolated from the rest of the group by a reclining moulded insert in a large chair.
- He has difficulty with being moved.

This young man participated in a multisensory movement group in which he was positioned on beanbags with others in a circle (following the postural management programme). The use of brightly coloured props facilitated a very visible link between him and other group members.

He was able to feel the movement of others through props and participation in the group. One-to-one work within the context of the group involved him in stretching to touch stimulating props, playing eye contact games, turn-taking, feeling the contact of another through feet, hands and trunk, and receiving sensory stimulation from different colours and textures. During the session, a reduction of muscle tone was achieved through interactions and appropriate touch. He led some sound and rhythm games during which he introduced his own ideas and played with cause and effect in interaction.

Overall, this young man became animated beyond normal expectations and expressed sheer delight in the experience he was enjoying.

A group activity used by the general public

Tai Chi

The ancient Chinese art of Tai Chi is based on movements used for self-defence but is now practised in a slower, gentler form to promote and sustain good health. The philosophical roots of Tai Chi are based in Taoism and the fundamental principles of harmony and balance in nature. Much has been written about its origins and development. To use Tai Chi as a group exercise form, it is necessary for the physiotherapist to have some personal knowledge of the basic movements, through attending a club or community group. To learn the basic movements from books alone would be difficult, although reading about underlying principles is to be recommended.

The movement or 'form' consists of slow, gentle postures which flow together and can be suitable for most ability levels. Recent research in the USA has demonstrated that regular practice of Tai Chi can reduce the likelihood of falls in elderly people (Wolf et al., 1996) and reduce blood pressure measurements in patients recovering from myocardial infarction (Channer et al., 1996). Staff at the Hong Kong Polytechnic University have now begun to investigate the possibility of using a sophisticated gait analysis system to analyse the body's balance during Tai Chi (Kirtley, 1999).

As an exercise modality, Tai Chi embraces one of the core skills of the physiotherapist.

Place

This is a day centre room large enough to accommodate participants standing to exercise. No equipment is needed other than a tape recorder, if music is required to create the right atmosphere. The group size may need to be tailored to the space available.

Participants

Tai Chi can encompass diverse ability levels. Although it is useful to aim for some uniformity of ability within the group, this is not necessary, as can be seen in many community groups where people with widely differing ability ranges practise Tai Chi together. It has been described as a journey, and all participants are at different stages of the journey, progressing in their own individual way. Participants' physical ability level needs to be 2 or 1 on the Hoffer scale or fully independent.

Staff

These include one physiotherapist plus the number of carers and volunteers required to assist individual participants.

Programme

- Sessions always begin with warm-up and gentle breathing exercises.
- The movement or 'form'.
  - Joints are moved slowly and rhythmically, within comfortable ranges.
  - Soft tissue is not over-stretched; all movements take place within each individual's own existing ranges. The importance of this must be stressed to the group at the beginning of each session, to prevent over-enthusiastic or competitive movements.
  - Weight is transferred from one foot to the other throughout the exercises.
  - Each limb moves independently, and there is heightened awareness of how the individual movements of each part of the body come together to form whole movements, which flow in an uninterrupted sequence.
  - Tai Chi requires balance and coordination.

There is scope for improvement and development in all these areas as the group progresses.

Clients who are enthusiastic and have gained some confidence may choose to join a community Tai Chi group in order to develop their skills further. This may be facilitated by the physiotherapist, with continuous support given by family, friends or volunteers. With the recent increase in interest in the martial arts in the West, groups can be found in most areas; local libraries are a good source of information.

Practising Tai Chi is both a calming and relaxing experience and can help to reduce stress. It is said to unify the mind and the body, allowing the 'chi' or vital energy to flow freely. It is a highly enjoyable form of group exercise through which many physiotherapy goals can be achieved.

Conclusion

Improving physical ability through participating in a group is fun and can improve the participant's ability to communicate and build relationships with others. Participants may learn how to work together, their concentration may improve, their feeling of achievement may be heightened, and their skills may develop sufficiently to allow them to participate in a similar group in the community. However, it is important that people who have been referred to therapists for a specific reason should be assessed, assigned to the appropriate group and reassessed at pre-planned intervals. This should in no way detract from the enjoyment of the group or from the additional health and social gains.

CHAPTER 15

Sport and outdoor pursuits

ANGELA JOHNSON, JONATHON GRAY AND IAN SILKSTONE

This chapter shows how skills learnt during the type of group work described in Chapter 14 may be developed further by using them in community environments where clients are expected to build on their ability. It explains how new skills must be tailored to fit individual needs and wishes adapting to individual abilities.

Sport as rehabilitation for people with disabilities was introduced by Dr Ludwig Guttman at the National Spinal Injuries Centre, Stoke Mandeville in 1944 (Cashmore, 1990). In the 1960s, recreation became recognised as an important element in rehabilitation programmes and in the constructive and creative use of leisure time for people with learning disabilities. Remedial gymnasts began to work in institutions for people with learning disabilities, where they encouraged participation in sporting activities, creating opportunities for team work, improved social interaction and increased tolerance of exercise (Luckey and Shapiro, 1974; Odumnbaku Auty, 1991).

The words sport, outdoor pursuits, leisure and recreation are freely interchanged in conversation meaning one and the same thing to many people. They have been described as follows.

Sport is:

> . . . an individual or group activity pursued for exercise or for pleasure, often taking competitive form, any pastime indulged for pleasure, to remove oneself in outdoor recreation. (Collins, 1994)

Leisure is a time in which:

> . . . there is opportunity for choice . . . an activity apart from the obligations of work, family and society to which the individual turns at will for either relaxation, diversion or broadening of experience. (Honeybourne et al., 1996)

Recreation is:

> . . . activity voluntarily engaged in during leisure and motivated by the personal
> satisfactions which result from it . . . a tool for mental and physical therapy.
> (Honeybourne et al., 1996)

The value of sport, outdoor pursuits, leisure and recreation is rarely
fully understood or recognised (Malin, 1995), and research into its value is
neglected. Many people still view recreation as a supplementary pursuit
that fills in gaps when an individual is not working or learning. At best it is
seen as fun, at worst it is regarded as idle time (Roggenbuck et al., 1990).

Opportunities for people with learning disabilities

The professional craft knowledge (Higgs and Titchen, 1995; see Chapter
5) of physiotherapists using recreational therapy daily has shown that
sport, outdoor pursuits and games provide an educational experience for
people with learning disabilities. Physical participation at any level can
have an impact upon sensorimotor systems, cognition and social aspects
of an individual's life (see Table 15.1 page 251). Organised sport and
outdoor pursuits provide constructive use of leisure time allowing opportunities for personal achievement whilst also helping to rechannel excess
energy and aggression by preventing boredom and loneliness.

According to Kennedy et al. (1991) and McConkey et al. (1981), people
with learning disabilities would like to enjoy the same recreational activities
pursued by the wider population but rarely have the opportunity to do so
(Wertheimer, 1983; Cheseldine and Jeffrey, 1981; McConkey et al., 1981).
In recent years, opportunities for participation have increased as a result of
the recognition of the rights of disabled people (see Chapter 1) but many
are still unaware of what is available and have not learned how to access
sporting facilities (Grey, 1996).

Kennedy et al. (1991) believe that the low participation rate by people
with learning disabilities in community recreation is a result of both
intrinsic and extrinsic barriers.

Intrinsic barriers

- Social ineffectiveness
- Health problems
- Physical and psychological difficulties
- Lack of skills/knowledge.

Extrinsic barriers

- Attitudes of others: there is a widespread apprehension towards people
  with disabilities (Barnes, 1991). Some sports centres fear that the

presence of people with disabilities may discourage non-disabled people from participating in the same social settings. Attitudes are reflected in the provision of hostile environments and structural boundaries (Finklestein, 1990).
- Lack of appropriate recreational facilities (Cheseldine and Jeffree, 1981).
- Few qualified instructors (Luckey and Shapiro, 1974).
- Dependence on parents and carers, lack of transport.
- Architectural barriers.
- Lack of communication, exclusion and omission.
- Personal economic limitations.

The role of a physiotherapist

Professionals in the field of sport and recreation are often unprepared for the challenge associated with learning disabilities. This is where a team of physiotherapists can play a major role in the lives of people with learning disabilities.

Physiotherapists, occupational therapists and speech and language therapists working with people with learning disabilities have embraced the principles of normalisation (Wolfensberger, 1972), which provide a guiding philosophy designed to increase individual competence, socialisation and social acceptance (see Chapter 1).

Previously, people with disabilities have been critical of the ways in which professionals, especially physiotherapists, have undervalued and underestimated their abilities (Tilstone, 1991). They have accused physiotherapists of acting as 'stigma coaches', reinforcing negative stereotypes and focusing on impairment rather than seeking to enable people who are already limited by social and personal attitudes (Rousch, 1986) to live independently (Johnson, 1993). Professionals are further criticised for taking control and imposing choices once an activity becomes a 'treatment' or 'therapy'. However, this should not and need not be the case.

The Chartered Society of Physiotherapy (1991) states that:

Chartered physiotherapists have an important role to play in the prevention of further disability and in helping disabled people to achieve their maximum potential for mobility and independence.

Recreation and therapeutic recreation as two separate entities do overlap. Therapeutic recreation offers therapy with the accompanying benefit of an enjoyable recreational experience.

Physiotherapists, using their knowledge and skills in conjunction with a holistic approach, have a vital role to play in maintaining optimum

Table 15.1 Benefits and development through sport and outdoor pursuits

Physical
Improves heart function
Improves circulation
Improves muscular and skeletal systems
Improves flexibility
Improves balance
Improves coordination
Improves fine and gross motor skills
Improves exercise tolerance
Improves reflex reactions
Improves manual dexterity
Improves body awareness
Improves agility
Improves postural awareness
Improves spatial awareness
Assists weight reduction

Psychological
Promotes confidence
Provides motivation to mobilise
Improves self-image
Increases self-esteem
Improves listening skills
Improves concentration
Improves directional sense
Increases perception
Helps to decrease behavioural problems

Social
Provides opportunity for contact with peers
Provides opportunity for social interaction
Provides opportunity for social integration
Provides opportunity for community integration
Provides opportunity for new experiences
Provides opportunity for fun and enjoyment

physical function and can provide positive psychological support towards independence.

The selected activities should be within the individual's capabilities and fit into lifestyles within the community. Some people prefer individual pursuits or dislike competition, so activities can be selected that provide support and companionship. Studies have shown that fun and enjoyment are the most important reasons for taking part in recreation and sport and in maintaining long-term involvement (Wankel and Berger, 1990).

Group work has been criticised in the past as dehumanising and taking away individual rights and dignity, but the disadvantages are usually the result of the following:

- Faulty selection of clients
- Poor communication with individuals
- Inappropriate selection of individuals for certain groups
- Overcrowding and poor techniques
- Low expectations of staff
- Lack of appropriate activities

(Gardiner, 1971; Jahoda and Cattermole, 1995)

Experience has shown that teaching in a group allows opportunity for clients to achieve personal recognition with peers and acquire skills, whilst being provided with help, encouragement and supervision. Well-planned classes can meet individual needs and expectations. Kennedy et al. (1991) suggested that the success of therapeutic recreation is dependent on the skills, qualities and attributes of the therapist, which include:

- Stamina and physical energy
- Enthusiasm and a sense of humour
- Positive attitude and understanding of societal attitudes
- Ingenuity, resourcefulness, creativity, ability to innovate
- Capacity to accept limited, slow progress
- Commitment
- Willingness to experiment

Before selecting a sport or activity it is necessary to assess individual needs, taking into account any medical conditions that may prevent participation, e.g. severe heart defects or exercise-induced epilepsy. Goals and objectives are then set. At intervals, there must be analysis and evaluation of progress which will allow modification if necessary.

Teaching points for success

- Always follow safety regulations
- Keep things simple
- Never underestimate the participants' capability
- Keep jargon and uncommon words to a minimum; good communication skills are vital, both verbal and non-verbal
- Break skills down
- Ensure sequential delivery of skills, allowing plenty of repetition of techniques

- Provide a variety of activities to prevent boredom
- Progress skills according to the needs of the group
- Use voice modulation to motivate and encourage
- Give good demonstrations
- Remember that failure to prepare is preparation for failure
- Adapt to the individual needs of the group
- Be enthusiastic, positive in approach
- Observe, give feedback, be consistent
- Involve participants in the coaching

The responsibility of the physiotherapist is to rehabilitate individuals to allow them to take their place as independent members of society and not to make them more 'normal' (Appleby and Wright, 1980). It is recognised that the Hoffer scale measures physical ability and this has been used to accommodate the variety of chapters in this book. However, in practice, therapists should also consider personal choice, learning ability, behaviour and psychological state in their assessments and adapt recreation accordingly.

- An individual's level of competence must not be presumed because of a label.
- Capability levels should not be seen as static.

Physiotherapists can provide an increasing range of opportunities and can teach skills that allow individuals to be as self-determining as possible. Appropriate dress for sport is very important. It provides a positive image and symbolises to others what the wearer does and enjoys. The positive responses of others through leisure identification reaffirm acceptance of an individual's true self (Haggard and Williams, 1992; Samdahl, 1992). Interventions must be positive, useful and fulfilling. Practising monotonous skills for hours on end cannot enhance quality of life and, if the skill gained is minimal, time has been wasted that could have been spent in more pleasurable ways.

Individual sports

There are many sports and outdoor pursuits to choose from. A small number of sports that are not normally considered suitable for people with learning disabilities have been selected for this chapter. Some sporting activities and recreational leisure pursuits have their own unique benefits, adaptations and in some cases contraindications. The selected sports are: rambling, volleyball, gymnastics, athletics, circuit training and cycling.

It is recommended that the following summaries are read in conjunction with their source material.

Rambling

(Hoffer scale suitability: fully ambulant and Hoffer scale 1–4 and entirely dependent.)

Rambling is one of the most popular outdoor pursuits today (Cotton, 1981; Ward and Rippe, 1988). It originated in the late eighteenth and early nineteenth centuries during the Industrial Revolution, when industrial workers left the smoke-filled towns and cities in search of fresh air and exercise (Channel 4, 1994; Honeybourne et al., 1996). Rambling clubs were set up and a nation-wide network of public footpaths and bridleways was created. Improvement in transport allowed easier access to the countryside and coastal areas. Few activities can be safer than rambling. It is an outdoor pursuit that can be adapted to suit any lifestyle, age, need and ability. This adaptability makes it accessible for life. In Australia, rambling has been included in the 'programmes for pleasure' for the over-50s because it combines fitness, activity and pleasure (Wilson, 1990).

Unique features of rambling (Environ Organisation, 1996)

- Can be done anywhere, e.g. trails, footpaths, parks, shopping centres
- Little risk of injury
- Inexpensive, requires little equipment (only shoes, socks and motivation)
- Quality time allowing communication and time to develop friendships
- Opportunity to work as part of a group
- Sense of adventure
- Educational

Adaptations of rambling

- Making the challenge easy or difficult depending on the needs and wishes of the ramblers
- Varying the distance walked
- Selecting areas of different terrain
- Back-packing for the more able

Contraindications

Non-specific.

Volleyball

(Hoffer scale suitability: fully ambulant and Hoffer scale 1–4.)

In 1985, WG Morgani invented volleyball to provide recreation and relaxation for overweight business men (Bertucci, 1987). Since then, the game has become popular and is now an Olympic and Special Olympic sport. Volleyball can be highly competitive, requiring high levels of skill, fitness, agility and coordination, or it can be relaxing recreation adapted to any level. It is ideal as a therapeutic exercise because it requires short bursts of energy followed by periods of rest. Physiotherapists do not need special training, but it is helpful to have some background knowledge of the game. The aim is to improve individual physical, psychological and social skills, and to provide opportunities to participate in a recognised, valued sport within a non-threatening environment.

Unique features of volleyball

- Simple, clear rules
- Non-contact sport
- Played indoors and outdoors
- Suitable for all ages
- Suitable for most abilities
- Requires little space or equipment
- Twelve players can play at any one time, so it is time- and cost-effective
- Allows individual flare even though it is a team sport
- Unified i.e. players integrated with non-disabled players

Skills to teach

- The Dig
- The Volley
- The Spike
- The Serve

Adaptations of volleyball

- Reducing the size of the court
- Allowing the ball to bounce before contact
- Varying the size and weight of the ball
- Playing mini volleyball – four per side
- Lowering the net
- Playing seated.

Contraindications

Osteoporosis, haemophilia.

Gymnastics

(Hoffer scale suitability: fully ambulant and Hoffer scale 1–4.)

Gymnastics has been regarded as a popular and positive sport for many years and is defined as 'practice or training in exercises that develop physical strength and agility or mental capacity' (Collins, 1994).

The primary aim is to develop motor development skills and promote general fitness, but the overall philosophy also includes positive psychological, social and emotional development. Gymnastics can be adapted for many individuals and used by physiotherapists as an enjoyable, appropriate activity to achieve assessment goals. As a physiotherapy intervention it allows individuals to achieve increasing self-esteem in individual performance by means of movement. It also develops the necessary, appropriate discipline and behaviour involved in taking part in the sport. Sessions can take place within community facilities or within any safe environment that has space to allow movement. All equipment must be of high quality and in excellent repair.

Although gymnastics is suitable for individuals assessed from fully ambulant to Hoffer scale 4, it can be adapted to suit all levels of learning ability. Training in special needs gymnastics is essential and can be arranged through the British Amateur Gymnastics Association. Knowledge of basic gymnastics, combined with physiotherapy knowledge, allows the therapist to observe movement and break down the acquisition of skills into readily understood stages. When given positive encouragement within an appropriate environment, gymnastics enables the individual to reach his or her full potential both physically and mentally.

Unique features of gymnastics

- Skills can be broken down to allow continuous achievement
- The gymnast/coach relationship is close
- The individual is a gymnast throughout the whole session whether performing or awaiting his or her turn
- Postures and movements have clear simple rules
- Sessions are focused and involve working together
- Teaches discipline and set codes of behaviour expected in gymnastics even when not performing
- Simple specific spoken language and demonstrations
- Teaches directional sense

Skills to teach

- Listening skills
- To stand like a gymnast
- To sit like a gymnast
- Gymnastic postures and terminology, e.g. straddle, squat, stretch
- Names of equipment
- Concepts of movement and direction

Gymnasts can be given brief, specific and technically correct advice to correct poor techniques and prevent bad habits forming.

All gymnastics revolves around straight, pike or tucked shapes.

Adaptations of gymnastics

- Floor work: mats
- Equipment: beam, box, springboard
- Planning the position of the equipment
- Altering the height of the equipment
- Varying the size of the work area
- Working in pairs or groups

Award schemes

The British Amateur Gymnastics Association runs an award scheme for various grades of gymnastics. Each grade has 10 elements to be completed. These awards can be adapted by breaking them down further to suit a group's need.

Contraindications

Atlantoaxial instability.

Athletics

(Hoffer scale suitability: fully ambulant and Hoffer scale 1–4.)

The term 'athletics' covers a wide variety of events rather than a single one (Devon County Council, 1993). Athletics includes events in both track and field. In a broader plain, it can cover road runs, cross country and tug of war (North West Council for Sport, 1992–1996). This variation allows physiotherapists tremendous scope to meet individual needs in a positive and valued way. Some individuals may aim for competitive events but for the majority the physiotherapist can use athletics to meet individually set goals in an enjoyable and fun way.

Athletics can be adapted to suit all levels of physical and learning ability. Special training in athletics coaching is not essential, but it is useful to have knowledge of the scope of events available.

Unique features of athletics

- Can take place indoors or outdoors within a safe area, in a variety of settings, e.g. athletics stadium, gymnasium, playing field
- Allows natural talent to flourish, e.g. for those who are continually on the move, running may be a suitable pursuit to channel natural skills in a positive and valued way
- Activities can be simplified
- Athletics has visual boundaries
- Creates discipline and control
- Inexpensive
- Has measurable markers for improvement which provides immediate feedback to the individual and others

Skills to teach

(Devon County Council, 1993; North West Council for Sport, 1992–1996)

- Running
- Jumping
- Throwing
- Boundaries
- Commands, e.g. go, start, stop

Contraindications

Non-specific.

Circuit training

(Hoffer scale suitability: fully ambulant and Hoffer scale 1–4.)

Circuit training was developed in the 1960s by Morgan and Adamson (Colson and Collinson, 1983) to provide a system of exercise that would maintain and improve fitness levels. A circuit involves a series of exercises (about 10 exercise stations) in sequence that ensure that the main muscle groups are worked in turn. A circuit can be adapted to suit all ability levels, with the aim to progressively improve endurance, strength, cardiorespiratory efficiency and functional skills (Hart and Hart, 1987; Bartlett, 1990). Fitness gains are of secondary importance to the psychological, physical and social effects. Exercises in the circuit must be within the capabilities of each individual.

There are a variety of circuits but the following are the two most suitable for people with impaired physical and learning ability.

A general circuit

Clients can work individually or in pairs. The aim is to achieve all-round fitness. Exercises can involve equipment (e.g. ball for throwing and catching) or be stationary (e.g. running, press-ups, step-ups).

A functional circuit

This concentrates on functional movements encountered in daily activities. It is designed to enhance functional skills by repetition. Exercises may include sitting to standing, rolling, climbing stairs, walking on uneven ground (Latto and Norrice, 1989).

Unique features of circuit training

- A circuit follows a definite structure or routine, which allows familiarity and decreases uncertainty
- The exercises are simple and adaptable to all capabilities and fitness levels
- A circuit allows periods of rest and periods of fitness, which can be altered according to fitness levels
- Working for a set time, e.g. 1 minute, at each station prevents the need to count the number of repetitions
- Everyone exercises and rests at the same time, allowing the therapist control and observation of the group
- Several people with varying ability and fitness levels can work together in the same group
- A circuit can be designed to fit a variety of settings and room sizes
- Improvement is measurable

Teaching points

- Each exercise must be demonstrated and practised fully
- Individuals must follow the same sequence of exercise

Adaptations of circuits

- Changing the time periods of the rests
- Counting repetitions
- Allowing individuals to work at their own pace
- Increasing or decreasing the number of exercises in a circuit
- Games circuits, skills circuits and integrated games can be included
- Equipment can be adapted to suit wheelchair users (e.g. sticks shortened in golf- and hockey-type exercises)

Contraindications

Non-specific.

Cycling

(Hoffer scale suitability: fully ambulant, Hoffer scale 1–4 and entirely dependent.)

Cycling can be a sporting activity, leisure activity or necessary mode of transport, and can facilitate therapeutically assessed needs. It allows experience, participation and presence within the local community and environment, at the same time providing pleasurable exercise on equal terms with non-disabled peers.

Cycles come in all shapes and sizes, allowing a greater number of people access to the activity. Static bicycles can be a good starting point for cycling. They require very little space and provide a stable base on which to teach the basic peddling. Three-wheeled trikes and tricycles allow progression, encouraging balance and posture during movement. Tricycles with two seats side by side allow for one-to-one supervision and physical and psychological support (Bartley, 1998). Adapted seating can be attached to some tricycles.

Cycling can be enjoyed in a variety of settings, e.g. parks, cycle paths, hospital grounds and in the countryside. Some clients may, in time, be able to use public highways, but this must be determined by the therapist through continuous assessment and education using the highway code.

It is now recognised that cycling has many therapeutic benefits and several therapists have produced literature to support this, including Geoff Bartley, Lancaster Hospital and Cybil Williams who was awarded the Front Line Excellence Award and Ann Russell Memorial Award of the ACPPLD for this work in 1998.

Unique features of cycling (Bartley, 1998)

- Different cycles are available to meet a variety of needs
- Body weight can be fully supported
- Little stress is placed on the joints
- Provides a decrease in muscular tension
- Allows experience of independent movement
- Allows experience of movement in the elements – wind, sun, rain
- Non-sighted clients can experience cycling with unobtrusive one-to-one support
- Improves bilateral coordination
- Encourages a controlled pattern of movement
- Teaches road awareness

Adaptations of cycling

- Changing the type of cycle
- Increasing the distance cycled
- Increasing or decreasing the amount of one-to-one support

Contraindications

Being overweight may be a problem when using two-seated tricycles.

Conclusion

Leisure provides freedom and the opportunity to make choices, and allows personal growth (Gold, 1989). Recreational activities such as sport and outdoor pursuits provide health gains while at the same time generating joy and satisfaction, which are crucial for people with learning disabilities, who often face boredom, loneliness and isolation. Fulfilling leisure experiences can help to improve quality of life (Johnson, 1997). All professionals must realise that people with learning disabilities are as diverse as others in society and have varying interests, attitudes, skills and talents. If people are to be enabled to make an informed choice, it is necessary to offer them a variety of experiences in a supportive setting. Physiotherapists should be innovative and creative with their own personal qualities and skills to ensure that they are being effective. Quality contact must be on an equal status and each individual should be consulted about what they want and need.

It is vital that all professionals, parents, carers, educators and friends promote a positive image; the ultimate goal of leisure must be towards total integration within community-based leisure experiences. Physiotherapists must encourage, educate, motivate and support clients by highlighting ability rather than disability.

CHAPTER 16

Complementary therapies

LIBBY DAVIES AND JANE BRUCE

There has been much debate about the definition and interpretation of the term 'complementary therapy', as well as the scope and variety of practices that may be encompassed by the use of such a term.

In the broadest sense, complementary therapy may be thought of as a specific modality applied in its own right or as anything adjunctive to any other given modality. Whether a specific entity or adjunctive practice, one area that is not commonly given adequate account is that of how the therapist sets up the environment – physical or non-physical – for what is to happen. The way the therapist moves and expresses him- or herself and handles any client (in terms of positioning as well as the more direct therapeutic intervention) will have major effects – positive or negative – and implications for the client and on the therapeutic process.

There are many defined complementary therapies; although each tends to have its own concept, philosophy and defined method(s) of delivery, all are in the main united by a common core philosophy of holistic and systemic health care. Tai Chi is mentioned in Chapter 15.

Selection and application of complementary therapies will be governed by certain factors: the knowledge base and experience of the therapist will ultimately be the major screening process. Other screening processes will of necessity be client based, in the sense of knowledge and recognition of what is acceptable to any given client, their likes and dislikes, level of cognition, and behavioural, attitudinal and social factors.

Many more people are delivering or using defined complementary therapies. This chapter aims to introduce those working with people with learning disabilities to two of them: aromatherapy and reflexology. These two therapies are particularly beneficial to this client group because they involve a lot of physical contact between therapist and client, thus helping to build trusting relationships. The introduction to each therapy outlines the basic concept; the case studies illustrate ways in which the therapies can be used to benefit the client, and show the valuable part that they play in the overall treatment of people with learning disabilities.

Reflexology

Like so many complementary therapies, the practice of reflexology has its roots in ancient times. It is a holistic method of treatment concentrating on the whole person and not just on an illness or symptom.

As the feet represent a microcosm of the body, all organs, glands and other parts of the body are laid out in a similar arrangement on the feet (Dougans and Ellis, 1992).The reflex foot massage is a specific pressure technique which works on precise reflex points on the feet. Using the thumb to 'caterpillar walk' across the foot with even pressure, subtle energy flows are worked on; these energies revitalise the body so that the natural healing mechanisms of the body can do their work. Hence, reflexology can initiate and accelerate healing in the corresponding part of the body and restore homoeostasis.

Reflexology cannot diagnose a problem. It may help to confirm what is already known and also alert the therapist and client to imbalances within the body, so helping to bring about an increased sense of well-being and relaxation, reduce stress, improve circulation, cleanse the body and balance the system. It is a wonderful, deeply relaxing treatment. It is not a painful therapy, although slight discomfort may be felt as the therapist works on an area of imbalance.

The role of reflexology in the treatment of people with learning disabilities is therefore useful not only for the aforementioned, but also in locating imbalances that they are unable to explain and comprehend. It can also be used as an assessment before an aromatherapy treatment and help in the selection of oils that will be of most benefit and value to the client.

Aromatherapy

Aromatherapy is a natural treatment using essential oils extracted from flowers, leaves, bark, berries and fruit of a wide variety of aromatic plants. The essential oil is not a single substance, but consists of a number of complex components. It is this that gives each oil a range of therapeutic properties. These oils can be introduced to the body in different ways, such as through inhalation, compresses, baths or massage (Price, 1983). The oils are highly concentrated and it is important to use the correct concentration and combination of oils to suit the needs of each individual client.

For the purposes of this chapter, the essential oils are used in conjunction with massage and should be diluted with a carrier oil such as almond or grapeseed oil. When the oils are used with massage, they help to enhance the physical effect of massage. The oils enter the body through the skin and also through the olfactory system. They can help build up the immune system, calm or lift the spirits, invigorate, or they may be used to treat a specific symptom such as a sore head or stomach. An aromatherapy treatment will balance the body, mind and spirit.

People with learning disabilities can benefit from aromatherapy in many ways. Ideally, the treatment should be carried out in quiet, warm surroundings using a plinth or bed, although this is not always possible in adult training centres or schools. It can be used to complement other treatments by, for example, helping to relax a client before a physiotherapy session, or by using it along with a behaviour modification programme as seen in case study 3. Although it appears that aromatherapy is beneficial, it is usually difficult to receive true and accurate feedback from the clients themselves. The most commonly used method of evaluation is by asking the carers to monitor any physical changes or changes in behaviour after treatment and how long these changes last.

The following case studies will help to illustrate the above concepts. The names of clients have been changed to ensure confidentiality.

Case studies

Case study 1: Liz

This study helps to illustrate how the combination of aromatherapy and reflexology can work together to treat a particular symptom and how reflexology can confirm the therapists' initial assessment and help in the choice of oils.

Liz is a 24-year-old woman with cerebral palsy and mental impairment. She has a moderate-to-severe learning disability. Her epilepsy is under control. She is ambulant with a rollator and communicates through signing and using a Walker Talker.

Liz attends sessions approximately once a month, although this can be more frequent if required. She thoroughly enjoys her sessions and is an active participant in her treatment. She enjoys smelling the oils and helps to blend the final mix. She is not able to understand the properties of the oils, but knows that they will help her. Liz is able to undress and dress with minimal assistance; this she enjoys doing independently.

Aims of treatment

- To promote relaxation
- To treat the presenting problem

Treatment

Liz has a full body massage during which she is very relaxed and content. At times, towards the end of the session, she can become quite emotional. This can often be linked to her menstrual cycle. The oils used are dependent on how Liz presents on that particular day and through feedback from the centre staff. She has a diary that goes between the centre and the care staff in her flat, which helps with communication. Added to this, a reflexology assessment will help in the choice of oils and also help to monitor the progress of her treatment.

Treatment example

Liz has been sneezing and coughing (dry) today. She was not her usual happy self. She was, however, keen to come for treatment. Her foot reflexes showed imbalances in the respiratory and upper lymphatic areas.

Liz was relaxed throughout. She did not sneeze and only coughed at the end when sitting up. She was also a little emotional but was easily calmed (Table 16.1).

Table 16.1 Oils used in case study 1

Oil	Plant origin	Relevant properties
Sandalwood	Santalum albumen	Antiseptic
Niaouli	Melaleuca virdifolia	Analgesic, antiseptic, bactericidal, balsamic, expectorant, stimulant (immune system)
Lavendin	Lavendula intermedia	Antiviral, antiseptic, decongestant (lymphatic system); this oil was chosen in preference to lavender because the properties, although similar, are more penetrating and therefore more suitable for respiratory conditions
Eucalyptus	Eucalyptus smithii	Analgesic, antiseptic, antiviral, balsamic, decongestant, expectorant

Outcome

During the afternoon, the staff reported that Liz appeared brighter. At her flat, the staff reported that Liz felt much better.

She was seen again one week later. She had had a good week and the cough and cold were better; the foot reflexes still showed some imbalances. The same mix was chosen and Liz was relaxed throughout her treatment.

Continuing aims of treatment

- To promote relaxation
- To alleviate PMT

Plan

To continue to see Liz monthly before her menstrual period or as necessary.

Case study 2: David

In this study, the properties and benefits of the oils are brought together to build up the immune system and strengthen the body's resistance to disease.

David is 21 years old and has epilepsy and also a metabolic disease. He lives at home with his mother and step-father. David is a young man who is multiply handicapped and has severe learning disabilities. He is wheel-chair-bound, totally dependent and unable to communicate verbally. He can be distressed and tense, which can sometimes be alleviated with a change in position. He is prone to respiratory infections and constipation.

David attends a centre based on the Rudolph Steiner ethos. He is seen weekly for treatment, the session lasting about 40 minutes. He always smiles and shows recognition and acceptance of the therapist.

A short reflexology assessment is carried out before the oils are blended. The staff keep the therapist up to date with David's condition, and a diary facilitates communication between his parents and the centre. David enjoys smelling the final blend.

Aims of treatment

- To promote relaxation
- To increase circulation
- To improve and strengthen the immune system
- To prevent and treat any infection
- To alleviate constipation
- To reduce tone

David has physiotherapy shortly after treatment.

Treatment

The areas massaged are the feet, legs, back, stomach and hands. During the session, David's position is frequently changed. The centre is provided with blends so that massage can continue through the week. Oils are also burnt in the room where David spends some of his day (Table 16.2).

Table 16.2 Oils used in case study 2

Oil	Plant origin	Relevant properties
Lavender	Lavendula angustifolia	Analgesic, antiseptic, antispasmodic, rubefacient
Tea tree	Melaleuca alternifolia	Anti-infectious, anti-inflammatory, antiseptic, antiviral, bactericidal, expectorant, immunostimulant
Eucalyptus	Eucalyptus smithii	Antiseptic, antispasmodic, antiviral, decongestant, expectorant, rubefacient, stimulant
Sweet margoram	Origanum margorana	Antiseptic, antispasmodic, bactericidal, expectorant, laxative, sedative
Juniper	Juniperus communis	Antiseptic, antispasmodic, rubefacient, sedative
Black pepper	Piper nigram	Antimicrobial, antiseptic, antispasmodic, laxative, bactericidal, stimulant (nervous, digestive, circulatory)
	Citrus retulata	Antiseptic, antispasmodic, mild laxative, sedative, stimulant (digestive and lymphatic)

Outcome

David has had less infections and therefore the need for antibiotics has been less.

- In 1996: six infections, five treated with antibiotics
- In 1997: five infections, two treated with antibiotics
- In 1998: one infection, treated with antibiotics to date (August 1998)

Plan

To continue to see weekly and monitor his health as before.

Case study 3: Kevin

This case study helps to illustrate how aromatherapy and reflexology can be adapted to include modification programmes and also benefit the client.

Kevin is 21 years old and has epilepsy and a severe learning disability and short attention span. He is ambulant when using a rollator and assistance. He has an ataxic gait. Kevin has no speech, but uses signs for 'please' and 'thank you'. Kevin's moods can fluctuate and he can become frustrated and bite his sleeve and can, on occasions, kick out. He can also become excitable; he will laugh, shriek, clap his hands, and bounce up and down.

Aims of treatment

- To promote relaxation
- To treat Kevin initially sitting on a chair, progressing to treating him on the floor at the end of the session

Treatment

Kevin is treated weekly. He is always willing to be treated and can be quite excitable. He is usually very accepting and interacts well with the therapist.

Kevin has to sit on a chair in the resource centre to be able to participate in activities. This is carried over into the treatment situation, in that the session starts with Kevin in a chair for a reflexology assessment and aromatherapy foot massage. Kevin is then allowed onto the floor for a back massage which he thoroughly enjoys. For this he must sit up and be still during the first part of the session. Should he lie down, the massage is stopped and Kevin is asked to sit up if he wants the massage to continue. Obviously, Kevin's mood and willingness to cooperate are crucial (Table 16.3).

Table 16.3 Oils used in case study 3

Oil	Plant origin	Relevant properties
Geranium	Pelargonium graveolens	Relaxing, balancing
Lavender	Lavendula angustifolia	Relaxing, balancing
Sandalwood	Santalum albumen	Relaxing, balancing

Other oils may be introduced should the therapist feel it necessary to treat a specific condition.

Outcome

By incorporating the appropriate element of Kevin's behaviour programme, the consistency in handling has made it possible to achieve a good working therapeutic relationship with Kevin. On the whole, the same level of calmness and control is carried throughout the day.

Plan

To continue seeing Kevin as before and instruct the staff on the use of a prescribed blend of oils.

Case study 4: Mandy

The purpose of this study is to convey how the main aim of relaxation may be obtained.

Mandy is a 19-year-old woman. She has cerebral palsy with a right-sided hemiparesis and a moderate-to-severe learning disability. She has no speech but vocalises, uses gross gestures, formal and modified Makaton and some idiosyncratic signs. She generally sits in her wheelchair but can weight-bear with a walker. She is always keen to come to her sessions. The first time she was treated was while on holiday with her school. She elected to have her neck and shoulders massaged. During her treatment only lavender was used and Mandy remained in her wheelchair. She thoroughly enjoyed her treatment and, although she did not totally relax, there was a noticeable reduction in the tone around the shoulder area.

Mandy now has a placement at the centre where aromatherapy and reflexology are available weekly. She attends therapy two to three times a month.

Aims of treatment

- To promote relaxation
- To reduce tone
- To contain hyperexcitability
- To improve Mandy's balance reactions while dressing and undressing

Treatment

A full body massage is carried out. Mandy's hyperexcitability tends to increase her tone and she does not fully relax. During the massage while in the prone position, she insists on leaning on her elbows with her head up, but does, however, relax more in the supine position. Alternatively, when a plinth is available, Mandy can be positioned with her arms over the end of the plinth (Table 16.4).

Table 16.4 Oils used in case study 4

Oil	Plant origin	Relevant properties
Sweet margoram	Origanum margorana	Calming, sedative
Lavender	Lavendula angustifolia	Astringent, sedative
Juniper	Juniperis communis	Astringent
Black pepper	Piper nigram	Circulatory stimulant

Outcome

There is some reduction in Mandy's tone but she does not totally relax yet.

Plan

- To continue treatment with the aim of achieving greater relaxation.
- Mandy suffers from a spotty back and it is planned, in the future after discussion with her parents, to use cleansing oils to try to improve this condition.

Conclusion

The aim of this chapter was to provide an insight into how complementary therapies can be used and adapted to benefit people with learning disabilities using aromatherapy and reflexology as examples.

As may be seen from the case studies, all the clients enjoyed and benefited from the therapies. Specific results were noted in some cases, for instance: Liz's symptoms improved and there was a reduction in Mandy's tone. In David's case more long-term results were noted; over 2 years there is positive evidence that his general health has improved. The main aim in most cases is to promote relaxation – a relaxed body is a healthy body.

Kevin's case, where the behaviour modification programme was carried through to therapy, illustrates the fact that these therapies are complementary and should therefore not be seen in isolation but as part of the ongoing programme.

Further reading

Chapter 1

Chartered Society of Physiotherapy (1992) Legal Work Pack. London: CSP.

Diamond B (1995) Legal Aspects of Nursing, 2nd edn. London: Prentice Hall.

Diamond B (1997) Legal Aspects of Occupational Therapy. Oxford: Blackwell Science Ltd.

Diamond B (1998) Physiotherapy in a changing legal context. Founders' Lecture delivered at The Royal Society of Arts. Chartered Society of Physiotherapy, London.

Diamond B (1999) Legal Aspects of Physiotherapy. Oxford: Blackwell Science Ltd.

Ward AD (1990) The Power to Act – the Development of Scots Law for Mentally Handicapped People. Glasgow: Scottish Society for the Mentally Handicapped.

Chapter 2

Portwood M (1999) Developmental Dyspraxia Identification and Intervention: A manual for parents and professionals. London: David Fulton Publishers Ltd.

Chapter 3

Barr ML, Kiernan JA (1983) The Human Nervous System. Philadelphia: Harper & Row Press.

Bazire S (1998) Psychotropic Drug Directory 1998. London: Mark Allen Publishing Ltd.

British Medical Association and the Royal Pharmaceutical Society of Great Britain (1998) British National Formulary, 36th edn. London: BMJ and Royal Pharmaceutical Printing.

Buck JA, Sprague RL (1989) Psychotropic medications of mentally retarded residents in community long term care facilities. American Journal of Mental Retardation 93: 618–23.

Buckley P, Bird J, Harrison G (1995) Psychiatry: A Postgraduate Text, 3rd edn. London: Butterworth-Heinemann.

Deb S (1998) Self injurious behaviour as part of genetic syndromes. British Journal of Psychiatry 172: 385–8.

Fraser WI, Nolan M (1994) Psychiatric disorders in mental retardation. In: Bouras N, ed. Mental Health in Mental Retardation: Recent advances and practices. Cambridge: Cambridge University Press.

Gerlach J (1991) Current views on tardive dyskinesia. Symposium. Atypical antipsychotics: clinical advantages. Pharmacopsychiatry 24: 47.

Gilbert P (1996) The A–Z Reference Book of Syndromes and Inherited Disorders, 2nd edn. Cheltenham: Stanley Thornes Ltd.

Gillberg C (1998) Asperger syndrome and high functioning autism. British Journal of Psychiatry 172: 200–9.

Hemmings H (1984) Psychotropic medication needs of mentally retarded adults before and after transfer from institutions to small units. In: Berg JM, ed. Perspectives and Progress in Mental Retardation, Vol. 2. Baltimore, MD: Park Press.

Howlin P (1997) Interventions for people with autism: recent advances. Advances in Psychiatric Treatment 3: 94–102.

Kanner L (1943) Autistic disturbances of affective contact. Nervous Child 2: 217–50.

Kaplan HI, Sadock BJ (1993) Psychotropic Drug Treatment. Baltimore, MD: Williams & Wilkins.

Linaker OM (1990) Frequency of and determinants for psychotropic drug use in an institution for mentally retarded. British Journal of Psychiatry 156: 525–30.

Ozonoff S (1991) Asperger syndrome, evidence of empirical distinction from high functioning autism. Journal of Child Psychology and Psychiatry and Allied Disciplines 32: 1107–22.

Ozonoff S (1991) Executive function deficit in high functioning autism. Journal of Child Psychology and Psychiatry and Allied Disciplines 32: 1081–105.

Ryan M (1991) Drug use in NSW institutions, innovation for inertia. Australia and New Zealand Journal of Developmental Disabilities 17: 177.

Thomas C, Lewis S (1998) Which atypical antipsychotic. British Journal of Psychiatry 172: 106–10.

Chapter 5

Emerson E (1998) Working with people with challenging behaviour. In: Emerson E, Caine A, Hatton C, Bromley J, eds. Clinical Psychology and People with Intellectual Disability. Chichester: Wiley.

Fripp S, Carroll J (1997) Prioritisation and case weighting. Luton and Dunstable Physiotherapy Department: Presented as a reviewed poster at CSP. Conference, Edinburgh.

Law M, Baptiste S, Carswell A, McColl MA, Polatajlo H, Pollock N (1994) Canadian Occupational Performance Measures, 2nd edn. Toronto: Canadian Association of Occupational Therapists Publications.

Ovretueit J (1993) Co-ordinating Community Care. Buckingham: Open University Press.

Rushfirth S (1985) Community physiotherapy services for people with mental handicap. Physiotherapy 71: 119–23.

Spalding NJ (1997) Rationing our therapy services: is it rightful and reasonable? British Journal of Therapy and Rehabilitation 4: 448–53.

Chapter 6

Bradley H (1991) Assessing Communication Together. York: Mental Handicap Nurses Association, MHNA Publications.

Carke-Keahoe A (1992) Towards effective communication. In: Brown H, Benson S, eds. A Practical Guide to Working with People with Learning Disability. London: Hawker Publishers, pp. 31–40.

Goldbart J, Warner J, Mount H (1994) The Development of Early Communication and Feeding for People who have Profound and Multiple Disabilities – a Workshop Training Package for Parents and Carers. London: MENCAP PIMD.

Knight C (1991) Developing communication through interaction. In: Watson J, ed. Innovatory Practice and Severe Learning Difficulties. Edinburgh: Moray House Publications, pp. 13–24.

Royal National Institute for the Blind (1993) Challenging Behaviour in Visually and Learning Disabled Adults. London: RNIB.

Royal National Institute for the Blind (1993) Stereotypical Behaviour in People with Visual and Learning Disabilities. London: RNIB.

Chapter 7

Hare Association for Physical Abilities. Booklet. 3 Melton Grove, West Bridgford, Nottingham, UK. See Appendix II.

State University of New York (1994) Functional Independence Measure (FIM). Buffalo, NY: State University of New York at Buffalo.

Steiner D, Norman G (1989) Health Measurement Scales: A Practical Guide to their Development and Use. Oxford: Oxford Medical Publications.

Swain J, French S (1999) Therapy and Learning Difficulties: Advocacy, Participation and Partnership. Oxford: Butterworth-Heinemann.

Wise JR (1998) Notes for Chartered Physiotherapists: Working with People with Learning Disabilities. Joyce R Wise, The Stables, College Square, Stokesley TS9 5DN.

Chapter 10

Bobath B (1969) The treatment of neuromuscular disorders by improving patterns of co-ordination. Physiotherapy 55: 18–21.

Bobath B (1978) Adult Hemiplegia: Evaluation and Treatment. London: William Heinemann Medical Books.

Caldwell M, Calder J, Aitken S, Millar S (1995) Use of personal passports with deaf–blind people. Talking Sense Autumn: 9–12.

Fraser BA, Galka G, Hensinger RN (1983) Managing Physical Handicaps: A practical guide for parents, care providers and educators. Baltimore, MD: Paul H Brookes Publishing Co.

Fraser BA, Hensinger RN, Phelps JA (1987) Physical Management of Multiple Handicaps. A professional's guide. Baltimore, MD: Paul H Brookes Publishing Co.

Lacey P, Ouvrey C, eds (1998) People with Profound and Multiple Learning Disorders: A collaborative approach to meeting complex needs. London: David Fulton Publishers Ltd.

Pope PM (1996) Postural management and special seating. In: Edwards S, ed. Neurological Physiotherapy, A Problem Solving Approach. New York: Churchill Livingstone.

Chapter 11

Association of Swimming Therapy (1981) Swimming for the Disabled. London: A & C Black.

Feil N (1992) Validation of the Feil Method – How to Help Disorientated Old. Ohio, IL: Edward Feil Productions.

Hydrotherapy Association of Chartered Society of Physiotherapy (1993) Standards of Good Practice. London: Chartered Society of Physiotherapy.

Reid Campion M, ed. (1997) Hydrotherapy Principles and Practice. Oxford: Butterworth-Heinemann.

Chapter 13

Anderson E (1987) Movement education for children with severe disabilities. British Journal of Physical Education 18: 5.

Hartley E, Rushton C (1984) The therapeutic use of the trampoline in inhibiting abnormal reflex reactions and facilitating normal patterns of movements in some cerebral palsied children. Journal of the Society of Remedial Gymnastics and Recreational Therapy 113: 6–11.

Chapter 14

Houston G (1990) The Red Book of Groups. Norfolk, CT: Rouchester Foundation.

Noorderhaven NG (1999) Intercultural differences – consequences for the physical therapy profession. Physiotherapy 85: 504–10.

Fitness groups

Hunt P, Hillsdon M (1996) Changing Eating and Exercise Behaviour. Oxford: Blackwell Science Ltd.

JABADAO

Chodrow J (1991) Dance Therapy and Depth Psychology. London: Routledge.

Penfield K (1996) Laban movement analysis and group process in dance movement therapy. Movement and Dance Quarterly.

Tai Chi

Panter J, Davis R (1990) The art of Taoist Tai Chi (cultivating mind and body), The Taoist Tai Chi Society of Canada. Toronto: Canadian Cataloguing in Publication Data.

Chapter 16

Sanderson H, Harrison J, with Price S (1991) Aromatherapy and Massage for People with Learning Disabilities. Birmingham: Hands-On Publishing.

Useful addresses

Chapter 2

Cerebral palsy
Capability Scotland
Advice Service Capability Scotland
(ASCS)
11 Ellersly Road
Edinburgh
Scotland

SCOPE
12 Park Crescent
London W1N 4EQ

Down's syndrome
Down's Syndrome Association
155 Mitcham Road
London SW17 9PG

Dyspraxia
The Dyspraxia Trust
8 West Alley
Hitchin
Herts SG5 1EG

Epilepsy
British Epilepsy Association
Anstey House
40 Hanover Square
Leeds LS3 1BE

Chapter 3

Rett Syndrome
UK Rett Syndrome Association
Hartspool
Golden Valley
Castlemorton
Malvern
Worcestershire WR13 6AA

Chapter 6

Autism and Asperger's syndrome
The Scottish Society for Autistic Children
Hilton House
Alloa Business Park
The Whinns
Alloa
Clackmannanshire FK10 3SA

The National Autistic Society
276 Willesden Lane
London NW2 5RB

Communication problems
The Makaton Vocabulary Development Project
31 Firwood Drive
Camberley GU15 3QD

Learning disability
MENCAP
4 Swan Courtyard
Coventry Road
Birmingham B26 1BU

Working with people who have a hearing problem
RAD (Royal Association in aid of Deaf People)
27 Old Oak Road
London W3 7HN

The National Deaf Children's Society
15 Dufferin Street
London EC1Y 8PD

The Royal National Institute for Deaf People (RNID)
19–23 Featherstone Street
London EC1Y 8SL

Working with people who have a visual problem
The Partially Sighted Society
62 Salusbury Road
London NW6 6NS

The Royal National Institute for the Blind (RNIB)
224 Great Portland Street
London W1N 6AA

Chapter 7

Face Profile Learning Disability Walnut Assessment
Devised by PI Clifford,
British Psychological Society

Centre for Outcomes, Research and Effectiveness
Sub-department of Clinical Health Psychology
UCL
Gower Street
London WC1E 6BT

AA Le Roux
TELER Information Pack
TELER PO Box 699
Sheffield S17 3YG

Mary Marlborough Lodge Assessment
Mary Marlborough Disability Centre
Headington
Oxford OX3 7LD

Mobility Opportunities via Education (MOVE)
1990 publication
The office of Kelly F Branton
Kern County Superintendent of Schools
Bakersfield, CA
USA

MOVE International (Europe)
Training and Development Director
University of Wolverhampton
Gorway Road
Walsall WS1 3BD

The OK Health Check
(ISBN 0 95 3001 105)
Fairfield Publications
14 Kingshaven Drive
Penwortham
Preston PR1 9BS

Chapter 9

Hare Association for Physical Abilities
3 Melton Grove
West Bridgford
Nottingham

Chapter 10

Equipment is specific to individual clients and several firms may have to be approached before the most appropriate piece is found.

Many areas have a centre where a range of equipment from different firms can be tried by individual clients. The centre staff will know which equipment can be supplied through Health and Social Services and which needs to be privately purchased.

The NAIDEX exhibitions held throughout the UK are a good opportunity to see and compare latest developments from a range of suppliers.

Comprehensive information about independently assessed equipment can be obtained from the following.

Disability Scotland
Princes House
Shandwick Place
Edinburgh EH2

The Disability Information Trust
Mary Marlborough Centre
Nuffield Orthopaedic Centre
Headington
Oxford OX3 7LD

The following is a small selection of well-known equipment suppliers.

Range of rehabilitation equipment including daily living, seating, positioning, soft play, multisensory – from different firms.

Nottingham Rehab Suppliers – A division of Novora Group Limited
Reg. Office: Ludlow Hill Road
West Bridgford
Nottingham NG2 6HD
(Supply the Bayreuth Standing Frame)

Theraplay Limited
32 Welbeck Road
Darnley Industrial Estate
Glasgow G53 7SD
(Supply the ARROW Walker)

Hoists and mobility aids
ARJO Ltd
St Catherine Street
Gloucester GL1 2SL

Chiltern Invadex
Chiltern House
Wedgwood Road
Bicester
Oxon OX6 7UL

Munro Rehab Ltd
8–10 Dunrobin Court
North Avenue
Clydebank Business Park
Clydebank G81 2QP

Sunrise Medical Ltd
High Street
Wollaston
West Midlands DY8 4PS

Positioning
Active Design
68K Wyrley Road
Witton
Birmingham B6 7BN

Pressure-relieving systems
Qbitus Products
Unit 12, Victoria Park
Lightower Road
Halifax HX1 5WD

Spenco Healthcare International Ltd
Burrell Road
Haywards Heath
West Sussex RH16 1TW

Seating and positioning
*Bioengineering Centre (for
Edinburgh Harness)*
Princess Margaret Rose Hospital
Edinburgh EH10 7ED
(Described by Rennie and Flynn,
1992)

James Leckey Design
Kilwee Industrial Park
Dunmurry BT17 0HD

The Kirton Health Group Ltd
23 Rookwood Way
Haverhill
Suffolk CB9 8PB

Rifton Equipment
Robertsbridge
East Sussex TN32 5DR

Symmetrikit
A Division of the Helping Hand
Company
Unit 9L
Bromyard Road Trading Estate
Ledbury HR8 1NS

Seating, sensory and postural
Jenx Ltd (primarily for children)
Nutwood 28
Limestone Cottage Lane
Sheffield S6 1NJ

Chapter 12

Hon. Sec. for ACPTR
Miss GM Walker, FCSP
The Orchard
Broadlands
Lower Paice Lane
Medstead
Hants GU34 5PX
Tel: 01420 562638

*Course Co-ordinator and
Chairman of ACPTR Course
Planning Committee*
Miss REJ Lane, MBE, FCSP, DIPTP
92 Craigton Road
Aberdeen AB15 7UJ
Tel: 01224 316595

Chapter 13

ACPPLD (via Chartered Society of
Physiotherapy, London, UK) can
supply information on standards
and opportunities for training.

Chapter 14

JABADAO workshops
JABADAO
Branch House
18 Branch Road
Armley
Leeds

Tai Chi
Suitable tapes are available and can
be accessed through 'new age'
outlets.

Sensory equipment
Hope Education Special Needs
Orb Mill
Huddersfield Road
Waterhead
Oldham OO4 2ST

ROMPA
Goyt Side Road
Chesterfield
Derbyshire S40 2PH

SpaceKraft Ltd
Crowgill House
Rosse Street
Shipley
West Yorkshire BD18 3SW

Chapter 15

British Sports Association for the Disabled (BSAD)
Solecast House
13–27 Brunswick Place
London N1 6DX

Special Olympics UK
The Otis Building
43–59 Clapham Road
London SW9 0JZ

Athletics
UK Athletics
30A Harborne Road
Edgbaston
Birmingham B15 3AA

Gymnastics
Special Needs Gymnastics
Wingate House
Wrenbury Hall Drive
Wrenbury, Nantwich
Cheshire CW5 8ES

Outdoor pursuits
Calvert Trust
Kielder Water
Hexham
Northumberland NE48 1BS

Badaguish
Cairngorm Outdoor Centre
Aviemore
Inverness-shire

Rambling
The Fieldfare Trust
67A The Wicker
Sheffield S3 8HT

Volleyball
English Volleyball Association
13 Rectory Road
West Bridgford
Nottingham

Jon Hall (volleyball coach)
Special Olympics NW and GB
Transplant Team
PE Department
Thorn Cross YOI
Appleton Thorn
Warrington
Cheshire

Chapter 16

ISPA (International Society of Professional Aromatherapists)
ISPA House
82 Ashby Road
Hinckley
Leicester LE10 1SN

Acts

Chronically Sick and Disabled Persons Act 1970. London: HMSO.

County Asylums Act 1808. London: HMSO.

Disabled Persons Act (Tom Clarke Bill) 1986. London: HMSO.

Education Act 1981. London: HMSO.

Education (Scotland) Act 1981. London: HMSO.

Health Act 1999. London: HMSO.

Madhouse Act 1774. London: HMSO.

Mental Deficiency Act 1913. London: HMSO.

Mental Deficiency Act 1914. London: HMSO.

Mental Deficiency Act 1927. London: HMSO.

Mental Health Act 1959. London: HMSO.

Mental Health Act (Scotland) 1984. London: HMSO.

Mental Health Act for England and Wales 1983. London: HMSO.

National Health Service Act 1946. London: HMSO.

National Health Service Act (as amended) 1948. London: HMSO.

National Health Service and Community Care Act 1990. London: HMSO.

Vagrancy Acts 1713 and 1714. London: HMSO.

References

Accardo PJ, Capute AJ (1998) Mental retardations. Mental Retardation and Developmental Disabilities Research Reviews 4: 2–5.

ACPPLD Rebound Therapy Working Party (1997) Good Practice in Rebound Therapy. Association of Chartered Physiotherapists for People with Learning Disabilities. London: Chartered Society of Physiotherapy.

Allan P, Pahl J, Quine L (1990) Care Staff in Transition – The Impact on Staff of Changing Services for People with Mental Handicaps. London: HMSO.

American Psychiatric Association (1994) Diagnostic and Statistical Manual of Mental Disorders, 4th edn. Washington, DC: APA.

Appleby KA, Wright A (1980) The technology of self control. Physiotherapy 66: 403–5.

Atkinson J (1994) Physiotherapy in the field of learning disabilities. A study of attitudes. BSc Honours project, unpublished, University of Central England, Birmingham.

Ayres AJ (1972) Sensory Integration and Learning Disabilities. Los Angeles: Western Psychological Services.

Baker EA (1993) Back-riding techniques in therapy. In: Engel B, ed. Therapeutic Riding Programmes. Maddison, WI: Omnipress, pp. 558–62.

Baldry JA, Rossiter D (1995) Introduction of integrated care pathways to a neuro-rehabilitation unit. Physiotherapy 81: 432–4.

Band R (1998) The NHS – Health for All. London: Royal Society for Mentally Handicapped Children and Adults.

Barclay J (1994) In Good Hands. Oxford: Butterworth-Heinemann.

Barnes C (1991) Disabled People in Britain and Discrimination: A case for anti-discriminatory legislation. London: Hurst & Co.

Barnes J, Barrell A, Dennis C, Jenkins J (1993) Standards for Good Practice in Physiotherapy Services for People with Learning Disabilities. London: Association of Chartered Physiotherapists for People with Learning Disabilities, CSP.

Bartlett EG (1990) Weight Training. London: David Charles.

Bartley J (1998) Cycles for All: A therapy in leisure initiative. Lancaster Hospital.

Bell E, Watson A (1985) The prevention of deformity in cerebral palsy. Physiotherapy Practice 1: 86–92.

Bellefeuille-Reid D, Jakubek S (1989) Adaptive positioning intervention for premature infants: Issues for paediatric occupational therapy practice. British Journal of Occupational Therapy 52: 93–7.

Berger P, Luckman T (1987) The Social Construction of Reality, revised edn. London: Pelican Books.

Berquet KH (1977) Maskulare Kreuzschmerzen bei Haltungsschaden. In: Junghanns H, ed. Lumbalgie und Ischialgie. Stuttgart: Hippokrates-Veil, pp. S27–8.

Bertucci B (1987) The AVCA Volleyball Handbook. London: Master Press.

Betts T (1998) Epilepsy, Psychiatry and Learning Difficulty. London: Martin Dunitz.

Bhattacharya A, McCutcheon EP, Sharvtz E, Greenleaf JE (1980) Results from a NASA supported study. Journal of Applied Physiology 49(suppl): 881–7.

Bobath K, Bobath B (1975) Motor Development in the Different Types of Cerebral Palsy. London: Heinemann.

Bobath K, Bobath B (1984) The Neuro-development Treatment. London: The Bobath Centre for Children with Cerebral Palsy.

Bohannon RW (1989) Correlation of lower limb strengths and other variables with standing performance in stroke patients. Physiotherapy Canada 41: 198–202.

Brown DA, Effgen SK, Palisano RJ (1998) Performance following ability – focused physical therapy intervention in individuals with severely limited physical and cognitive abilities. Physical Therapy 78: 934–50.

Brown FR III, Aylward EH (1996) Introduction. In: Brown FR III, Aylward EH, Keogh BK, eds. Diagnosis and Management of Learning Disability. San Diego, London: Singular Publishing Group Inc., p. 2.

Brown J (1992) The residential setting in mental handicap: an overview of selected policy initiatives. In: Thompson T, Mathias P, eds. Standards and Mental Handicap. London: Baillière Tindall, pp. 106–22.

Bruce M (1988) Occupational therapy in group treatment. In: Scott DW, Katz N, eds. Occupational Therapy in Mental Health Principles and Practice. London: Taylor & Francis Ltd.

Carr JH, Shepherd RB (1987) Movement Science: Foundation for Physical Therapy in Rehabilitation. Rockville, MD: Aspen Publishers.

Cashmore E (1990) Making Sense of Sports, 2nd edn. London: Routledge.

Chadwick D, ed. (1997) The Encyclopaedia of Epilepsy, 2nd edn. Oxford: Alden Colour.

Channel 4 (1994) Go! London: Sports Council.

Channer KS, Barrow D, Barrow R, Osborne M, Ives G (1996) Changes in haemodynamic parameters following Tai Chi Chuan and aerobic exercise in patients recovering from myocardial infarction. Postgraduate Medical Journal 72: 349–51.

Chartered Society of Physiotherapy (1989) Physiotherapy helpers and community and other support workers. Physiotherapy 75: 289–91.

Chartered Society of Physiotherapy (1991) Disabled People and their Families (leaflet). London: Chartered Society of Physiotherapy.

Chartered Society of Physiotherapy (1996a) Standards of Physiotherapy Practice. London: Chartered Society of Physiotherapy.

Chartered Society of Physiotherapy (1996b) Information Paper PA6: The delegation of tasks to physiotherapy assistants and other workers. London: Chartered Society of Physiotherapy.

Cheseldine S (1991) Community mental handicap teams. In: Fraser WI, MacGillivray RC, Green A, eds. Hallas' Caring for People with Mental Handicaps. Oxford: Butterworth-Heinemann, pp. 215–24.

Cheseldine SE, Jeffree DM (1981) Mentally handicapped adolescents: their use of leisure time. Journal of Mental Deficiency 25: 49–59.

Citterio DN (1985) The influence of the horse in neuromotorial evolution. In: Proceedings of the 5th International Congress on Therapeutic Riding. Milan, Italy: ANIRE Association.

Cogher L, Savage E, Smith MF, eds (1992) Cerebral Palsy – The Child and Young Person. London: Chapman & Hall Medical.

College of Occupational Therapists (1995) Standards, Policies and Procedures Guidelines for Occupational Therapy Services for Clients with Learning Disabilities. SPP115A. London: College of Occupational Therapists.

College of Occupational Therapists (1996) The Role of Support Workers in the Delivery of Occupational Therapy Services. London: College of Occupational Therapists.

Collen FM, Wade DT, Robb GF, Bradshaw CM (1991) The Rivermead Mobility Index: A further development of the Rivermead Motor Assessment. International Disability Studies 13: 50–4.

Collins (1994) English Dictionary and Thesaurus. Glasgow: HarperCollins.

Colson JHC, Collinson FW (1983) Progressive Exercise Therapy in Rehabilitation and Physical Education. Bristol: Wright PSG.

Cooperman DR, Bartucci E, Dietrick E, Millar EA (1987) Hip dislocation in spastic cerebral palsy: long term consequences. Journal of Paediatric Orthopaedics 7: 268–276.

Corbett JA (1990) Psychiatric morbidity and mental retardation. In: James FE, Snaith RP, eds. Psychiatric Illness and Mental Handicap. London: Gaskell, pp. 397–407.

Cotton E (1970) Integration of treatment and education in cerebral palsy. Physiotherapy April: 143–7.

Cotton M (1981) Out of Doors with Handicapped People. London: Souvenir Press Ltd.

Coupe J, Goldbart J (1988) Communication before Speech – Normal Development and Impaired Communication. London: BIMH Publications, Chapman & Hall.

Crichton JU, Mackinnon M, White CP (1995) The life expectancy of persons with cerebral palsy. Developmental Medicine and Child Neurology 37: 567–76.

Croal I (1999) Effects of neuromuscular electrical stimulation (NMES) on spastic and non spastic muscle of children with cerebral palsy. Association of Paediatric Chartered Physiotherapists Journal 90: 34–48.

Crook P, Stott R, Rose M, Peters S, Salmon P, Stanley I (1998) Adherence to group exercise: physiotherapist-led experimental programmes. Physiotherapy 84: 366–72.

Cullen C (1991) Bridging the gap between the treatment techniques and service philosophy. In: Harris J, ed. Service Responses to People with Learning Difficulties and Challenging Behaviour. Kidderminster: British Institute of Mental Handicap, Cookley Printers Ltd, pp. 55–7.

Cyriax J (1982) Textbook of Orthopaedic Medicine, Vol. 1, 8th edn. London: Baillière Tindall.

Davis BC, Harrison RA (1988) Hydrotherapy in Practice. Edinburgh: Churchill Livingstone.

DeLubersac R (1985) The psychomotor mechanism, riding and the horse. In: Proceedings of the 5th International Congress of Therapeutic Riding, Milan, Italy.

Department of Education and Science (1978) Special Educational Needs (Warnock Report), Cmnd. 7212. London: HMSO.

Department of Health (1988) Community Care: Agenda for Action (Griffiths Report). London: HMSO.

Department of Health (1989) Caring for People: Community Care in the Next Decade and Beyond, Cmnd. 849. London: HMSO.

Department of Health (1995) The Health of the Nation – A Strategy for People with Learning Disabilities. Oldham: HMSO.

Department of Health (England) (1997) The New NHS: Modern, Dependable. London: The Stationery Office.

Department of Health (Wales) (1997) NHS Wales: Putting Patients First. London: The Stationery Office.

Department of Health and Social Security (1971) Better Services for the Mentally Handicapped, Cmnd. 4683. London: HMSO.

Department of Health and Social Security (1978) Development Team for the Mentally Handicapped: First Report – 1976–77. London: HMSO.

Department of Health and Social Security (1979) Report of the Committee of Enquiry into Mental Handicap Nursing and Care (Jay Report), Cmnd. 74681 (I) and 74681 (II). London: HMSO.

Department of Health and Social Security (1987) Mental Handicap: Progress, Problems and Priorities: A review of mental handicap services in England since the 1971 White Paper, Better Services for the Mentally Handicapped. London: HMSO.

Devon County Council (1993) The Devon Approach to Physical Education: Athletics. Exeter: Devon County Council.

Disability Services Commission – Western Australia (1998) Local Area Co-ordination – A New Approach to Service Delivery for People with Disabilities and Their Families. Submission for the 'Service Design – Delivery' category of 1998 Premier's Awards, Australia.

Dougans I, Ellis S (1992) The Art of Reflexology. Shaftsbury, Dorset: Element Books Ltd.

East C (1991) Intent to Communicate, unpublished, Southampton University.

Enderby P (1997) Therapy Outcome Measures. London: Singular Publishing Group Inc.

Environ Organisation (1996) Small Steps, Giant Leaps: A review of the feet first project. London: Environment and Transport 2000.

Ferber R (1986) Solve your Child's Sleep Problems. London: Dorling Kindersley.

Finklestein V (1990) Disability and the helper – helped relationships: an historical view. In: Brechin A, Liddiard P, Swain J, eds. Handicap in a Social World. Milton Keynes: Hodder & Stoughton, Open University Press, pp. 231–46.

Firth H, Rapley M (1990) From Acquaintance to Friendship: Issues for people with learning disabilities. Kidderminster: BIMH Publications.

Fisher AG, Murray EA, Bundy AC (1993) Sensory Integration: Theory and practice. Philadelphia: FA Davis & Co.

Fleck CA (1997) Hippotherapy: Mechanics of human walking and horseback riding. In: Engel B, ed. Rehabilitation with the Aid of the Horse: A collection of studies. Durango, CO: Therapy Services.

Fletcher B (1998) Moving and Handling for Chartered Physiotherapists. London: Chartered Society of Physiotherapy.

Fraser WI, Deb S (1994) The use of psychotropic medications in people with learning disabilities, toward rational prescribing. Human Psychopharmacology 9: 259–72.

Fraser WI, Green AM (1991) Changing perspectives on mental handicap. In: Fraser WI, MacGillivray RC, Green AM, eds. Hallas' Caring for People with Mental Handicaps. Oxford: Butterworth-Heinemann, pp. 1–7.

French S (1993) Disability, impairment or something in between. In: Swain J, Finklestein V, French S, Oliver M, eds. Disabling Barriers – Enabling Environments, 1st edn. London: Sage, pp. 17–25.

French S (1994) Attitudes of health professionals towards disabled people. Physiotherapy 80: 687–93.

Fryers T (1997) Impairment, disability and handicap: categories and classifications. In: Russell O, ed. The Psychiatry of Learning Disabilities. London: The Royal College of Psychiatrists, pp. 16–30.

Fryers T, Russell O (1997) Applied epidemiology. In: Russell O, ed. The Psychiatry of Learning Disabilities. London: The Royal College of Psychiatrists, pp. 31–47.

Fulford GE, Brown JK (1976) Position as a cause of deformity in children with cerebral palsy. Developmental Medicine and Child Neurology 18: 305–14.

Gaag A, ed. (1996) Communicating Quality. London: Royal College of Speech and Language Therapists.

Gage J (1991) Gait Analysis in Cerebral Palsy. London: MacKeith Press.

Gardiner D (1971) The Principles of Exercise Therapy (reprinted with additions). London: G Bell & Sons Ltd, pp. 230–4.

Gastason R (1985) Psychiatric illness among mentally retarded, a Swedish population study. Acta Psychiatrica Scandinavica Supplementum 71.

Gates B (1997) Learning Disabilities. Edinburgh: Churchill Livingstone.

Gething L (1993) Attitudes towards people with learning disabilities of physiotherapists and members of the general population. Australian Journal of Physiotherapy 39: 291–6.

Gillberg C (1986) Psychiatric disorders in mildly and severely mentally retarded urban children and adolescents. British Journal of Psychiatry 149: 68–74.

Gold D (1989) Putting leisure into life. Entourage 4: 10–11.

Goldfarb BJ, Simon SR (1984) Gait patterns in patients with amyotrophic lateral sclerosis. Archives of Physical Medicine and Rehabilitation 65: 61–5.

Golding R, Goldsmith L (1986) The Caring Persons Guide to Handling the Severely Multiply Handicapped. London: MacMillan Education Limited.

Goldsmith E, Golding RM, Garstang RA, Macrae AW (1992) A technique to measure windswept deformity. Physiotherapy 78: 235–42.

Goldsmith J, Goldsmith L (1996) Symmetrical Body Support: A Carer's Guide to the Management of Posture. Ledbury: The Helping Hand Company (Ledbury) Ltd.

Goldsmith J, Goldsmith L, Peters A, Hewitt L (1998) Postural Care Workshop for Families. Ledbury: The Helping Hand Company (Ledbury) Ltd.

Goodridge D, Shorvon S (1983) Epileptic seizures in a population of 6000. (1) Demography, diagnosis and classification and the role of the hospital services. (2) Treatment and prognosis. British Medical Journal 287: 641–7.

Gordon CT, State RC, Nelson JE, Hamburger SD, Rapoport JL (1993) A double blind comparison of clomipramine, desipramine and placebo in the treatment of autistic disorders. Archives of General Psychiatry 50: 441–7.

Green EM, Mulcahy CM, Pountney TE, Ablett RH (1993) The Chailey standing support for children and young adults with motor impairment: a developmental approach. British Journal of Occupational Therapy 56: 13–18.

Grey T (1996) Foreword in Sport and Leisure. Oxford: The Disability Information Trust.

Grossman HJ, ed. (1973) Manual on Terminology and Classification in Mental Retardation. Washington, DC: American Association on Mental Deficiency.

Haggard LM, Williams DR (1992) Identity affirmation through leisure activities: leisure symbols of the self. National Recreation and Park Association 24: 1–18.

Hallsworth M (1995) Positioning the preterm infant. Paediatric Nursing 8: 18–20.

Hamilton K (1997) An introduction to treatment with the use of the horse. In: Engel B, ed. Therapeutic Riding 11. Strategies for Rehabilitation. Maddison, WI: Omnipress.

Hardan A, Sahl R (1997) Psychopathology in children and adolescents with developmental disabilities. Research in Developmental Disabilities 18: 369–82.

Hari M, Akos K (1988) Conductive Education. London: Routledge.

Harris J, ed. (1991) Service Responses to People with Learning Difficulties and Challenging Behaviour. Kidderminster: British Institute of Mental Handicap, Cookley Printers.

Hart J, Hart L (1987) 100% Fitness. Surrey: Elliot Right Way Books.

Health Services Advisory Committee (1998) Manual Handling in the Health Services, Health and Safety Commission. London: HMSO.

Henderson Sir DK (1964) The Evolution of Psychiatry in Scotland. Edinburgh: E & S Livingstone Ltd.

Herge EA, Campbell JE (1998) The role of the occupational and physical therapist in the rehabilitation of the older adult with mental retardation. Topics in Geriatric Rehabilitation 13(4): 12–21.

Hewett D (1994) Access to Communication. London: David Fulton.

Hewett D (1996) How to do intensive interaction. In: Collis M, Lacy P, eds. Interactive Approaches to Teaching – A Framework for INSET. London: David Fulton.

Hewitt L, Peters A, Goldsmith S (1998) Provision of a night time postural care service within a community setting. Physiotherapy in press.

Higgs J, Titchen A (1995a) The nature, generation and verification of knowledge. Physiotherapy 81: 521–9.

Higgs J, Titchen A (1995b) Propositional, professional and personal knowledge in clinical reasoning. In: Higgs J, Jones M, eds. Clinical Reasoning in the Health Professions. Oxford: Butterworth-Heinemann, pp. 129–46.

Hoffer M and associates (1973) Functional ambulation in patients with myelomeningocele. Journal of Bone and Joint Surgery 55A: 137–48.

Hollins S (1985) The dynamics of teamwork. In: Craft M, Bicknell J, Hollins S, eds. Mental Handicap. Eastbourne: Baillière Tindall, pp. 281–7.

Hollins S, Esterhuyzen A (1997) Bereavement and grief in adults with learning disabilities. British Journal of Psychiatry 170: 497–501.

Honeybourne J, Hill M, Moors H (1996) Advanced Physical Education and Sport. London: Stanley Thornes.

Horak FB (1987) Clinical measurement of postural control in adults. Physical Therapy 67: 1881–5.

Illingworth RS (1987) The Development of the Infant and Young Child, Normal and Abnormal, 9th edn. Edinburgh: Churchill Livingstone.

Ingram TTS (1964) Paediatric Aspects of Cerebral Palsy. Edinburgh: Livingstone.

International League Against Epilepsy (1981) Commission on Classification and Terminology. A proposal for a revised seizure classification. Epilepsia 22: 489–501.

Jahoda A, Cattermole M (1995) Activities of people with severe learning disabilities: living with purpose or just killing time? Disability and Society 10: 2.

Jamieson N (1989) Hand contractures in mental illness. Physiotherapy 75: 496–9.

Jan JE, Estezel H, Appleton RE (1994) The treatment of sleep disorders with melatonin. Developmental Medicine and Child Neurology 36: 97–107.

Jenkins J, Felce D, Mansell J, de Kock U (1983) Bereweeke Skill-Teaching System Handbook. Berkshire: NFER-Nelson.

Johnson A (1997) Cor I was over the hills: the benefits of walking as viewed through the eyes of people with learning disabilities. Unpublished dissertation for Master's Degree, Sheffield University.

Johnson R (1993) Attitudes don't just hang in the air . . . disabled people's perceptions of physiotherapists. Physiotherapy 79: 619–27.

Johnstone M (1987) Restoration of Motor Function in the Stroke Patient: A physiotherapist's approach, 3rd edn. Edinburgh: Churchill Livingstone.

Kanner L (1964) A History of the Care and Study of the Mentally Retarded. Springfield, IL: Charles C Thomas.

Kay B, Rose S, Turnbull J (1995) Continuing the Commitment. The Report of Learning Disability Project. London: Department of Health.

Kennedy DW, Smith RW, Austin DR (1991) Special Recreation: Opportunities for Persons with Disabilities. Dubuque, Iowa: WC Brown.

Kerr M, Fraser W, Felce D (1996) Primary health care for people with a learning disability: a keynote review. British Journal of Learning Disabilities 24: 2–8.

Kiresuk TJ, Smith A, Cardillo JE, eds (1994) Goal Attainment Scaling: Applications, theory and measurement. Hillsdale, NJ: Lawrence Erlbaum.

Kirtley C (1999) East meets West in Hong Kong. The Standard, Vicon Motion System, 1, 1–2, Oxford Metrics Ltd, Oxford (US subsidiary Vicon Motions System, Tustin).

Klenerman P, Sander J, Shorvon S (1993) Mortality in patients with epilepsy: a study of patients in long-term residential care. Journal of Neurology, Neurosurgery, and Psychiatry 52: 659–62.

Kotagel S, Gibbons VP, Stith JA (1994) Sleep abnormalities in patients with severe cerebral palsy. Developmental Medicine and Child Neurology 36: 304–11.

Kristiansen K, Ness NE (1987) Hjelpesystenet: Igar, I dag I morgan. Trondheim.

Lane H (1977) The Wild Boy of Aveyron. London: George Allen & Unwin Ltd.

Latto K, Norrice B (1987) Give Us a Chance. London: Disabled Living Foundation.

Le Roux AA (1993) TELER: the concept. Physiotherapy 79: 755–8.

Levitt S (1977) Treatment of Cerebral Palsy and Motor Delay. Oxford: Blackwell.

Lindsey M (1998) Signposts for success. In: Commissioning and Providing Health Services for People with Learning Disabilities. London: Department of Health.

Loudon JB (Chairman) (1992) The Future of Mental Handicap Hospital Services in Scotland. Edinburgh: HMSO.

Lowe K, Felce D (1995) The definition of challenging behaviour in practice. British Journal of Mental Disability 23: 118–23.

Lowthian P (1997) Notes on the pathogenesis of serious pressure sores. British Journal of Nursing 6: 907–12.

Luckasson R, Coulter DL, Polloway EA et al. (1992) Mental Retardation: Definition, Classification and Systems of Support. Washington, DC: American Association on Mental Retardation.

Luckey RE, Shapiro IG (1974) Recreation: An essential aspect of habilitative programming. Mental Retardation October: 33–5.

Lund J (1985a) Epilepsy and psychiatric disorder in the mentally retarded adult. Acta Psychiatrica Scandinavica 72: 557.

Lund J (1985b) The prevalence of psychiatric morbidity in the mentally retarded adult. Acta Psychiatrica Scandinavica 72: 563.

Macadam M, Rodgers J (1997) A multi-disciplinary, multi-agency approach. In: O'Hara J, Sperlinger A, eds. Adults with Learning Disabilities. Chichester: John Wiley & Sons, pp. 187–204.

McConkey R, Walsh J, Mulcahy M (1981) The recreational pursuits of mentally handicapped adults. International Journal of Rehabilitation Research 4: 493–9.

McEwen C, Millar S (1993) Communication Passports. Augmentative Communication in Practice: Scotland. Collected Papers: Study Day. CALL Centre, University of Edinburgh.

McGibbon NH (1994) Motor learning: The common denominator. In: Proceedings of the 8th International Therapeutic Riding Conference, New Zealand, pp. 94–6.

McKay C (1998) Appendix to Restraint of Residents with Mental Impairment in Care Homes and Hospitals. Edinburgh: Mental Welfare Commission for Scotland.

McKenzie RA (1981) The Lumbar Spine, Mechanical Diagnosis and Therapy. New Zealand: Spinal Publications.

Mahoney FI, Barthel DW (1965) Functional evaluation – The Barthel Index. Maryland State Medical Journal 14: 61–5.

Maitland GD (1986) Vertebral Manipulation, 5th edn. Oxford: Butterworth-Heinemann.

Malin N (1995) Services for People with Learning Disabilities. London: Routledge.

Malloy E (1998) A patient with mental retardation and possible panic disorder. Psychiatric Services 49: 105–6.

Mandal AC (1984) The Correct Height of School Furniture. Physiotherapy 70(2): 48–53.

Martin J (1981) The Halliwick Method. Physiotherapy 67: 296–7.

Maslow A (1962) Towards a Psychology of Being. Princeton: Van Nostrand Reinhold.

Mathews D, Hegarty J (1997) The OK Health Check: A health assessment checklist for people with learning disabilities. British Journal for Learning Disabilities 25: 138–43.

Medical Devices Agency (1995) Upholstered chairs for children: a comparative evaluation. Disability equipment assessment no. A16.

Mesibov GB (1990) Normalisation and its relevance today. Journal of Autism and Developmental Disorders 20: 379–90.

Minear WL (1956) A classification of cerebral palsy. Paediatrics 18: 841.

Mittler P (1979) People not Patients: Problems and Policies in Mental Handicap. Cambridge: Methuen & Co Ltd.

Morris J (1991) Pride against Prejudice. Transforming Attitudes to Disability. London: Women's Press.

Morris P (1969) Put Away. London: Routledge & Kegan Paul.

Muir WJ (1998) Learning disability. In: Johnstone EC, Freeman CPL, Zealley AK, eds. Companion to Psychiatric Studies. Edinburgh: Churchill Livingstone, pp. 597–647.

Mulcahy CM (1986) An approach to the assessment of sitting ability for the prescription of seating. Occupational Therapy November: 367–8.

Mulcahy CM, Pountney TE, Nelham RL, Green EM, Billington GD (1988) Adaptive seating for motor handicap: Problems, a solution, assessment and prescription. British Journal of Occupational Therapy 51: 347–52.

Murphy C, Boyle C, Schendel D, Decoufle P, Yeargin-Allsopp M (1998) Epidemiology of mental retardation in children. Mental Retardation and Developmental Disabilities Research Reviews 4: 6–13.

National Health Services Executive (1999) Clinical Governance, Quality in the New NHS. Bristol: NHSE.

Nelham RL (1984) Principles and practice in manufacture of seating for the handicapped. Physiotherapy 70: 54–8.

Nirje B (1969) The normalisation principle and its human management implications. In: Kugel R, Wolfensberger W, eds. Changing Patterns in Residential Services for the Mentally Retarded. President's Committee on Mental Retardation 179–195 (b), Washington.

North West Council for Sport (1992–1996) Focus on Sport – Athletics North West. Warrington, Cheshire.

Novosel S (1984) Psychiatric disorder in adults admitted to hospital. British Journal of Mental Subnormality 30: 54–8.

O'Connor and Tizard, quoted by Morris P (1969) Put Away. London: Routledge & Keegan Paul, p. 7.

O'Dwyer NJ, Nelson PD, Nash J (1989) Mechanism of muscle growth related to muscle contracture in cerebral palsy. Developmental Medicine and Child Neurology 31: 543–52.

Ockleford A (1994) Objects of Reference. Promoting Communication Skills with Visually Impaired Children who have Other Disabilities. London: Royal National Institute for the Blind.

Odumnbaku Auty PM (1990) Hydrotherapy – Evaluating and Costing a Physiotherapy Intervention (Modality) in the Service for People with Learning Disabilities using Hydrotherapy as an Example. Is it a cost effective resource? London: Chartered Society of Physiotherapy.

Odumnbaku Auty PM (1991) Physiotherapy for People with Learning Disabilities. London: Woodhead Faulkener.

Okawa M, Takahashi K, Sasaki H (1986) Disturbance in circadian rhythms in severely brain damaged patients correlated with CT findings. Journal of Neurology 233: 274–82.

Oliver M (1993) Redefining Disability a challenge to research. In: Swain J, Finklestein V, French S, Oliver M, eds. Disabling Barriers – Enabling Environments, 1st edn. London: Sage, pp. 61–7.

Oppenheim AN (1992) Questionnaire Design, Interviewing and Attitude Measurements. London: Pinter Publisher.

Papathanasiou I, Lyon-Maris SJ (1997) Outcome measurements and case weightings in physiotherapy services for people with learning disabilities. Physiotherapy 84: 633–8.

Parry R, Vass C (1997) Training and assessment of physiotherapy assistants. Physiotherapy 83: 33–40.

Partridge C (1994) Meeting physical needs of adults with learning disabilities and their carers: a neglected area. Journal of the Royal Society of Medicine 87: 365–6.

Patel P, Goldberg D, Mass S (1994) Psychiatric morbidity in older people with moderate and severe learning disability: II The prevalence study. British Journal of Psychiatry 163: 481–91.

Peterson V (1981) Variations on a G Force. Article received from 1240, East 800 North, Utah 84097.

Pountney TE, Mulcahy C, Green E (1990) Early development of postural control. Physiotherapy 76: 799–802.

Price S (1983) Practical Aromatherapy. London: Thorsous.

Reid A, Chesson R (1998) Goal Attainment Scaling: Is it appropriate for stroke patients and their physiotherapists? Physiotherapy 84: 136–44.

Reid Campion M (1991) Hydrotherapy in Paediatrics, 2nd edn. Oxford: Butterworth-Heinemann.

Rennie J, Flynn M (1992) A prototype seating harness for people with severe learning disability and physical handicap. Physiotherapy 78: 740–4.

Richardson S, Katz M, Koller H, McLaren J, Rubenstine B (1979) Some characteristics of a population of mentally retarded young adults in a British city. Journal of Mental Deficiency Research 23: 275–87.

Riede D (1988) Physiotherapy on the Horse. Translated and edited by G Tebay. Washington, DC: Delta Society.

RNIB (1995) Improving environments for people with visual and learning disabilities. Focus Fact sheets, January. London: Royal National Institute for the Blind.

Robb JE (1994) Orthopaedic management of cerebral palsy. In: Benson MKD, Fixsen JA, Macnicol MF, eds. Children's Orthopaedics and Fractures. Edinburgh: Churchill Livingstone, pp. 255–75.

Roggenbuck JW, Loomis RJ, Dagostino J (1990) Learning the benefits of leisure. Journal of Leisure Research 22: 112–24.

Rosser RM (1976) Recent studies using a global approach to measuring illness. Medical Care 14 (suppl 5).

Rousch SE (1986) Health professionals as contributors to attitudes towards persons with disabilities. Physical Therapy 66: 241.

Russell D and associates (1989) Gross Motor Function Measure, a means to evaluate the effects of physical therapy. Developmental Medicine and Child Neurology 31: 341–52.

Rutter M, Tizard J, Yale W, Graham P, Whitmore K (1976) Isle of Wight studies 1964–1974. Psychological Medicine 6: 313–32.

Samdahl DM (1992) Leisure in our lives: exploring the common leisure occasion. Journal of Leisure Research 24: 19–32.

Sander J, Hart Y, Johnston A et al. (1990) National General Practice Study of Epilepsy: newly diagnosed epilepsy seizures in the general population. Lancet 336: 1267–71.

Saunders L (1997a) Issues involved in delegation to assistants. Physiotherapy 83: 141–6.

Saunders L (1997b) A systematic approach to delegation in out-patient physiotherapy. Physiotherapy 83: 582–9.

Savage DR (1970) Intellectual assessment. In: Mitler P, ed. The Psychological Assessment of Mental and Physical Handicaps. London: Methuen.

Scheerenberger RC (1987) A History of Mental Retardation. Baltimore, MD: Paul H Brooks Publishing Co. Inc.

Schwarz C (1993) Chambers Dictionary. Edinburgh: Chambers Harrap Publishers Ltd.

Scottish Health Service Planning Council – Scottish Home and Health Department (1980) Scottish Health Authorities Priorities for the Eighties. Edinburgh: HMSO, pp. 69–73, 19–20, chap. V1, p. 17, chap. V11 (ii).

Scottish Health Service Planning Council – Scottish Home and Health Department (1988) Scottish Health Authorities Review of Priorities for the Eighties and Nineties. Edinburgh: HMSO.

Scottish Home and Health Department (1970) The Staffing of Mental Deficiency Hospitals. Edinburgh: HMSO.

The Scottish Office (1997) Designed to Care (Scotland). Edinburgh: The Stationary Office.

Scrivens E (1986) The National Health Service: origins and issues. In: Patrick DL, Scambler G, eds. Sociology as Applied to Medicine. London: Baillière Tindall, pp. 204–10.

Skinner AT, Thomson AM, eds (1983) Duffield's Exercises in Water, 3rd edn. London: Baillière Tindall.

Smith S, Cook D (1990) A study in the use of rebound therapy for adults with special needs. Physiotherapy 76: 734–5.

Swain J (1993) Taught helplessness? Or a say for disabled students in schools. In: Swain J, Finklestein V, French S, Oliver M, eds. Disabling Barriers – Enabling Environments. London: Sage, pp. 155–62.

Szymanski LS, Crocker AC (1989) Mental retardation. In: Kaplan HI, Sadock BJ, eds. Comprehensive Textbook of Psychiatry. Baltimore, MD: Williams & Wilkins, pp. 1653–71.

Tardieu R, Lespargot A, Tabary C, Bret MD (1988) How long must the soleus muscle be stretched each day to prevent contractures. Developmental Medicine and Child Neurology 30: 3–10.

Thomas A, Bax M, Smyth D (1987) The Provision of Support Services for the Handicapped Young Adult. London: Department of Child Health, Charing Cross and Westminster Medical School.

Tilstone C (1991) Teaching Children with Severe Learning Disabilities. London: David Fulton Publishers Ltd.

Tredgold (1908) Textbook on Mental Deficiency.

Tredgold (1909) The feeble-minded: a social danger. Eugenics Review.

Trent JW (1994) Inventing the Feeble Mind – A History of Mental Retardation in the United States. Berkeley, CA: University of California Press.

Turner S, Sweeney D, Hayes L (1995) Developments in Community Care for Adults with Learning Disabilities: A review of 1993/94 Community Care Plans. Hester Adrian Research Centre, University of Manchester. London: HMSO.

Turrill S (1992) Supported positioning in intensive care. Paediatric Nursing May: 24–7.

Tyne A, O'Brien J (1981) The Principles of Normalisation. London: Campaign for Mentally Handicapped People/Campaign for Mental Handicap Education and Research Association (CMH/CMHERA).

United Kingdom Central Council for Nursing, Midwifery and Health Visiting (1998a) Code of Professional Conduct. London: UKCC.

United Kingdom Central Council for Nursing, Midwifery and Health Visiting (1998b) Guidelines for Mental Health and Learning Disability Nursing. London: UKCC.

United Nations Declaration on the Rights of Mentally Retarded Persons (1971) General Assembly Resolution 2865 (XXVI) of December 20, 1971.

United Nations Declaration on the Rights of Disabled Persons (1975) General Assembly Resolution 3447 (XXX) of December 9, 1975.

Vitiello B, Behar D (1992) Mental retardation and psychiatric illness. Hospital and Community Psychiatry 43: 494.

Wade DT (1992) Measurement in Neurological Rehabilitation. Oxford: Oxford University Press.

Wade DT, Parker V, Langton Hewer R (1986) Memory disturbance after stroke: frequency and associated losses. International Rehabilitation Medicine 8: 60–4.

Walker M (1970) The Makaton Vocabulary Development Project, 31 Firwood Drive, Camberley, Surrey.

Wankel LM, Berger BG (1990) The psychological and social benefits of sport and physical activity. Journal of Leisure Research 22: 167–82.

Ward A, Rippe J (1988) Walking for Health and Fitness. London: JB Lippincott.

Welsh Office (1983) All Wales Strategy for the Development of Services for Mentally Handicapped People. London: HMSO.

Wertheim A (1983) Leisure. London: Values into Action.

WHO (1980) International Classification of Impairments, Disabilities and Handicaps. Geneva: World Health Organization.

WHO (1992) The ICD-10 Classification of Mental and Behavioural Disorders. Clinical descriptions and diagnostic guidelines. Geneva: World Health Organization.

WHO (1993) The ICD-10 Classification of Mental and Behavioural Disorders. Diagnostic criteria for research. Geneva: World Health Organization.

Williams J (1991) Calculating Staffing Levels in Physiotherapy Services. Rotherham: Pampas Publications.

Willoughby C, Polatajko H (1995) Motor problems in children with developmental co-ordination disorder: review of literature. American Journal of Occupational Therapy 49: 787–93.

Wilson C (1990) Programmes for pleasure: combine fitness with enjoyment in Australia. Ageing International, Winter Edition.

Wise JR (1998) Notes for Chartered Physiotherapists: Working with People with Learning Disabilities. Joyce R Wise, The Stables, College Square, Stokesley TS9 5DN.

Wolf SL, Barnhart HX, Kutner NG, McNeely E, Coogler C, Xu T (1996) The Atlanta FICST Study: reducing frailty and falls in older persons: an investigation of Tai Chi and computerised balance training. Journal of the American Geriatric Society 44: 489–97.

Wolfensberger W (1972) The Principle of Normalisation in Human Services. Toronto: National Institute on Mental Retardation through Leonard Crainford.

Wolfensberger W (1992) A Brief Introduction to Social Role Valorisation as a High-order Concept for Structuring Human Services, revised edn. Syracuse, NY: Training Institute for Human Service Planning, Leadership and Changing Agentry (Syracuse University).

Wolfensberger W, Thomas S (1983) PASSING (Programme Analysis of Service Systems' Implementation of Normalisation Goals): Normalisation Criteria and Ratings Manual, 2nd edn. Toronto: National Institute on Mental Retardation.

Young A, Chesson R (1998) Goal Attainment Scaling as a method of measuring clinical outcome for children with learning disabilities. British Journal of Occupational Therapy 60: 111–14.

Young J (1992) The use of specialised beds and mattresses. Journal of Tissue Viability 2: 79–81.

Index